Alternative to Extinction

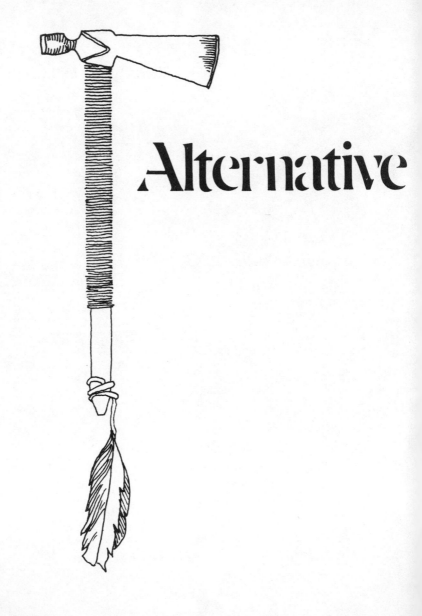

Alternative

Robert A. Trennert, Jr.

to Extinction

Federal Indian Policy
and the Beginnings of the
Reservation System,
1846-51

Temple University Press
Philadelphia

Temple University Press, Philadelphia 19122
© 1975 by Temple University. All rights reserved
Published 1975
Printed in the United States of America
International Standard Book Number: 0-87722-030-1
Library of Congress Catalog Card Number: 74-83203

Contents

Preface   vii

1. The Barrier and the Indian   1

2. William Medill and
Federal Indian Policy, 1845–48   16

3. Toward a Reservation System:
Whig Indian Policy, 1849–51   40

4. Reservations or Removal:
Texas and the Government   61

5. Military and Civilian Policy:
New Mexico, 1846–52   94

6. Across the Emigrant's Path:
The Border Tribes   131

7. End of the Indian Barrier:
The Central Plains   160

8. Epilogue   193

Notes   199
Bibliography   239
Index   255

Preface

Federal Indian policy in the period between 1846 and 1851 is significant primarily because the nation found itself confronted with an Indian problem that demanded new answers to the question of how the white and Indian might live together in peace. These were the years of Manifest Destiny, when America acquired large parts of the Far West, and, unexpectedly, a new Indian frontier. Within this new territory—Texas, New Mexico, California, Oregon, Utah—were scores of tribes, whose incorporation into the nation changed the entire scope of federal Indian responsibilities. Although the Indians of all the newly acquired lands presented unique problems, by far the most significant portion of this frontier involved the geographical area from the Rocky Mountains to the Missouri and from the Platte to New Mexico. This was the domain of the most powerful Indian nations on the continent, the mounted tribes of the plains and Southwest. As a consequence of the confrontation with these tribes, the United States government ended the "barrier" policy of confining Indians to the vast area west of the Mississippi. What emerged instead was a policy conforming more with the inevitabilities of expansion, one whose most important aspect envisioned a system of reservations, in which the Indians were to be separated from the whites in restricted and well-defined areas. The modern reservation system, which fully developed after the Civil War, has its philosophical origins in this period.

The roots of the modern reservation system have not been fully explored by historians of Indian policy. Both Alban W. Hoopes and James C. Malin, the two major authorities on this period, though demonstrating that the period of expansion necessitated a new policy, have passed over the historical implications for a reservation policy.[1] Hoopes, to be sure, attributes the first modern reservation to California in 1852, but he fails to recognize that the ideas employed had been conceived and experimented with by officials of the Indian Office between 1846 and 1851 in an effort to find an alternative to what seemed to be the inevitable extinction of the Indian. This study is directed to exploring this effort, as well as to the various influences that affected the formulation of Indian policy.

Nothing was more confusing and perplexing than the formulation of Indian policy during this expansive era. So many factors other than the welfare of the Indians entered into the fundamental decisions that the results, despite good intentions, often tended to be inconclusive and ineffective. The difficulties in devising a workable policy were overwhelming. The nation faced conditions which changed so fast that neither government nor the people could cope with them.[2] Those responsible for Indian policy found it necessary to make immediate decisions about scores of frontier tribes, previously without much contact with whites, whose lands were invaded by American citizens. The national interest required prompt action to protect the settlements of New Mexico, to establish peace with the Indians of Texas, to safeguard the western emigrant routes, and to guard the widely scattered frontier posts. Moreover, the government felt an obligation to shield the various tribes on the frontier from the usual adverse effects of contact with the white men. Thus the United States was confronted with a complex and somewhat dichotomous problem of providing for the safety of its citizens and at the same time preventing the destruction of the aboriginal population.

I am deeply indebted to many people and institutions who have shared their knowledge and expertise with me. Thanks must especially go to the numerous professional research staffs in the various libraries and archives; particularly to Jane Smith and Robert Kvasnica of the Social and Economics Records Division of the National Archives. I should also extend thanks to Elmer

Parker, the Military Records Division of the National Archives; Bernard Bernier and Roy P. Basler, Library of Congress; Mary I. Fry, Henry E. Huntington Library; Anne McDonnell, Kentucky Historical Society; James R. Bently, The Filson Club; Mrs. Frances H. Stadler and Mrs. Arthur W. Felt, Missouri Historical Society; Mrs. Gordon E. Gatherum, Ohio Historical Society; and Mrs. Frances B. Macdonald, Indiana Division, Indiana State Library.

Additional expressions of gratitude must go to Russell F. Weigley and Francis Paul Prucha for reading portions of the manuscript and making invaluable suggestions. Wilbur R. Jacobs, who initially recommended the subject, has been a guiding light throughout. Finally, I am especially grateful to my wife Linda, whose patience and encouragement assured that I would finish the project.

Alternative to Extinction

1

The Barrier and the Indian

❧ We sometimes fail to realize that the formulation of all Indian policies in American history, even the most just, has been based on certain attitudes that could best be described as racial. Those white officials who took it upon themselves to try to solve problems rising out of the confrontation between white and Indian looked at things from an ethnocentric point of view. This does not necessarily mean that their desire to help the Indian should be discredited. Many simply accepted the superiority of Anglo-American institutions as a fact; to them, as to most Americans, the question was one of "civilization over savagism."[1] There was no appreciation or even awareness that Indian culture had a value in itself. Accordingly, every legitimate Indian policy devised by this nation has had one goal—to help the Indian by acculturating him into the mainstream of American life.

The policy of the United States government during the late 1840's and early 1850's based itself upon this premise. It was not founded so much on ethnic hostility as on an attempt to work out an acceptable solution to a racial dilemma. The government wanted to prevent Indian interference with the activities of the "civilized" race while at the same time exercising a benevolent paternalism to assure the survival of at least part of the native population, albeit under controlled conditions.

1

From the time the nation acquired Louisiana in 1803, some government officials, most notably Thomas Jefferson, had seen in the trans-Mississippi country a possible solution to the Indian problems facing the nation. The basic premise of their argument revolved around the belief that white contact with the Indian was degrading to the native and the cause of most interracial difficulties. The goal of the government was to end such problems peacefully, and this seemed best accomplished by civilizing, educating, and assimilating the native population in such a manner that the Indian would adopt only the virtues of white civilization.[2] The newly acquired western lands appeared ideally suited to such a purpose. Here the Indian could be isolated from white society until he was ready for assimilation. The government had no intention of transplanting the eastern tribes into the "Great American Desert," lands unfit for habitation.[3] They were to be given the good lands lying just west of Missouri and Arkansas where agricultural pursuits might easily be adopted. The belief that the Indian could be separated from the white therefore rested not so much on the idea that whites would find the Indian country undesirable as on the concept that the land to the west was so vast that white encroachment would not be significant for a long time. By then, it was hoped, the Indians would be ready to integrate into American society without serious disturbance. Meanwhile, the Indian population would be located on the farthest reaches of the national domain, allowing life to go on undisturbed in the rest of the country.

These ideas were put into effect with the creation of the removal policy and the Indian barrier philosophy of the twenties and thirties. James Monroe, who did much to give the ideas currency, expressed the benefits of separation in his message to Congress in 1824: "Experience has shown that unless the tribes be civilized, they can never be incorporated into our system, in any form whatever," but in the "vast territory" between the present states and the Rocky Mountains, the Indians might reside in peace until they became civilized. Monroe's secretary of war, John C. Calhoun, backed the same policy and proposed to guarantee tranquility by giving the Indians "the strongest and most solemn assurances that the country given them should be theirs as a permanent home for themselves and their posterity, without being disturbed by encroachments of our citizens." Thus crystallized the policy of removal which culminated in the act of May 28, 1830, providing for the removal west of the Mississippi of all Indians and guaranteeing them their new homes.[4] The dream of a permanent barrier seemed to become a reality as the various tribes, having been given sincere assurances this would be their last move, began their westward migration.

The removal policy does not mark the beginning of a general reservation system although the War Department did mark out some rough tribal boundaries and assign agents to several of the transplanted and indigenous tribes.[5] The concept of reservations, of course, was known at this time, and indeed since the Puritan era Americans had been setting aside defined lands where the Indians could be forcibly civilized. However, reservations never became general policy as long as land remained for removal, a fact well demonstrated in the removals of the 1830's and the construction of the Indian barrier, a line behind which all the nation's Indian population would remain. Here they would need protection from white invasion but little supervision while the slow process of acculturation took place. Thus the tribes were not restricted from coming and going as they pleased, agents and teachers were few and ineffective, and no provisions were made for restricting and integrating the native tribes already on the prairies. Only in a few selected places were more restrictive reservations attempted, and these proved failures as long as the Indians had any choice in the matter. In 1832, for instance, a reservation was created along the Iowa River for some of the Sac and Fox. These people quickly expressed their dissatisfaction with the little plot of land assigned them and in 1836 they returned the land to the government and went west to join their less restricted relatives.[6]

Removal necessitated a general reorganization of federal Indian policy, and in 1834 a complete revamping was undertaken, in light of the fact that soon all the Indians would be located west of the Mississippi. The laws passed in 1834 reflected the

influence of the barrier philosophy by attemptng to institution-
alize the "permanent" settlement of racial problems. Since the
prairie lands were to be Indian territory there seemed no reason
to provide much flexibility in meeting future changes. The barrier
seemed to resolve the Indian dilemma, and only the task of protecting and civilizing the aboriginal population remained.

The most significant changes came in the congressional action
to reorganize the Indian service, which until this date had functioned in a haphazard manner with very little legal basis for
many of its activities. Congress therefore defined its duties and
relationships between the various categories of Indian administrators. At the top of the pyramid of responsibility remained
the secretary of war, who had officiated over Indian affairs
since 1789. Directly under him, the commissioner of Indian
affairs, an office created in 1832, was charged with actual Indian
relations and the day-to-day operations of the Indian Office. The
various field officers—superintendents, agents, and subagents—remained, but with considerable modifications. Two categories of
superintendents continued to be employed. Governors served as
ex officio superintendents in organized territories with an Indian
population. Special or full superintendents such as the one at
St. Louis handled the tribes beyond the reach of organized government (thus embracing most of the tribes on the frontier). To
define the somewhat ambiguous responsibilities of these officers,
Congress authorized them to "exercise a general supervision and
control over the official conduct and accounts of all [subordinate]
officers and persons employed by the government."[7]

Reorganization made its greatest impact on Indian agents by
institutionalizing their responsibilities. The general duties of the
agents had consisted primarily of arbitrating disputes between
whites and Indians, paying annuities to the tribes, settling intertribal difficulties, and supervising the civilizing and educational efforts of the government. These duties were extended by
the law of 1834 and a uniform salary fixed. One significant additional responsibility assigned agents was their control over
traders in the form of power to issue and revoke licenses. This
change came about because of complaints from Indians that they

were being cheated and maltreated by traders. Prior to 1834 the government had "considered that every person (whatever might be his character) was entitled to a license on offering his bond." Agents were now allowed to refuse or revoke the licenses of men of bad character.[8]

Congress presumed that the responsibilities of the Indian Office were now fixed and, as removal became a reality, the duties of agents would diminish. Accordingly, the reorganization provided for twelve agencies, which could be discontinued as they became unnecessary; it further stipulated that no more agencies could "in the future be established without the sanction of Congress." The only section of the law having any flexibility for meeting increased responsibilities came in the provision which allowed the president to determine the number of subagents.[9] Subagents, however, drew a rather small salary and were not designed—or able—to meet the needs of the sudden expansion of the 1840's. Consequently, the reorganization of the Office of Indian Affairs, which became law on June 30, 1834, provided little opportunity for the federal government to meet any rapid change in the nature of the Indian frontier without enacting major legislative revisions. As it turned out, when expansion came, Congress took five years to make the necessary changes.

Congress also passed a comprehensive intercourse act in 1834 to improve the regulation of trade and commerce with the Indians. For some time it had been clearly evident that the various laws designed to protect the Indian from the whites were ineffective. Whiskey peddlers evaded the law with disturbing regularity, whites invaded Indian sanctuaries, and numerous frauds and crimes were committed against the native population. Since the success of removal depended on separation, the intercourse act officially defined the unorganized territory west of the Mississippi as "Indian Country." In this territory federal laws were strengthened to safeguard the new Indian homeland. Most of the provisions simply elaborated on past laws, but taken together they show the intent of Congress: the licensing system for traders was tightened, no whites were permitted to hunt or trap in the Indian country, no persons could settle or inhabit any land guaranteed to the Indians, and the government would forcibly remove anyone violating these laws.[10] As far as legally possible the Indians would be separated from the deleterious effects of white contact.

Another bill recommended by the Committee on Indian Affairs sought to confirm the special status of the Indian lands by establishing a "Western Territory." The United States was asked to guarantee this land to the tribesmen forever, to provide a territorial form of government in which the Indians would actively participate, and to work toward the eventual admission of the territory into the Union. But Congress was not ready for such a radical step and quickly defeated the proposal. So while the acts of 1834 reorganized the laws to conform to the Indian frontier, the nation failed to protect that frontier by creating a permanent homeland. It is quite likely of course, as many congressmen believed, that such an Indian state at that time was impractical and the legal complications would have been overwhelming.[11] Without it, however, there was even less guarantee that whites could be kept out of Indian country.

The entire reorganization of 1834 thus attempted to bring the operations of the federal government into line with the believed reality of a great Indian barrier to the west. Since the government could not visualize future changes, the outlines of Indian policy were rather rigidly set. Many of the reforms were indeed necessary and the changes themselves cannot be criticized, but in providing for future contingencies the entire plan was remarkably silent. The logic of the time seemed to dictate that the nation's Indian population could be kept out of the way and eventually civilized without much expense or effort.

The idealism behind removal and the laws of 1834 remained virtually unchanged until Manifest Destiny brought expansion into the Indian lands. Most observers agreed that removal provided the perfect answer, and attempts were made to strengthen the idea of a government for the Native Americans. Once more in the thirties and again in 1846 a number of congressmen tried to create an Indian state, but the proposals met defeat from legislators unwilling to guarantee the Indians a territory of their own.[12] Despite this failure, the officers of the Indian Office attempted to carry out the logical consequences of removal by fostering civilization as soon as possible. In the 1840's a strong wave of reformism, inspired in part by the reform spirit of the Jacksonian age, swept Indian administrators. Attempts were made to bring education to the tribes behind the barrier and settle them down to an agricultural life. During the early part of the decade, Commissioner of Indian Affairs T. Hartley Crawford devoted a great deal of energy to promoting manual-labor schools among the transplanted tribes. He saw such schools as being "not only deserving of favor," but "indispensable to the civilization of the Indians." The government also actively encouraged religious societies to enter the Indian country and help bring civilization to the Indians. By 1842 some fifty-two schools, mostly operated by missionaries, were in existence with an enrollment of over 2,000 pupils.[13] Yet these attempts failed to achieve the desired progress. It soon became obvious that the barrier philosophy had certain weaknesses.

One problem was that the program was inherently too limited to reach most of the indigenous tribes of the prairies, particularly such people as the Sioux and Cheyenne who were free and powerful, and would not accept the white man's way unless forced to do so. These tribes also failed to accept the American logic that all Indians could live together in peace. They were not particularly pleased to see new tribes competing for their buffalo and used this as an excuse to raid the eastern tribes.

Most difficulties, however, came from the fact that the barrier failed to keep the evils of white society from contaminating the natives. In the decade following the passage of the intercourse laws the records of the Indian Office were filled with complaints that the Indians were being debauched by whites despite all the restrictions and attempts at enforcement. Most of the difficulty arose over the continual importation of liquor into the Indian country. In 1841, David Dawson Mitchell, superintendent at St. Louis, reported to Crawford:

I have ascertained that there has been One hundred and fifty barrels of Alcohol Smuggled into the Indian Country during the present year— equal to Three Hundred barrels of whiskey! And that during the preceding twelve months, upwards of One hundred and twenty Indians, mostly heads of families, have fallen in drunken broils! The evils end not here. Civil Wars being thus produced, the camps are broken up, into Small bands who Scatter themselver over the prairies —dreading their relations even more than their natural enemies. Hunting is neglected, for all their time and vigilance are required to guard against attacks, and the Indians Starve in the midst of plenty.

Such activities, of course, hindered the civilizing process. Commissioner Crawford reported in 1840 that as long as whiskey continued to flow to the Indians he saw little chance of bettering their condition.[14] Yet not much could be done until Congress could be persuaded to provide more effective restrictions.

Related to the alcohol problem was the question of the traders. The 1834 acts had not proved as effective as anticipated in restricting the abuses of the whites who came to trade with the Indians. Not only did these people continue to use whiskey as a tool of the trade, but they resorted to numerous other measures to defraud the natives. Traders found it relatively easy to circumvent most of the limitations and they continued to indebt the Indian, overcharge him, and collect most of the annuity money due the tribes. Moreover, the attempt at restricting licenses to men of good character did not work in practice. Licenses were easily obtainable, and those unable to get one simply conducted business without legal sanction. As long as the Indian department lacked any effective means of enforcement these abuses continued, making it even more difficult to gain much headway with the process of civilizing the Indian.

The army was also charged with responsibility on the Indian frontier, especially for assuring the peace and tranquility of the Indians. Like the civilian branch of the government, the military found itself unprepared to meet the changes of the forties. Several factors influenced the condition of the army prior to 1846. Of primary importance was the persistent inclination of military leaders and government to ignore the need for an effective army establishment on the frontier. "Preoccupied with the next foreign war rather than the current domestic conflict," notes Robert Utley, "they rarely stepped from the pathways marked out by the military intellects of Europe to explore more than superficially the doctrinal implications of continuing warfare with a primitive people."[15] Moreover, the philosophy of the Indian barrier implied that the Indians would need little federal protection, that they would be able to live among themselves in peace while becoming civilized, and therefore the military would play a relatively minor role once the Indian country was established. Dictates of economy also argued against a strong military establishment. In an age of limited governmental expenditures, Congress kept an eye out for any unnecessary costs; and expenses were substantially increased on the frontier. Sources of supply were further away, transportation of goods and materials more difficult, and the nature of the terrain required the use of cavalry, which were considerably more expensive than infantry to maintain.[16]

A few attempts were made in the years before 1846 to improve the military position on the frontier. Most of the impetus came from officers in the frontier service or settlers who were keenly aware of the need. Although in 1832 and 1836 Congress did create battalions of dragoons to be used specifically on the frontier, other proposals to build up the military establishment met defeat from a Congress reluctant to approve any more than the bare necessities.[17]

In this fashion the nation entered into the age of expansion. Within the short period of three years during the mid-1840's the United States acquired, as President James K. Polk told Congress in 1848, "One million and ninty-three thousand and sixty-one square miles, . . . [or] a country more than half as large as all that which was held by the United States before their acquisition."[18] Waiting in this area were the tribes that would force an end to the barrier idea and demonstrate to government administrators that a policy of reservations would be the only practical solution, from the white man's viewpoint, to deal with a drastically altered Indian frontier.

Before we enter into a discussion of Indian policy, it is appropriate to discuss the tribes that occupied this new frontier. With the exception of some of the transplanted eastern tribes that lived along the border, the peoples that confronted the nation during this period were substantially different from the forest Indians that had influenced past policy. In this region lived the nomadic and mounted tribes of the prairies and mountains, including the so-called "plains Indians."

The Indian tribes that were to have the major impact on federal policy lived in the large area that included the Great Plains and portions of the Southwest.[19] Part of this region had been on the farthest reaches of the nation's frontier and the rest was acquired from expansion into Mexican territory. Perhaps more than a quarter million natives occupied the area.[20] This frontier is divided geographically into four separate areas. Nearest the frontier settlements of Missouri and Iowa ranged a group of peoples called the border tribes: the Pawnee, Omaha, Oto, Ponca, Kansa. These Siouan-speaking peoples, relatively few in numbers, lived in established villages, but in most other respects were similar to the more nomadic tribes farther out on the plains. To the west of the border Indians, on the central plains, were found the more formidable Brulé and Oglala Sioux, Cheyenne, Arapaho, and Shoshoni. Here were the typical plains Indians, whose life and economy were dictated by the nomadic chase of the buffalo. In the Southwest, from the Santa Fe road to New Mexico, the Comanche, Ute, Navajo, and several bands of the Apache roamed the countryside. The tribes in this area varied considerably in cultural background, but all were mounted and powerful warriors. Finally, the plains of northern and western Texas served as the homeland of the Kiowa, Wichita, Lipan Apache, and southern Comanche, who presented a formidable obstacle to the expansionistic tendencies of Texans.[21]

Though differing in significant details, the frontier tribes had certain features in common. All of the native societies, to a greater or lesser extent, were already experiencing cultural changes induced by the spread of European influences, which, sweeping ahead of the white man like a tidal wave, altered the biotic and cultural environment. The Indian's ability to live in harmony with his natural environment was slowly being destroyed, although most Indians had seen few if any white men and certainly could not visualize the impact of the changes. Alcohol, disease, and trade brought major changes in life patterns, acquisition of the horse and gun modified ecological relationships. In the Southwest, Spanish contact produced additional alterations in native cultures. Edward H. Spicer, in his study of white impact on Indian civilizations, has demonstrated that native communities were disrupted and radically changed—new economic, social, and religious patterns emerged from the symbiotic relationship of the Spaniard and the Indian.[22]

Undoubtedly the most significant feature of these tribes was the horse and gun culture which reached its apex about the time of American expansion in the 1840's. Not until the introduction of the horse by the Spanish in the sixteenth century had it been possible for the plains and Southwestern tribes to emerge from their rather stable existence to become highly mobile, nomadic, and warlike societies. The horse became the focal point of their culture. Acquisition of these animals meant wealth, made extended warfare possible, and allowed easy pursuit and capture of the buffalo. By the middle of the nineteenth century most Indians on the plains had changed their way of life and had truly become the "Lords of the Soil."[23]

Compared with eastern peoples, the horse tribes have generally been considered to be physically among the finest on the North American continent. They were usually taller and stronger than most of the other American Indian population. Their characteristics impressed observers from the beginning, helping stereotype these peoples in the popular mind as the "typical" American Indian. In 1834, for instance, artist George Catlin saw much of the noble savage in the Cheyenne when he observed:

There is no finer race of men than these in North America, and more superior in stature, excepting the Osages; scarcely a man of the tribe, full grown, who is less than six feet in height. The Shiennes are undoubtedly the richest in horses of any tribe on the Continent, living in a country as they do, where the greatest numbers of wild horses are grazing on the prairies. . . . These people are the most desperate set of horsemen, and warriors also, having carried on almost unceasing wars with the Pawnees and Blackfeet, time out of mind.

This description, with certain individual variations, could well have applied to all the Indians living along the plains frontier.[24]

With the exception of some of the New Mexican Indians, all of these tribes depended upon the buffalo. Even the relatively sedentary border tribes like the Oto and Omaha, who by 1846 were growing crops and living in rather permanent villages, persistently spent their summer months on the plains hunting buffalo. An abundance of evidence testifies to the reliance placed on the buffalo. "They varied their diet with the flesh of deer, antelope, elk, and occasionally bear," observes Wayne Gard, "but buffalo—fresh or dried—was their staple."[25] Of course, the buffalo was more than just food; it provided all the necessities of life. Francis Parkman succinctly explained the dependence on this animal in his classic description of the Oglala Sioux:

The Western Dahcotahs have no fixed habitations. Hunting and fighting they wander incessantly, through the summer and winter. Some follow the herds of buffalo over the waste of prairie; others traverse the Black Hills, through the dark gulfs and sombre gorges, and emerging at last upon the "Parks" those beautiful but most perilous hunting grounds. The buffalo supplies them with the necessities of life; with habitations, food, clothing, bed, and fuel; strings for their bows, glue, thread, cordage, trailropes for their horses, coverings for their saddles, vessels to hold water, boats to cross streams, and the means of purchasing all they want from the traders. When the buffalo are extinct, they too must dwindle away.[26]

Cultural alterations occurred when the tribes became mounted. Inevitably the tribesman became more of an individualist as his mobility increased. Systems of tribal government were accordingly organized in an extremely democratic manner, so much so that the term "tribe" is something of a misnomer. Tribes were not, as Americans often believed, comparable to "nations." Most tribes had no specific leadership but rather a series of loosely organized bands under the personal influence of individual chiefs. Even these chiefs maintained a most tenuous hold over their bands and could rarely enforce an unpopular decision.[27] This fact makes clear one reason that the Americans had such difficulty in concluding binding treaties with these Indians: the tribal organizations were so diffuse that no agreement could truly bind more than those who made their mark on the designated piece of paper. Unfortunately for both the Indians and the United States, whites generally refused to accept this fact.

The horse tribes were most noted for their superiority in war. War, in fact, was a way of life, and it is no exaggeration to describe these Indians as perpetually involved in fighting one another. As General S. L. A. Marshall has so aptly noted, "The Spirit of live-and-let-live wasn't there." Most Indian young men directed their lives toward becoming brave and courageous warriors. Not surprisingly, all the plains tribes were excellent horsemen, often described, as individuals, as the "finest light cavalry in the world."[28] The Comanche, perhaps, outdid them all. Captain Randolph B. Marcy, who was on the plains in this era, gives this description of a Comanche warrior:

His only ambition consists in being able to cope successfully with his enemy in war and in managing his steed with unfailing adroitness. He is in the saddle from boyhood to old age, and his favorite horse is his constant companion. It is when mounted that the prairie warrior exhibits himself to the best advantage; here he is at home, and his skill in various manoeuvres which he makes available in battle—such as throwing himself entirely upon one side of his horse and discharging his arrows with great rapidity toward the opposite side from beneath the animal's neck while he is at full speed—is truly astonishing.[29]

Use of the horse tended to intensify tribal warfare. The mobility provided by mounted warriors increased intertribal contact and, as raiding provided the major method of acquiring horses, accelerated the frequency of hostilities. Yet such warfare seldom, if ever, was motivated by a desire to exterminate the opponent, but rather by revenge, honor, or a desire to obtain material wealth (horses). As often as not war was looked upon as a means of gaining social prestige: the most distinguishing feature of the plains war "complex" was a graded set of honors based on bravery—counting a coup (touching an enemy and getting away without harm) generally received the highest honor.[30]

Only occasionally did significant losses occur and usually only when an enemy was taken by surprise or overrun by a large group. In fact, "war parties set out with a particular end in view and victory lay in the accomplishment of that purpose and in the safe return of the party."[31] Not until the white man began moving on the plains and driving the buffalo away did the tribes find it necessary to launch wars of extermination. Then hunger became a motivation for killing: "they must scatter about their country in small bands," noted Father DeSmet, "like hungry wolves, in search of food frequently following the prey of their more powerful neighbors and cruel foes, who slaughter indiscriminately old men, women, and children. . . . The Sioux must necessarily encroach on the lands of the Arickeras, Crows, Assiniboins, Cheyennes and Pawnees—the Crows and Assiniboins on the Blackfeet and vice versa, and thus endless struggles, and murderous and cruel wars [are] daily perpetrated and multiplied."[32]

Well armed, mounted, and trained in the arts of war, the horse Indians were potentially the most deadly Indian opponents the Americans had yet encountered. Some anthropologists even considered that the greatest impact of the horse on these tribes was to give them a war potential which served as a major block to white invasion. There were, of course, certain disadvantages to the Indian mode of warfare. Indian war parties were generally small in number and more suited to counting a coup or stealing horses than fighting an efficiently organized and led army; individualism tended to rule Indian warfare as it did many other aspects of their culture.[33] Despite these disadvantages, however, the warriors had a great deal in their favor. Being generally nomadic, they moved easily from one location to another, had no permanent villages or agricultural fields for whites to destroy, and were usually able to choose between battle and retreat as the situation demanded. The Indian and his pony were well adapted to their environment and this gave them a noticeable advantage over American dragoons. The experience of Major Enoch Steen with the Apache was all too common:

When these Indians start a marauding expedition they come mounted on their best horses (which are equal to any of ours) and at the same time have relays waiting for them at Twenty five or thirty miles distant. They do their mischief and get off with several miles . . . [head] start—come up on their relays and thus are mounted with fresh animals and can snap their fingers at us whose horses are broken down by the long chase.[34]

Thus, most of the Indians facing the United States during the era of expansion differed significantly from the eastern Indians. They needed to be handled differently, and since they could not be removed in the same way as their eastern brethren, a new program was necessary to assure peace. But it took some time for the federal government to realize that many aspects of the old policy were being outdated.

2

William Medill and
Federal Indian Policy, 1845-48

❧ Indian policy during the period of Manifest Destiny came to the forefront only when it affected matters most Americans considered more important. Even then it surfaced with unusual difficulty. The American people found themselves first engaged in a controversial war with Mexico and then in an increasingly dangerous dispute over the issue of slavery. Such urgent issues naturally took precedence over the seemingly minor question of dealing with an aboriginal population on the edge of the frontier. To be sure, citizens and their representatives in Washington did not completely ignore Indian affairs, but all too often other issues became entangled with questions of policy or forced suspension of critical decisions. These circumstances tended to frustrate and delay the formulation of an effective policy to cope with the Indian problems that confronted an expanding nation.

The solution to these problems required prompt attention. Changes created by the acquisition of nearly half a continent containing a considerable Indian population necessitated a complete reassessment of Indian policy to prevent the conflict that might be expected. Travelers and settlers in the new territory needed effective protection. Contact had to be established with the tribes and arrangements made to maintain peaceable relations with white Americans. Measures were urgently needed to

16

protect the weaker tribes, some of them recent transplants from the eastern United States, from their more hostile Indian neighbors. Abuses of frontier trade and intercourse with the natives also demanded correction before they led to an explosion. In attempting to provide solutions to these difficulties and to establish a workable Indian policy for the frontier the government found itself faced with confusion, political bickering, sectional scheming, and outright opposition. That anything was accomplished was due mostly to the work of a few individuals who were seriously concerned with solving the newly created confrontation before the frontier erupted in war.

At the commencement of the period of expansion in 1846, William L. Marcy, Polk's secretary of war, was technically responsible for Indian affairs. Although Marcy was a man of ability, the Mexican War and the political duties of a cabinet member diverted his attention to other matters, leaving the responsibility for determining Indian policy to the commissioner of Indian affairs, William Medill. Handsome, full-bearded, politically ambitious, and with somewhat of a reputation as a reformer, Medill was just forty years old when, on October 29, 1845, President Polk promoted him to the top post in the Indian bureau. Like many of his predecessors he had absolutely no prior experience in dealing with Indians. His qualifications consisted solely of his being a prominent Van Buren Democrat from Ohio who was nominated for the position by the state machine as a means of demonstrating that the president harbored no hostile attitude toward Van Buren men and of placing a representative of Ohio in the high councils of government.[1] Upon entering office, Medill inherited accountability for the general goals of protecting, civilizing, and educating the Indians so long advocated by the government. He also inherited a department unchanged in scope and outlook since 1834. Medill quickly threw all his energies into the task of permanently resolving some of the Indian problems besetting the nation. He made himself aware of the reforming philosophy of his predecessor, T. Hartley Crawford, and he concluded that the Indian department must be ruled with a firm hand if any significant changes were to be made. Unfortunately, his political philosophy occasionally limited his vision.

Before the events that brought the United States the great areas of the Far West—the annexation of Texas, the Mexican War, and the settlement of the Oregon boundary dispute—the operations of the Office of Indian Affairs, as have been noted, were assumed to be adequate to handle the Indians within the limits of the nation. Medill's department was operating near the full strength provided for it by the laws of 1834. Even at this time, however, the departmental organization was unequal to the task. Of the four Indian superintendencies, only one, the St. Louis office, functioned as a "full superintendency." Henry Dodge, governor of Wisconsin, acted as ex officio superintendent in that Territory, while agents performed the duties of superintendents in the Michigan and Western (Oklahoma) offices. In 1834, Congress had authorized a maximum of twelve agents, and eleven of these posts were filled in 1846. While a number of the agencies were near the frontier, most of the agents were concerned only with helping the transplanted tribes adjust to removal. An additional thirteen subagents were spread across the country. Most of the field officers owed their appointments to the good graces of the Democratic administration. Although some of the agents were able men, all too many contributed nothing more than required to retain office. It also is noteworthy that only one agency, the Upper Missouri Agency, dealt with the more powerful tribes of the plains and Rockies. Yet even this agency was concerned primarily with overseeing the fur trade and thus was too far north to be of much benefit in handling the main thrust of expansion.

First congressional interest in exercising more control over the western tribes came in early 1846. Leading the drive were a number of expansionists, largely western Democrats, who were keenly aware of the increasing emigration to Oregon and California and the role these settlers might play in annexing that territory. The travelers needed protection to reach their destination and the expansionists determined to give it to them. Much of the concern centered upon the proposal to establish military forces on the Oregon Trail, which finally culminated, May 13, 1846, in a

bill authorizing a chain of forts along the route.[2] As none of the
lands beyond the Rockies yet belonged to the United States, Indian agents could not be appointed past the continental divide.
However, the Indian bureau could expand its operations out
onto the plains, an action strongly recommended by Senator
Thomas Hart Benton of Missouri. In particular, Benton suggested that an agency be created to handle the dangerous tribes
roaming the Platte and Arkansas valleys, with whom the nation
had no treaties, in order to provide protection for the passing
emigrant trains. Congress responded favorably on June 27 by
creating the Upper Platte Agency, and a month later appointed
Thomas Fitzpatrick as agent, thus giving the United States its
first agency among the tribes to be affected by expansion.[3]

Other proposals for improving the Indian service were introduced into both houses of Congress during the following months.
On August 10, 1846, the House of Representatives asked the
commissioner of Indian affairs to provide suggestions for their
consideration.[4] Medill responded eagerly to this resolution. He
had begun to realize that the Indian service must be enlarged
as soon as it became evident that expansion would bring many
new tribes under governmental control. Exactly how to accomplish this task remained a problem, but when Medill sent a circular on the subject to his field officers, many replies favored extending the area of government control. Thomas H. Harvey, the
superintendent at St. Louis, suggested that several of the existing
agencies were no longer effective. Some of the tribes standing
directly across the path of American expansion resided hundreds
of miles from the nearest agency. Now, wrote Harvey, *the interest of the Whites upon the prairies, in my opinion, call loudly
upon the Government for the location of an efficient officer among
them.*" From New Mexico, which had passed into American
hands, provisional governor Charles Bent also reported to Medill
that agents were absolutely necessary to control the various tribes
in that quarter.[5] Informants in Texas and elsewhere generally
recommended the same.

Medill was even more alive to the fact that the trade and intercourse provisions of the act of 1834 were ineffective. Two chronic
problems drew the commissioner's attention: the illegal liquor

trade and the manner of paying annuity funds to the frontier tribes already bound to the United States by treaty. Under the existing laws a fine of $500 and forfeiture of goods were the only penalties imposed on anyone convicted of introducing "spirituous liquor" into Indian country. These restrictions were notoriously weak; so much whiskey made its way to the frontier that a national scandal had developed. British traders smuggled liquor down from Canada, Mexicans brought it up from Santa Fe, and, more significant, American frontiersmen imported liquor from the adjoining states. For nearly ten years almost every official along the frontier had noted the prevalence of whiskey sellers and the resultant effects on the Indians. In 1846, things seemed worse. "Some efficient steps should be taken," pleaded subagent Robert B. Mitchell at Council Bluffs, "to prevent the frequent use, and the ease of obtaining and introducing whiskey to this nation. The article is kept in great abundance near the [Iowa] State line, where squaws and young men exchange horses, guns, blankets, and other articles that they can get on credit from the traders, for whiskey."[6]

Such activities outraged Medill and he minced no words when it came to the use of alcohol among the Indians. His main concern was that whiskey was undermining the government's attempt to improve the condition of the Indians. "I cannot too strongly impress upon you," he wrote to one agent, "the importance of the duty imposed upon you. The prevention of the use of strong drink has almost been the one thing needful to ensure the prosperity of the Indian race and its advancement in civilization. The use of it has tended more to the demoralization of the Indians than all other causes combined." In his annual report for 1846 the commissioner again underlined his concern: "Whiskey is the greatest obstacle to their [the Indians] rapid moral and social elevation, and no means should be spared to break up the traffic in it, now and heretofore so extensively and injuriously carried on among the Indians." One means of making improvements seemed to be that of changing the law: "Under the present laws, the only penalty for introducing liquor into the Indian country, and selling or bartering it to the Indians, is, in the former case, a forfeiture of the article if found, and in the latter a fine if convicted of the offense. The profits of the trade are so great that the risk of detection and loss of the article is, and will be incurred without hesitation."[7]

Similar problems arose in connecton with annuity payments. In 1834 Congress had decided to stop giving funds to heads of families and began the practice of supplying the annuities to the chiefs for distribution. Supposedly this system would end the perpetration of fraud and allow the chiefs to apply the funds "to the expenses of their Government, to the purpose of education, or to some object of general concern." But paying annuities to the chiefs and headmen failed to improve the condition of the Indians. Entrusting a large amont of money to a few Indians proved a windfall for unscrupulous traders. The chiefs, finding the temptation to run up huge debts too much to resist, charged their purchases to tribal funds, leaving little or no money for the rest of the tribe. These debts thus became tribal debts and the government soon found itself making annuity payments directly to the traders to satisfy the personal accounts of a few tribesmen. Then, too, once the chiefs and principal men became indebted to the traders, they were forced to act as the traders desired or lose their credit. The private trading companies consequently held enormous power over the tribes—a power which could be used against the Indian Office if necessary.[8]

Numerous reports reached the commissioner's office enumerating the abuses perpetrated under the annuity system.[9] By early 1847, Medill had decided on the advisability of several changes. First, annuities must be kept under tight control to prevent the degradation that he saw accompanying the accumulation of too much money in the hands of a few tribesmen. From the commissioner's viewpoint, the Indian, "who is naturally improvident and has little regard for money when it comes into his possession, after supplying his temporary wants, has the means of living for a time, independent of industry or exertion, in idleness and profligacy, until the indisposition to labor or the habit of intemperance becomes so strong, that he degenerates into a wretched outcast." Two other proposals were made at the same time. One suggestion would have made a cut in the size of the annuity should the tribe decrease in number, and the other proposed that "goods and provisions" should be furnished in lieu of cash if the tribes would agree.[10] These changes were all intended to reduce the amount of money available to the tribes and thus eliminate the temptation for whiskey sellers and traders to cheat and debauch the Indian.

Medill discovered also that some trading companies were actively working against the efforts of Indian agents to help the tribes. He found that if agents were overzealous in trying to protect the Indians from fraud, the traders used their political power in Congress to have the objectionable men replaced. One correspondent wrote Medill to warn him that "the most active representatives of the Indian traders" were presently using such threats to force Thomas H. Harvey, Medill's superintendent at St. Louis, to moderate his attempts to prosecute several companies for fraud and liquor smuggling. The traders, continued the letter, "are men of great means, activity, and determination in procuring the removal of agents of the Government connected with Indian affairs; and although *not seen* often in such efforts are generally prime movers in asking a change when the government agents unite energy and high character for integrity."[11] Such information troubled Medill. He soon determined to correct the situation and this resolve developed into a crusade against the traders.

Until Congress could be urged into taking legislative action, Medill's ability to change the system was severely limited. He did, however, do all in his power to limit the abuses. Agents were directed to be especially active in halting the liquor trade. "There are but few whites residing in the district of country referred to," noted one of his instructions, "except at distant and widely separate trading points: and over these traders and their employees it will be your duty to keep a watchful eye."[12] Although traders were occasionally caught and prosecuted as a result of this surveillance, the illegal activities continued much as before—the largeness of the Indian country and the paucity of agents assuring the traders of relative immunity. Quite a few cases of fraud were also uncovered, but the larger trading outfits usually managed to evade punishment. Prominent frontier companies like Chouteau's American Fur Company and W. G. & G. W. Ewing were often found to be cheating the tribesmen out of annuities, charging higher prices, and smuggling liquor.[13] These companies, however, operated an effective lobby in Washington, especially among the Missouri delegation to Congress. By appealing to the president, the secretary of war, and Congress, and if necessary by bribing witnesses, they usually managed to cloud the issue sufficiently to escape conviction. Clearly, then, new laws and impartial enforcement were necessary if the tribes were to be protected.

Medill submitted his proposals to Congress through the secretary of war on December 30, 1846. The report was confined to reorganizing the department (his views on liquor and annuities having already been published in his annual report). The commissioner told the legislators that since the last reorganization of the department in 1834, "the condition of things has become so changed as to require material and corresponding alterations in the organization then prescribed."[14] Yet the "alterations" he proposed seemed to contradict logic by tending to restrict the already limited Indian Office just at the time concern should have been for expansion.

From the commissioner's viewpoint, however, there existed two logical reasons for his decision. First, although all of the Far West had now been occupied by Americans, Congress had yet to decide on a form of civilian government. Consequently, with the exception of Texas where other problems existed, military governments ruled over the new lands and the Polk administration considered it illegal to place civilian agencies in any of the possessions without congressional approval. Secondly, Medill was looking for reform. In Ohio he had earned a reputation for his views on hard money and strict economy, and these ideas he transferred to the Indian Office. Since the department could not expand, he concentrated his efforts on improving the existing system. He saw that the low salaries paid by the government failed to attract qualified public servants and he recommended higher wages, particularly for subagents, who were then receiving only $700 per year. In order to do this and save money, the number of people employed by the department needed reduction. This maneuver was to be accomplished by eliminating a number of agents and subagents on the ground that most of the Indians had now been removed west of the Mississippi. As many of these tribes lived next to each other, "it is believed that their affairs could be as well and satisfactorily, and certainly more economically managed by one intelligent and efficient agent, as if there were one agent or sub-agent for each." More specifically, the commissioner proposed three full superintendencies (two west of the Mississippi), eight agents, and four subagents. Even at a higher rate of pay, the reduction of personnel promised an annual saving of $11,650 for a department already spending under $30,000 a year on its field officers.[15]

Congress rapidly took up the issue of revising Indian policy. On February 9, the House Committee on Indian Affairs reported a bill to make major amendments in the laws of the 1830's. The committee proposed changes in the trade and intercourse laws as well as the modifications in departmental organization proposed by Medill. The bill consequently contained two parts: first, providing that the number of field personnel be combined and reduced, and second, providing that annuities be paid to the heads of families and heavier penalties be imposed for violations of the liquor laws. However, congressional dissatisfaction with the proposed reduction of personnel (and undoubtedly dissatisfaction over loss of the patronage that went with these jobs) soon became evident and Medill, deciding the bill had no chance of passage in its present form, reluctantly yielded to the opposition and agreed to strike out the proposed reorganization in order to obtain the other reforms.[16]

The Indian Intercourse Act which became law on March 3, 1847, consequently did not make any great organizational changes in the Office of Indian Affairs. Only the appointment of a temporary agent for Texas made any concession to the expansion of the nation (Chapter 4).[17] The most significant features of the act, therefore, came in a modification of the annuity provisions and a tightening up of the liquor trade. Section II of the act imposed two years' imprisonment in addition to the existing fines for any person convicted of selling or bartering liquor to the Indians. The bill further provided that annuities be paid to heads of families at the discretion of the president, that debts of individual Indians would no longer be considered as binding on the tribe, and that annuities, where sufficiently large, be paid semi-annually. In an attempt to dampen the Indians' thirst, annuity money could also be withheld from those natives under the influence of alcohol or refusing to cooperate with the government in preventing the use of ardent spirits.

Medill was pleased with the text of the reforms. "It is probably one of the most salutary laws affectng our Indian relations that has ever been passed," he wrote to Thomas Harvey. The new annuity provisions in particular seemed to promise great improvements for the Indians. In the past

it was too often the case that the upright and well disposed reaped little or no benefits . . . whatever; the idle and profligate recklessly incurring large debts on the faith of them, which through improper influences [of traders] the chiefs would be induced to recognize and sanction as national or binding on the whole tribe, and order to be paid out of their annuities, thus robbing the better class to make good the improvidence of the worse.

Now, the commissioner confidently predicted, everyone would receive "his just and proper share of the bounty of the government."[18] Before he discovered otherwise his attention was drawn to other events transpiring on the frontier.

One of the foremost problems centered upon difficulty with the Indians along the trails to the Pacific. Beyond the Missouri resided a conglomerate of warlike tribes—Sioux, Cheyenne, Pawnee—under only nominal control of the overtaxed Indian bureau. These tribes proved extremely annoying to the emigrants and settlers—stealing property, killing an occasional traveler, and generally making themselves obnoxious to the whites. Inevitably this state of affairs led to more pressure on Washington to do something about this situation. "We have a large body of Indians on our frontier," noted the St. Louis *Daily Union,* "without the means of protection from the Government, and we are surprised that more depredations are not committed . . . upon the settlers on the frontier."[19] Even where agents were in evidence, frontiersmen often complained that the officers were derelict in their duties and ineffective. What the frontier populace wanted, aside from military protection (which was not yet in evidence either), was an effective federal organization that would keep the Indians at peace and under control. They were prepared to push these demands by any means available.

A serious outbreak of intertribal warfare early in 1847 also brought down a flood of criticism upon the Indian bureau. In particular, the Yancton and Brulé Sioux carried out a series of devastating raids on the defenseless border tribes (Chapter 6), most of whom were supposedly under the protection of the United States.[20] The increasing intensity and brutality of the well-publicized massacres caused many people to question the effectiveness of government policy. Whig newspapers used the opportunity to condemn the Polk administration. "There must be a criminal remissness on the part of the government, or those having more immediate charge of Indian affairs," said the St. Louis *Missouri Republican*, "to allow these scenes among the tribes. This state of things has existed for several months, and yet no means have been attempted to check the refractory conduct of these tribes." Other Whig papers took similar positions, charging that Indian policy was neither just nor humane.[21]

These accusations caused a great deal of consternation at the Indian Office, forcing Medill into an uncritical defense of Indian policy. Thomas Ritchie, acting as the administration's spokesman through the pages of his Washington *Daily Union*, spoke for the commissioner. In answering the charges, however, Ritchie found some difficulty in justifying the government's inability to bring peace to the frontier, and so confined himself to rather feeble excuses. How, he asked, did the Whigs know what measures had been taken anyway? Was it the government's fault if the Indians violated treaties or the Mexican War caused a reduction of troop strength along the frontier? The best he could offer in the way of remedies were some rather vague promises: "We learn . . . that measures have been taken to prevent future outrages, and to compel the marauding bands to observe peaceful relations hereafter. We shall not specify them; but time will fully develop them, and we have no doubt, to the general satisfaction of the country."[22] Noticeably absent was any suggestion of expanding the services of the Indian bureau.

Giving the commissioner even more headaches were the trading companies, which were becoming increasingly angry over the trade and intercourse provisions of the act of March 3, 1847. Medill, as author of the act, received most of their fury. Aiding the companies' own powerful lobbyists were a number of influential politicians, including Thomas Hart Benton and Daniel Webster.[23] Because the traders knew they lacked moral grounds for attacking the liquor restrictions and there was little chance for repeal, they concentrated on blocking the annuity provisions. But Medill did not intend to be swayed from his determination to break the hold of the traders over the Indians. Whenever a lobbyist approached him asking that some provision of the law not be enforced lest the companies lose money, he turned them down with ill-disguised hostility. The traders, consequently, attempted to go over the commissioner's head. Pierre Chouteau, William G. and George W. Ewing, and others fired off strong letters to Marcy defending the old system of annuities on both economic and humanitarian grounds. The traders claimed the law would ruin their business. A number of tribes had run up substantial debts and the companies feared they would not be collectable according to the new annuity provision: "If the payment of annuities are to be made, not as usual to the Chiefs, but to 'heads of families,' it follows that the Chiefs, head men and braves, whose obligations we hold, can never meet them, and the traders must bear consequences enormously injurious to them."[24]

Unable immediately to frustrate the implementation of this new provision, the traders turned their attention to making sure that existing debts were not declared null and void. Several companies held substantial claims dating prior to the enactment of the 1847 law; the Potawatomi, for example, were said to owe $74,000.[25] Should the notes be held invalid, the traders said, the government would be in a position of imposing ex post facto laws. At least one firm also contended that the trading companies were doing more than the government to insure the survival of many tribes. George W. Ewing wrote to Marcy that while "trade with the border tribes has been *adverse* and even *disastrous*," his company had generously continued to serve the natives because "during the long interval between the payment of annuities these destitute people fall back on their traders and demand credit and have always got it. Without it they would perish and suffer." Using such reasoning, the trading houses asked the government to suspend the act of 1847 until such a time as no injustice would be worked against them. In essence they wanted payment of all claims on the books prior to March 3, 1847, whether legitimate or not. Benton and others hinted to Medill that such would be a prudent policy.[26]

Still the commissioner refused to be influenced by the trading companies and persisted in trying to break their powers. The feud, of course, soon became public knowledge. Medill hastened to assure all interested parties that no injustice would result and that the law did not operate retroactively. But he also made it abundantly clear that the Indian Office had no intention of paying any fraudulent claims, no matter when they were incurred. On August 30, 1847, the companies were instructed to submit all claims to the department before April 1848 for a decision as to whether the debts were of a truly tribal character or had been incurred by individual Indians. Only those claims found to be valid would be paid out of tribal funds. The companies readily submitted their claims. At the same time realizing that Medill held the key to their success, they also launched an attack on the commissioner, denouncing him in the press, working to convince members of Congress that he was prejudiced against the private trading companies, and attempting to have him removed from office.[27]

William G. Ewing, senior partner of W. G. & G. W. Ewing Company, even made an unsuccessful bid for Congress, which was as least partly based on the hope of giving the company influence. Medill retaliated by allowing the Washington *Daily Union* to print from his files "a few specimens of the dealing of traders with

Indians." These letters were particularly critical of the Chouteau and Ewing operations, stating among other things that the old annuity system had "left the way open, if it did not offer, inducements to their [chiefs] being bribed to allow unjust and unfounded claims against the tribe."[28] As a result, by the end of 1847 the Indian commissioner and the private companies were at loggerheads.

Coincidentally, the Indian Office began to see a relationship between its efforts to reform trade and intercourse and the idea of establishing a series of limited reservations for the Indians of the Far West. As has been seen earlier, the idea of reservations was not altogether new, but from the beginning of the removal policy most governmental emphasis had been on a permanent Indian country beyond the Mississippi where the tribes could live without much restriction. American expansion utterly destroyed this possibility. Clearly now all the tribes could not live in their own "state" and whites had reason to enter the Indian refuge. There would soon be pressure to open large segments of the West once inhabited only by Indians and trappers. Under such circumstances officials of the Indian department began to see that two changes were necessary for the future survival of the tribes; they must be concentrated in smaller areas to make way for the advancing whites, and they must be closely supervised and isolated by the government until they learned the white man's ways. From these ideas were born the rudiments of the reservation system. Only the idea of racial segregation lingered on from the Indian barrier philosophy. It was still believed the two races could not live together in harmony.

The concept of moving the Indians away from possible areas of white expansion did not mature immediately—indeed, it had been brewing for some years. Moreover, the initiative came from field officers and was adopted by the commissioner only after he began to see it as part of a larger scheme. Thomas Harvey first brought the idea to Medill's attention in 1845 when he proposed clearing routes through some of the border tribes along the Missouri as the best means of keeping things quiet on the frontier (Chapter 6).[29] Obtaining rights of way through the Indian country appeared to have advantages for both sides. Moving the Indians away from the trails would safeguard the emigrants, while at the same time keeping the tribesmen away from the degrading influences of the American frontiersmen and enabling the Indian Office to concentrate on the civilization program.

Harvey's recommendations were not acted upon immediately. By early 1847, however, the commissioner was coming more and more to accept the theory that some of the frontier Indians must be removed elsewhere for their own good.[30] The continued intertribal warfare along the borders of Missouri and Iowa undoubtedly strengthened his concern. After one particularly gruesome Sioux massacre agent John Miller mournfully asked: "What will these poor Omahas do—will the Government do nothing for them?" The missionaries on the frontier also expressed concern for the fate of their wards, and their voices were something to be reckoned with. Edward McKinney, a worker among the Oto, wrote that unless the government acted soon, "their progress in civilization, or even their continued existence, is impossible." Although Medill took no immediate steps to bring relief to the stricken tribes he did commence working on a master plan for saving the border Indians.[31] Not only must they be moved, but something had to be done to provide permanent protection.

The emergence of a plan for Indian reservations, although at this time pertaining primarily to the border tribes, became public in Medill's annual report for 1848. It contained all the necessary ingredients: economy, humane concern for the Indians, segregation, and a safe route to the West.[32] The proposal renounced the concept of a barrier state and all the implications that went with it, except separation of the races. Medill suggested two reservations (called colonies) for the tribes standing in the way of expansion: "one north, on the headwaters of the Mississippi and the other south, on the western borders of Missouri and Arkansas." Establishment of the reservations would thus provide a gigantic corridor "opened for our population that may incline to pass or expand in that direction," and clear the desirable lands of the lower Platte valley of its native population. The report naturally stressed the advantages to the Indians. By colonizing the tribes away from the white population and confining them on small tracts of land their future survival would be assured. In line with most humanitarians of the day, the commissioner firmly believed in assimilation as the ultimate solution to the Indian problem. Thus on reservations, with no opportunity to pursue the old life, the adults could be gradually forced into agricultural pursuits. An educational system, in the form of manual labor schools, would also be imposed on the restricted people until they became civilized enough to be adopted into the mainstream of American life. These ideas, adopted officially in the 1848 report, mark the first major step on the way to a general policy of reservations. If such a system proved practical, the next step might be a similar plan for the more dangerous tribes of the high plains, and eventually the tribes of California, New Mexico, and Oregon when they officially came under the jurisdiction of the Indian Office.

A closer reading of Medill's solution to the Indian dilemma shows that the scheme also fitted a number of political considerations, and the proposed colonies were not designed solely to benefit the red men. The commissioner's reforms had won considerable praise in some Democratic circles and he had even been mentioned as a vice-presidential candidate.[33] Stress on economy in the new plan certainly promised to enhance his reputation. As a result, in proposing the reservations, Medill referred back to his earlier proposals for economies, stating that grouping the border tribes together in compact units "would admit of the discontinuance of a number of agents and subagents and thus lead to a considerable reduction in the amount paid for salaries, contingent expenses for agents, & c." By concentrating the Indians and also allowing the missionary societies more participation in the civilizing effort—and a number of religious groups were eager to assume more responsibility for the tribes—the government obligations and expenses could be further reduced. As Medill's philosophy in general equated good government with cheap government, the planned colonies thus coincided with his desire to serve the party.

Removing the border tribes from the lower Platte and Kansas valleys also agreed with the schemes of several influential western

senators, especially David R. Atchison of Missouri and Stephen
A. Douglas of Illinois, to secure a northern route for the contemplated Pacific railroad. To acquire the coveted route it seemed
clear that the lands west of Missouri and Iowa needed territorial
status. Since Congress was not likely to sponsor a route through
unorganized Indian country, some parts of the Indian barrier
must be removed. Those who favored this move had already
made their views known to the Indian department, and as time
went on they became more influential.[34] So while the colonization
idea stemmed partly from a concern for the welfare of the Indians, it also offered a solution well designed to further the interests of several important politicians. Here again emerges the fact
that such a policy would soon have to be expanded westward to
be effective. The lands inhabited by the powerful tribes further
up the Platte route must also be cleared before building a railroad.

The commissioner, enthralled with his reservations plan,
wasted no time trying to implement the financial aspects of it,
though without the knowledge of most congressmen. He prevailed upon Democratic Congressman James J. McKay of South
Carolina, to add a proviso to the Indian Appropriation Act of
1848 reducing the size of the Indian department. It read, in part:

That, for the Indians east of the Rocky Mountains, there shall be two
superintendencies of Indian affairs. . . . And the organization prescribed
by that act [1834] be further so modified that the number of agents
shall not exceed nine, and the number of sub-agents six, for all the
Indians east of the Rocky Mountains, except the Indians of Texas.[35]

But Medill put the cart before the horse by trying to reduce the
Indian department before actually solving the Indian difficulties
besetting the nation and by ignoring the fact that with the Mexican War now at an end all of the Southwest was now under
American control. The significant factor is not that the administration would fail to consider expanding the Indian service but
that some congressmen were incensed at such a proposal and
clearly hoped for more positive action.

When the representatives of the western states discovered Medill's attempt to limit the department they unleashed a furious attack on Indian policy. The frontiersmen wanted an effective organization designed to keep peace and were disturbed that no western sentiment had been consulted by the commissioner. On July 6, 1848, Robert W. Johnson, a Democrat from Arkansas, speaking for "those deeply concerned in this issue," rose to deliver in the House of Representatives a scathing denunciation of both the proposal and the commissioner. Johnson noted that a cutback in the Indian bureau opposed the trend of events. "Many additional tribes, by recent acquisition are thrown within our borders; many others, already ours, are in daily contact with our people upon the track of emigration to the shores of the Pacific. Our supervision for the security of our people should be extended, our agencies increased; yet this is a proposition to cut down the number, from twenty-nine to fifteen." Fewer agents, the frontier congressman thought, increased the possibility of hostilities erupting among the tribes as well as lessening protection for the new territories. Furthermore, fewer civilian officers meant more reliance on military force, and "where our intercourse had been conducted and sustained by force, bloodshed and war had been the consequence; and it had become apparent that the benign influences of a policy dictated in peace, were far best for the Indian, as well as preferable to us."[36]

The Arkansas Democrat also accused Medill of misconduct in office and having interests other than the welfare of the Indians. Johnson claimed that Medill's primary concern was his own political ambition and not conditions among the tribes. In particular, he said, the commissioner seemed quite willing to allow utter confusion on the frontier just so he could save his superiors the paltry sum of $11,650. Other western representatives, including Richard W. Thompson and William Rockhill of Indiana, and Frederick P. Stanton of Tennessee (all Democrats except Thompson), added their voices to the opposition. "The saving of $10,000 or $12,000," stated Stanton, "in carrying on the relations between these Indian tribes surely was of too small im-

portance to induce us to excite the least unfriendly feelings on
the part of these tribes." The only vigorous support for Medill's
plan came from the South, particularly from James J. McKay
(Democrat) and Daniel M. Barranger (Whig) of North Carolina.
Their arguments, typical of southern concern for economy in
government, were based on the savings that could be effected and
the idea that a reduction of personnel would help curtail the
power of the central government by eliminating executive patronage.[37] Although all these statements were somewhat exaggerated,
they do show that even during this period, when party loyalties
were still strong, party rhetoric did not necessarily apply to the
question of Indian policy. Westerners thought economy must be
secondary to protection and that the control of Indian affairs
should not be in the hands of easterners, no matter what their
party.

Trader criticism of the commissioner also made its way into
the House debate on Medill's bill. Several of the western representatives who denounced Medill for his reorganization plan also
used the occasion to attack the annuity system and the commissioner's alleged attempt to break the companies. Johnson, who
may or may not have been influenced by the lobbyists, attacked
the new mode of payment on the grounds that it tended to
destroy tribal government and the powers of the chiefs, obliter-
ated their national existence, worked against the U.S. government by weakening the influence of agents over tribal leaders,
and actually did nothing for the individual Indian, whose portion
of the annuity might be as little as a dollar and a half. Thompson, who was partial to trading interests, repeated everything the
traders were saying, charging Medill with improperly enforcing
regulations, using the new law to drive legitimate traders out of
the Indian country, and attempting to put the companies that
opposed him out of business. The commissioner of Indian affairs,
observed the Indiana Whig, "exercised a power which should be
confined to no man under our free government." Medill was defended against these accusations by William Rockhill (the man
who defeated William Ewing for Congress). Rockhill reviewed
some of the frauds committed by the Ewings and then asked if

perhaps Thompson had "some personal and pecuniary interest" in the matter.[38]

The result of the debate proved something of an anticlimax. Medill's proposal sailed through the northern-dominated House on July 8, 1848, by a vote of 110 to 61. Undoubtedly the primary motivation of many congressmen to vote for a reduction in the Indian department was the administration's belief that Congress, as a result of the debate over slavery, was not immediately going to create civilian governments in California and New Mexico. By this time the question of the extension of slavery into the new territories had arisen to prominence in Congress. As debate grew more heated, it became increasingly clear that neither side would willingly admit new territories until the slavery question had been solved. This impasse seemingly meant a continuation of military governments in time of peace. Polk believed that peace-time military governments were legitimate and until Congress established other governments, he refused to allow any civilian agencies to operate in the territories. So according to administration theory the Indian Office had no legal way of expanding. The Senate, on the other hand, while agreeing that the department could not legally expand into the new territories, did not wish to make any cutback as expansion must inevitably occur soon. Therefore, at a joint conference on July 25, the Senate rejected Medill's proposal without substituting one of its own.[39] When the Indian appropriation bill became law on July 29, 1848, it remained silent on any proposal to alter or expand the Indian Office, or to create any reservations. Matters remained in essence where they were in 1846, and although neither side recognized it, the slavery issue would complicate Indian affairs even more in the next few years.

Meanwhile Medill continued his battle with the trading companies over fraudulent claims and the illegal liquor trade. By April of 1848 pressure on the commissioner had become intense for him to act favorably on the debts allegedly owed the companies. According to previous instructions, the firms had submitted to the Indian Office for adjudication claims of $163,000, which they classified as "national debts." The Ewing brothers as well as lobbyists for several other companies all flocked to Washington to see that the claims were paid to the fullest by pressuring Congress and Secretary Marcy for a favorable decision. They also used all other means at their disposal to coerce the administration. In one instance, for example, they convinced Governor James Whitcomb and the entire Indiana legislature (where the Ewings had considerable sway) to petition the president to act favorably on their claims.[40] The actions of some congressmen on Medill's proposal to reorganize the Indian department, just occuring at this time, also indicate the traders were using this issue to their advantage.

Even thought criticism of him continued, Medill was determined to persist in the matter, and he was not without support from reform-minded friends. When he began examining the claims submitted by the traders, he listened to the advice of men like Joseph Sinclair, a former agent from Fort Wayne who had long favored a per capita system and was well versed in the nefarious ways of the traders.[41] As a result, Medill was tough on the traders, placing upon them the absolute burden of proving the debts were legitimate. In most instances the traders came up short. For example, in the case of the claims of the Ewings and James Clymer against the Potawatomi for $4,773, Medill rejected nearly the entire sum. His justification was "There is no data upon which to judge whether the charges are reasonable, as in many cases quantities and dates are not stated, and there is nothing to indicate the particular kinds or quantities of articles. . . . Thus, of the whole amount charged, there is only some $830 of which there is any specification or explanation whatever." Nearly all of the other thirty-two cases were rejected for the same basic reasons; the companies either failed to prove the debts were legitimate or were of a national character. In announcing these decisions Medill also noted that over the last few years "the enormous sum" of $721,066 had been paid to traders from annuity funds. It seemed incredible to him now, "in any just and proper system of trade," the traders could still be asking for more money.[42]

Though some of the commissioner's decisions were undoubtedly just and earned Medill a great deal of respect in some quarters, they also provoked the trading companies into more opposition. William G. Ewing, who had just lost his license to trade with the Sac and Fox as well as his claim against the Potawatomi, Sac and Fox, and Miami, launched an attack on Medill in the press and elsewhere, charging prejudice against the companies, and proposing that all claims should be removed from his jurisdiction and given to an impartial committee. Ewing also agreed to act for several other St. Louis houses as well as himself in encouraging the secretary of war or the president in overriding the decision. If Ewing's tactics poved successful, as Medill well knew, the "Scoundrels" had things so shaped that a reversal could be claimed as a confirmation of the commissioner's unfitness, and that he ought to be removed from office. In the field, the traders worked to make the whole annuity system inoperative by persuading the tribes to reject individual payments and, in some cases, by bribing agents to pay tribal funds directly to the traders.[43] Despite these tactics, Medill remained firm, and he was upheld by his superiors. All the traders could do was wait for the upcoming 1848 election and hope the present administration was replaced by one more responsive to their monetary interests.

The department's attempt to halt the liquor trade experienced mixed success. Medill had anticipated that the addition of imprisonment to the fines already in existence would produce the desired results, and in some cases this appears true.[44] Yet reports continued to come in from the field that the law was generally ineffective and the prevalence of alcohol was as great as ever. The trading companies, of course, continued to smuggle alcohol; but part of the problem, as Harvey explained to Medill in his report for October 1848, was not so much with whites taking liquor into the Indian country as it was with the close proximity of white settlers to Indian lands. Indians were able to slip into the adjoining states of Missouri or Iowa where numerous stills operated right on the border and purchase all the whiskey they could carry away. Such procedures meant that whites were not guilty of taking liquor into the Indian country. And, said Harvey, "the existing laws of the State of Missouri [and Iowa] on this subject of selling to Indians are so ineffective that it is difficult to convict the seller, or to punish him effectually if convicted."[45]

Any attempt by the federal government to prevent the production and sale of liquor in the border states immediately incited the sensitive question of state sovereignty. The Indian Office did attempt to use its influence to persuade the border states to reform their laws. Secretary Marcy in July 1847 wrote a pointed letter to the governors of the border states intimating that greater vigilance was required. Medill, in his 1848 report, again brought the matter to attention. Liquor, he wrote, "can never be checked until the States adjoining the Indian country come forward and cooperate in the general effort against this unholy and iniquitous traffic, by passing stringent laws, restraining the evil disposed among their citizens on the frontier from engaging in it with the Indians."[46] As long as frontier citizens saw no pressing need to limit the activities of whiskey sellers, the Indian Office met only with apathy. Faced with obvious state inaction, Superintendent Harvey recommended attacking the problem where the bureau possessed some authority, with the Indians. He, therefore, suggested arresting all intoxicated Indians and putting them to hard labor. Those who did not learn their lesson the first time and continued to purchase liquor should then be prosecuted under the law of 1847 and sent to prison.[47] Medill definitely saw some merit in this procedure and recommended it to Secretary Marcy. A few weeks later, however, Zachary Taylor and the Whigs swept the national elections and the plan died.

Just prior to the election, the Polk administration managed to break the sectional deadlock long enough to organize Oregon as a territory. Although far north, Oregon had been involved in the issue from the beginning. Southerners opposed the organization of this freesoil area unless they could be compensated with slave territory in the Southwest; and of course, many northerners stood pat on the Wilmot Proviso, thus creating a stalemate. Stephen A. Douglas was finally able to break the impass, partly as a result of the massacre of Marcus Whitman and the resulting Cayuse War of 1848, by proposing that the Missouri Compromise line be extended to the Pacific for the sake of determining Oregon's status.[48] This eventually proved successful, and on August 14, 1848, Congress passed an act organizing the Territory of Oregon. Joseph Lane, who was named governor, became ex officio superintendent of Indian affairs. But he did not arrive until March 1849 and there is no indication that the Indian Office gave him any material aid. The Democrats tried extremely hard during the last few months before Taylor's inauguration to pass territorial bills for California and New Mexico, but the slavery issue made it impossible. Thus to the end of Polk's tenure the Indian Office did not extend itself into any of the new territories.

In retrospect, then, despite the great territorial acquisitions during the Polk years and the resultant changes in national responsibility for Indian relations, only limited changes were attempted by the Indian Office. Medill concentrated most of his energies on the reforms he felt were necessary and proper and did not attempt to use the Office in any imaginative way to meet the demands created by expansion. Though the commissioner could be a crusading and effective reformer when he was sure of his position, he refused to challenge Congress on the fuzzy question of assuming jurisdiction for all the new tribes just being brought under the spread eagle. However, the commissioner's report of 1848 outlining the general ideas for a reservation system, would have lasting significance by providing a guide for succeeding administrations to follow.

3

Toward a Reservation System:
Whig Indian Policy, 1849-51

❧ On March 4, 1849, the mantle of Indian responsibility was handed over to the Whig party, which in the past had earned something of a reputation for being more kindly disposed than the Democrats toward the red men. By the time the party managed to regain power the expansion of the 1840's had ended. Yet although the physical aspirations of the American people had been attained, none of the attendant complications of Indian-white relations even remotely approached solution. The Indians, once presenting an unbroken barrier against the advancing Americans, were now surrounded by whites and their country bisected by routes of travel. The Whigs were accordingly confronted with frontier citizens who wanted effective federal protection, an increasingly angry Indian population, and a number of special interest groups who hoped to use Indian policy to their advantage. Since the Whigs themselves had often been outspoken in their criticism of Indian affairs under the Democratic regime, they were also under considerable political pressure to provide a workable solution to Indian problems.

From the beginning the Taylor administration attempted to adjust Indian affairs to reality. Expansion was a fact and the frontier population needed protection, even if it meant bending the will of Congress. The Indians must be moved from the vicinity of white men lest they be exterminated. And the political status of California and New Mexico had to be determined before any regular Indian policy could operate in those territories. Although the changes proposed and carried out were not revolutionary or even original—in nearly every instance they stemmed from ideas proposed by the preceding administrations—some Whigs were at least willing to act, and the results constituted the first positive steps toward reorganizing the Indian department and the beginning of a policy of permanent Indian reservations.

Inauguration day also brought another new element to federal Indian affairs, the Department of the Interior. The idea of creating a home department and placing the Office of Indian Affairs under it originated during the last days of Polk's administration and quickly became a reality. On December 11, 1848, outgoing Secretary of the Treasury Robert J. Walker suggested to Congress that a new cabinet post be created to handle a variety of existing agencies. Influenced by an overoptimistic evaluation of the state of Indian relations, Walker believed the Indian bureau might be removed from the War Department, since the duties of the office should pertain more to peace than war.[1]

The Democrats quickly brought the bill before Congress. Though the proposal contained a number of controversial items and most of the debate centered on the question of how much patronage the new department created, Indian affairs did receive its share of discussion. Opposition to the proposal centered on the nature of the Indian problem. "Who," noted John C. Calhoun, "does not see that the Indian affairs are immediately connected with the War Department? Who does not see that the preservation of peace and harmony on our frontier, both between ourselves and the Indians, and between the Indian tribes themselves, depends upon the action of the War Department." Those favoring the new department believed that Indian warfare was drawing to an end and, as the Indians were transformed from enemies to wards of society, governmental responsibility rightly belonged in the hands of civilians.[2]

In a late night session on March 3, 1849, the Senate approved the creation of the Department of the Interior and transferred the Indian affairs to that office. The vote indicated that neither party saw any great objection to the department, although representatives of the frontier states, perhaps partly because of their proximity to Indian hostilities, generally cast their ballots in opposition.[3] Of course changing the administrative procedure did little to alter the basic foundation of Indian policy: in reality the Indian Office had always operated separately from the military branch, quite often in direct opposition. With the establishment of the Department of the Interior, the army retained primary responsibility for hostile tribes while the Indian Office concentrated on formulating general policy for peaceable or subdued tribes.

The Taylor administration pursued a more energetic Indian policy from the beginning. The selection of Thomas Ewing, "The Old Salt Boiler," as the first secretary of the interior placed a forceful personality in charge of Indian affairs. Ewing, a longtime Whig Senator from Ohio, was one of Taylor's strongest backers. Obese and somewhat fearful looking, he believed, like the president, that California and New Mexico ought to be brought into the Union without hesitation. He also fully approved of the spoils system.[4] Except for the month between the inauguration and the death of Harrison the Whigs had never really controlled government patronage. The party, with Ewing in the lead, was now ready to pay off past debts. And since he was directly responsible for the Indian Office it should not be surprising that changes there came with ruthless rapidity.

Ewing found himself under great pressure to make the "right" appointments. Representatives of the trading companies were in Washington to see that men favorable to their claims were employed. Most of the concern centered upon Medill's replacement, but men such as Superintendent Harvey were also on the traders' black list. Ewing responded to these requests and in the first month of the new administration nearly every significant field officer was replaced. Regrettably, this purge included most of the able men in the Indian service. But much to the consternation of the traders, Ewing did not remove Medill at once. "The Scamp Medill is not yet removed," wrote George Ewing from Washington in disgust.[5] The traders really had nothing to fear, however. With the Whigs in control, Medill's continuation in office was a matter of little significance since Secretary Ewing (he was distantly related to the Ewing brothers) intended to set policy for the Indian Office and not allow the commissioner the full responsibility he had enjoyed under the secretary of war. Therefore, Medill, whose job President Taylor wanted to keep open for political reasons, had the experience of remaining in office while Ewing began overturning his reforms.

Indeed, one of the first items on Ewing's agenda was the reopening of all the claim cases that Medill had declared null or fraudulent. The new czar of Indian affairs saw no reason to invite trader opposition to his policies. Thus on April 7, 1849, Ewing ordered Medill to deliver for additional investigation all papers and evidence concerning the claims of Pierre Chouteau, W. G. & G. W. Ewing, James Clymer, and the rest. The interior secretary himself reviewed the cases. His decision in nearly every instance was to overturn Medill's ruling and pay off the traders. Within a year all the claims were settled. Although the exact amount of the settlement is impossible to determine, most of the claims were adjusted to the pecuniary benefit of the trading companies. At the same time Ewing quietly dropped the provision that annuities be paid to heads of families, in effect allowing the trading companies to regain much of their old influence over the chiefs.[6]

The Whig changes in personnel were attended by other significant and far-reaching steps. On March 31, 1849, Ewing began the first of a series of moves to provide needed agents for the frontier. This also coincided with the attempts of Taylor to provide civil governments for the Mexican Cession without involving Congress or the issue of slavery. The president and many of his advisers believed that only a little encouragement from Washington was necessary for the citizens of California and New Mexico to proceed on their own, form a state government, draft a constitution, and then simply present themselves to Congress for admission to the Union. This process would allow the territories to decide for themselves the matter of slavery and perhaps avoid a disastrous discussion of the Wilmot Proviso in Congress. One means of subtly demonstrating official encouragement of this process would be for the administration to intervene in California and New Mexico to end total military authority and introduce civilian institutions of government. Ewing made just such a move through the Indian Office. By using the power implied in the act of June 30, 1834, he moved several of the existing Indian agencies westward. Within the first week of April the Upper Missouri Agency was transferred to Salt Lake in "California" and the Council Bluffs Agency moved to Santa Fe, New Mexico. The incumbent agents were retired and loyal Taylor men sent to the new outposts. Ewing, in addition, used the presidential prerogative of appointing a subagent for the Gila valley in New Mexico and two subagents for California.[7] These alterations provided the first civilian administrators for the lands of the Mexican Cession.

The blatant use of patronage in the Office of Indian Affairs and the placement of civilian officers in the Mexican Cession resulted in a flood of Democratic criticism. The ousted party quickly recalled that Taylor had campaigned on a nonpartisan approach, which seemingly implied the new administration would not be composed of spoilsmen. Now, they moaned (with some accuracy), the Whigs having attained office by deception all nonpartisan ideas were dropped and the Taylor regime was proceeding to decide all matters on strict party lines. Since Ewing was enthusiastically sweeping Democrats out of all the offices under his control, particular attention was drawn to the appointment of Indian agents. The Washington *Daily Union* said it would not be surprised if all disappointed Whigs who could not find an office elsewhere became Indian subagents: "There are the Sagahannocks, Woggoaches, Rootapoogies, and others, hundreds of wild Indians in Texas, New Mexico, California, and between the States and those countries, all of whom should have a Whig sub-agent or two."[8]

Ewing's expansion of the Indian department became a hot political issue during the summer of 1849. "The chief butcher of the cabinet," as the Democrats enjoyed calling the interior secretary, was roundly condemned for sending agents into territories not yet organized by Congress. Part of the attack was typically political in nature, simply charging that good men were being replaced by Whig rascals and incompetents. Another Democratic argument of the same sort, which in several embarrassing instances proved true, was that the administration was allowing Whigs to conduct "gold-mining expeditions" in California by paying their way as Indian agents.[9] Aside from these accusations, other more fundamental questions were brought forward. The real question, as the *Daily Union* pointed out, was whether the government could extend to the new territories the Indian trade and intercourse acts when other civilian laws did not yet apply. New Mexico and California, as everyone knew, remained unorganized due to the slavery stalemate and, to the Democrats as well as some southern Whigs, it appeared highly illegal to extend civilian control to those lands. "It is known to the country that there is no law in New Mexico and California but military law." The Democrats also questioned whether the Indian acts of 1834 gave anyone except Congress the power to transfer agents into territory acquired at a later date.[10] Under these circumstances the opposition did not believe that new agents, even if appointed, could be empowered to act on behalf of the national government.

The Taylor administration insisted that under various provisions of the acts of 1834 they had every right to transfer agencies.[11] However, the uncertain status of the new territories and the fact that many more agencies were needed caused Ewing to change his approach and begin constructing a legislative program authorizing legal expansion of the department.

In the meantime, Taylor named Orlando Brown of Kentucky to replace William Medill as commissioner of Indian affairs. The appointment became effective on June 30, 1849. Much like the case of Medill, Brown's appointment came for political reasons. Until the nomination, the Whig faction in Kentucky, led by John J. Crittenden, had been ignored in Washington. Since Brown was a close personal and political friend of the powerful Kentucky governor, he was expected to spend most of his term dispensing patronage and advising the president. In congratulating Brown on his placement as the *"great sachem,"* Crittenden took special pains to underline the political advantages Kentucky Whigs might secure from this office. Thus Orlando Brown's appointment had nothing to do with Indian affairs. The major difference between him and the outgoing Medill lay in ambition. Brown, a quiet, humble, and respected country gentleman, entertained few political aspirations.[12] Never, before his arrival in Washington, did he display any knowledge of or concern for Indian policy. Taking into account these circumstances it is not surprising to find that Ewing continued to formulate and execute Indian policy.

Despite the obvious fact that Ewing still ran Indian affairs, the selection of a new commissioner naturally pleased some and disturbed others. George Ewing wrote to Pierre Chouteau, Jr., on June 13, 1849, that "The *villain* Medill is *kicked* out, good— He & the hypocrite Harvey can now console each other in their retirement."[13] Undoubtedly Ewing spoke for most traders. Others stood up for Medill, praised his conduct, and hoped Brown would serve the nation half as well. The Cincinnati *Enquirer*, in particular, hoped Brown would be able to withstand "the brow-beatings of members of Congress, who are shameless enough to act as agents for claims against that Bureau."[14]

The activities of Secretary Ewing during his first few months in office made it abundantly clear that he was not interested in the types of reform that Medill had considered significant. Cracking down on traders would not solve the real problems. Other things seemed more important to the Whigs and when the administration settled down to implementing a policy the major emphasis was on separating the races and restricting the nomadic tendencies of the tribesmen. To this extent, however, they did adopt ideas first expressed by the preceding administration.

The question of how to deal with the powerful tribes living near the Rockies was the first to present itself. A few days before leaving office, Medill, in an official letter to Ewing, suggested a need for protecting the large body of emigrants heading for the gold fields of California via the Oregon and Santa Fe trails. Medill had undertaken the move at the behest of the new superintendent at St. Louis, David Dawson Mitchell, an old fur trader and Indian fighter, who was repeating much of what Harvey had contemplated for the past two years. The letter noted that the plains tribes were growing restless over the white invasion of their country and argued that a move on the part of the federal government had now become imperative. Concluding that the natural state of these Indians was one of war and that they could not be expected to abstain from molesting white travelers without some rather strong inducements, the outgoing commissioner recommended a generous treaty with the potentially hostile tribes to buy a right of way through their country.[15] If such a peaceful agreement were arranged, reasoned Medill, then perhaps hostilities could be avoided and the white advance might continue unimpeded.

Secretary Ewing agreed to the proposition and instructed Brown, who had just taken office, to carry it out. However, somewhere in the transition a new element was added. By mid-August Brown was discussing ideas that carried beyond Medill's original suggestions for the plains tribes. Of special notice in regard to the proposed treaty is the comment that "there should also be a clear and definite understanding as to the general boundaries of the sections of the country respectively claimed by them, as their residence & hunting grounds; & they should be required not to trespass upon those of each other without permission from the occupant tribes, or from the proper Agent or agents of the government."[16] In addition to the designated tribal lands, Brown thought a common hunting ground might be set aside for all tribes to use. These ideas were the first concrete proposals by federal policy makers for establishing a permanent reservation for the nomadic tribes of the prairie—for restricting them to well-defined lands instead of a vague general area.

The Indian bureau hoped the treaty for this purpose could be signed before the year ended, but circumstances made impossible any gathering of the tribes, and the commissioner decided to wait until the following summer before calling the great council. In the meantime, Mitchell received instructions to make all the necessary preparations, including the selection of twenty high-ranking chiefs who were to be given a grand tour of the United States upon conclusion of the treaty. By fall the scope of the proposed treaty was enlarged to include the Indians of Texas and New Mexico; this, if carried into effect, would have established permanent and well-defined lands for nearly all the plains tribes.[17]

As plans for the great council matured, the Indian department also revived former commissioner Medill's proposed northern and southern colonies for the border tribes of the Missouri. "The smaller tribes scattered along the frontier," wrote Brown in his annual report, "embracing the Sacs and Foxes of the Missouri, the Iowas, the Omahas, the Ottoes, and Missourias, the Poncas and if possible the Pawnees—should be moved down among the tribes of our southern colony, where suitable situations may be found for them, in connexion with other Indians of kindred stock."[18] If the two colonies could be put into operation a wide area of country along the middle Missouri would be opened to white expansion. The removal of the border tribes in conjunction with the assignment of specific lands to the plains tribes thus promised to protect the Indians from advancing Americans and to clear a path across the middle of the country to the Pacific.

In order to meet the added responsibilities such a program would entail, the commissioner and Secretary Ewing proposed a general reorganization and enlargement of the Indian department. In his 1849 report, Brown stressed the lack of changes since 1834. He stated that the department was utterly incapable of handling the duties now devolving on it, that responsibility for the tribes was much greater than before, that transactions with them had multiplied, and that "a large number have been added to our jurisdiction in Texas, Oregon, California, and New Mexico." A completely new system of superintendents seemed desirable to effect the necessary expansion. The only full superintendency then in existence, covering all the tribes west of the Mississippi, was entirely inadequate. The other superintendencies were either territorial governors or agents handling joint duties. Though such an arrangement might have been acceptable before expansion, the vast territory of the Far West called for several

independent superintendencies. Brown, therefore, suggested ending the practice of making governors ex officio superintendents.
Neither governors nor agents were capable of devoting full time
to the execution of these duties. He recommended instead "that
authority be given for the establishment of seven full and independent superintendencies: four for the Indians east of the
Rocky mountains, including those of Texas, . . . and one each
for the Territories of Oregon, California, and New Mexico."[19]

The current provisions for Indian agents were also deemed de-
fective. By law there could only be twelve agents and this number
was simply inadequate. However, since the size of the Indian population in much of the Far West had yet to be determined the
department decided not to make specific requests until more information could be gathered. All Brown asked at this point was
at least four agents for every territory plus two full agents for
Texas.[20]

Although this program was the first realistic approach to ac-
commodating the Indian bureau to the needs of the post-
expansion period, it was not destined to have smooth sailing.
Congress still had to give its stamp of approval, and Indian policy
was unfortunately involved with other controversial issues. Of
primary importance was the sectional conflict between the North
and South, at this time reaching a peak over the question of
slavery and civilian government in the newly acquired territories.
There was also the issue of the Pacific railroad. Americans, both
North and South, looked forward to the great day when rails
would stretch across the continent, but both sections wanted the
railroad to run through their territory. Since any northern railroad would have to run across Indian country, Indian policy
naturally became an issue of sectional concern. Thus when the
Thirty-First Congress convened in December 1849, the department's proposals for clearing routes through the Indian lands
and extending Indian regulations over the new territories became intertwined with the sectional debate.

Although the department realized the attitude of Congress was
not particularly favorable, it decided to present its plans and
hope for the best. One of the most pressing needs was to obtain

funds for the upcoming treaty with the plains tribes. Accordingly, Brown drew up a bill requesting $200,000 for presents and the other expenses concomitant to such a large undertaking and handed it to David R. Atchison of the Senate Committee on Indian Affairs, who had agreed to steer it through the Senate. Atchison presented the bill on March 18, 1850.[21]

David Atchison must surely have been pleased to see Brown's bill since it contained items of keen interest to him. Long an advocate of a Pacific railroad, the Missouri senator was at the time promoting the interests of the Hannibal and St. Joseph Railroad, which aspired to build westward into the Indian country (and perhaps to the Pacific).[22] A significant portion of that route would be opened to a railroad if the treaty with the tribes of the Platte were carried into effect. Other expansionists backed Atchison. For example, Stephen A. Douglas, chairman of the influential Senate Committee on Territories, and desirous of a railway from Chicago to the Pacific, had already proposed a similar treaty. Earlier in the session, on December 31, 1849, he had introduced a resolution requesting the Senate Indian Affairs Committee to inquire into the expediency of extinguishing Indian title to large sections of the Far West and establishing reservations where the "Indians may be permanently located and protected." Douglas' concern of course was more for clearing possible routes for a railroad than helping the Indians. Thus the Indian department's proposed treaty clearly fitted in with the plans for a northern railroad, a fact which Secretary Ewing well recognized.[23]

The treaty appropriation bill received enough support from northern Whigs and expansionist Democrats to pass the Senate on April 30, 1850. When the measure came to the House, Ohio Whig John Crowell took the lead and tried to get the bill passed by telling his colleagues that the treaty "would be attended with the most salutary results," and save the government millions by preventing an Indian war. By this time, however, the House was completely embroiled in the furious debate over the extension of slavery. As Congress hammered out the ingredients of the compromise of 1850 in an atmosphere of high emotions and short tempers, all issues of secondary importance were neglected. Consequently the House passed over the bill without taking action.[24] The Indian department was thus forced, much to its embarrassment, to postpone the treaty for another year. So the first part of Ewing's reform program foundered on the rocks of sectionalism.

At the same time the treaty bill was coming to naught, the Indian Office proceeded with the rest of its congressional program by drawing up several bills to reorganize the Indian service. Ewing was especially anxious for the passage of these bills both because he believed more agents were desperately needed and because he saw an opportunity to aid Taylor's plan for resolving sectional difficulties. As has been noted, both Taylor and Ewing favored encouraging the people of California and New Mexico to proceed by themselves in forming their own state constitutions and then seeking admission. Ewing had moved two Indian agencies west in 1849 to help foster this movement. Taylor then took up the matter by sending T. Butler King and Colonel George McCall as his personal representatives to encourage statehood.[25] Now the interior secretary saw another chance to help the president with the reorganization bill. If more Indian agencies could be established it might serve as a further demonstration of presidential support and encourage the people to continue their statemaking efforts. And, if Congress could be persuaded to approve these measures, it would be a victory for the hard-pressed administration forces and pave the way for congressional acceptance of the new states.

In writing the reorganization bills the Indian Office first needed to determine the exact number of agents and superintendents required, the geographical locations of the new offices, and other specific changes. Indian turmoil existed in all the new territories, and the few agents Ewing had sent out in 1849 were not able to do much more than report the depredations. In planning for the new agents Commissioner Brown was keenly aware of the role such officers must play in promoting peace and stability. While admitting that military force was still a necessity, he predicted that future peaceful relations with the Indians depended on effective agents. "It is by and through such officers," he told Hugh N. Smith of New Mexico, "that our Indian relations must be directly managed and controlled; and it is deemed that an adequate number be provided for by Congress as early as possible."[26]

Brown listened to the advice of his field officers as well as other experts in deciding on the exact number of new officers required. From New Mexico, for example, agent Calhoun sent word that at least one agent for each of the four major tribes was necessary. He also specifically recommended the establishment of well-defined reservations where the Indians could be kept under supervision. These proposals closely coincided with department thinking and undoubtedly strengthened the idea that reservations were a necessity. Consequently, the commissioner finally recommended five agents, who were to be assigned to individual tribes, and an independent superintendent for the territory to oversee all operations. Must the same happened with California and Oregon, and for each area the department sought three agents and a superintendent independent of the governor's office.[27] Texas presented additional difficulties. Continual Indian outrages there brought demands on the government to strengthen its inadequate peacekeeping efforts (Chapter 4). Mexican officials also put pressure upon the United States to restrain the Indians of Texas from crossing the international border in violation of the treaty of Guadalupe Hidalgo. As a result, the department finally recommended the appointment of two additional agents to supplement the one special agent already in Texas. To assure the effectiveness of these agents, a bill was introduced into the Senate to extend the Indian interourse laws to the Texas Indians.[28]

In all, then, the Indian Office asked for thirteen new agents, three superintendents, and the extension of the intercourse acts. The proposals were presented to Congress in early 1850 in the form of four bills, one each for Oregon, California, New Mexico, and Texas. Like the treaty appropriation request, these bills soon ran up against congressional opposition. Congressmen were too busy discussing the Wilmot Proviso and Henry Clay's proposed compromise to devote much time to Indian affairs, despite pressure from the administration. And, when they did consider the matter, the forces opposed to Taylor were able to muster enough strength to postpone departmental requests until the territorial issue was resolved. Congress was not going to have anything to do with Taylor's plan to resolve difficulties. The proof is overwhelming, said the Democratic Washington *Union*, that Taylor intended "to interfere with the political affairs of the people of New Mexico [and California, it might have added], with the view of inciting them to form a government prematurely, and apply for admission to the Union."[29] The sole victory for the department came in the one area completely removed from any sectional controversy. Oregon had been a territory since 1848 and its status was therefore not questioned when its bill came before Congress. Accordingly, an act on June 2, 1850, established an independent superintendency in Oregon, allowed up to three agents, and extended the Indian Intercourse Act of 1834 over the territory.[30] Since this bill embodied all the proposals so eagerly desired for New Mexico, California, and Texas, it is evident that there was little opposition to the proposals themselves, only to extending the agencies of the federal government before Congress acted on the slavery question.

As if the department did not have enough trouble in the spring of 1850, the question of claims also became a political issue. Actually, the matter had been brewing for some time. It had become public knowledge that Secretary Ewing intended to ignore the annuity provisions of the act of 1847. Almost as soon as he was settled in office he had begun paying old claims to the trading companies. In addition, he issued orders in May 1849 that tribes could have their annuities paid directly to traders upon request.[31] With many chiefs controlled by the traders, this was tantamount to allowing payment of the money at the traders' discretion. It was impossible to expect that the Democrats, still praising Medill for attempting to limit the abuses of trading companies, would let the issue pass.

Unfortunately, much of the criticism unjustly fell on Orlando Brown. Brown was unhappy in Washington from the start. He and Ewing never got along together. The interior secretary was distinctly cool to his subordinate, and the political power Brown hoped to use in Kentucky's interest was largely negated by Ewing's tight reign on departmental patronage. There are hints also that Brown did not much approve of Ewing's activities in regard to the trading companies, although he did not disagree in public. Brown's discomfort was made complete when the Cincinnati *Enquirer*, on September 8, 1849, charged the commissioner with incompetence and corruption because he had allowed payment of many of the claims rejected by Medill. Although Brown's friends came to his rescue by pointing out that the claims had been decided by Ewing, the impact served to disillusion the sensitive commissioner to the point where he was ready to submit his resignation. Only the pleadings of Crittenden and others not to desert "Old Zack" kept Brown in Washington.[32]

As it became increasingly evident that Ewing was responsible for paying off the companies, public attention focused more on him. In April 1850, the House, under the leadership of Democratic Congressman William A. Richardson of Illinois, initiated an investigation of Ewing on charges of corruption in office. One of the complaints was that the interior secretary had reopened a claim declared invalid by Medill and had paid the Ewing brothers, men who knew how to "perpetrate as gross frauds as any people in the world," some $77,000 in back claims. These charges were basically true, although the figure quoted by the Democrats was probably exaggerated. It is known, for example, that the department paid nearly $16,000, the entire Sac and Fox claim, to Chouteau and Ewing in March 1850. When the secretary appeared before Congress he denied the specific charges but did admit to paying the traders Indian annuity funds on other occasions. These actions he defended on grounds that the law of 1847 gave the president or secretary of war (now the secretary of the interior) discretion in such matters and that he simply used that prerogative in calling up the old claims.[33] While nothing came of the investigation, probably because Ewing's interpretation of the law was technically if not morally correct, the department's cooperation with the traders continued to give opponents an issue in opposing Indian policy.

Zachary Taylor died unexpectedly in July, and his passing opened the door for a break in the stalemate over Indian policy.

By September the Compromise of 1850 had settled the sectional issue, leaving Congress free to discuss other issues. At least one of the department's problems was solved by the Compromise itself. As part of the sectional package, the Utah Territorial Act and the New Mexico Territorial Act were signed into law on September 9, 1850.[34] According to the terms of both bills, the territorial governor also became ex officio superintendent of Indian affairs. Although this did not create the independent superintendencies desired by the department, at least the Office of Indian Affairs obtained for the first time congressional sanction for extending departmental responsibilities into the Mexican Cession. Unfortunately, Congress, in a rush to end the session after ten months of bitter debate, failed to make any provision for the appointment of agents.

Congress did do something about the Texas situation, however. One of its last acts before adjournment was to pass the much delayed Indian Appropriations Act of 1850. To this act the Indian department added an amendment granting two more special agents for Texas and an authorization to conclude a new treaty with the Indians of that state. The House and Senate concurred and the act became effective on September 30, 1850. On October 15, three commissioners were ordered to Texas to meet with the Indians. Once among the Indians they were to conclude a treaty and bring peace to that frontier. In addition, "the object is to look to you for all material to guide it [the department] in its future action in conducting its Indian and other relations in that country."[35] These instructions implied that the department wanted to establish reservations in Texas (Chapter 4).

By the end of 1850, then, only fragments of the Whig Indian policy had been achieved. During the latter half of that year a number of changes occurred in the leadership of the Indian department. Not unexpectedly, Orlando Brown departed first. By the end of June the commissioner of Indian affairs had taken all he could of life in Washington and resigned. Despite the fact that Crittenden wished to pick Brown's successor, the administration selected its own candidate, Luke Lea of Mississippi. Lea, a relatively unknown Whig politician who had failed in an at-

tempt to gain the governorship of Mississippi in 1849, had no experience with Indians. He assumed office on July 1, 1850, and his
penny-pinching attitude quickly brought him into disrepute
among some members of the department.[36] The second important change came immediately after Taylor's death, when Thomas
Ewing, seeing that his services in the Fillmore administration
were not required, resigned on July 22, 1850, to resume his Senate seat.[37] Alexander H. H. Stuart, a Virginia Whig, was named
as the new secretary of the interior. Although Ewing's departure
allowed the Indian commissioner to regain more control over Indian affairs, the changes brought no revolution in policy. Both
Stuart and Lea rapidly committed themselves to bringing to a
successful conclusion the proposals planned by Ewing and the department.

Lea quickly adopted the idea of reservations for all tribes on
the frontier. Only by forcing the Indians to cease their wandering
ways, the commissioner believed, could "the great work of regen-
erating the Indian race" be accomplished. In the most specific
plan to date—and one which indicates the adoption of a commitment to the idea of reservations—Lea spelled out the benefits of
restricting the frontier tribes in his annual report for 1850:

There should be assigned to each tribe, for a permanent home, a
country adapted to agriculture, of limited extent and well-defined
boundaries; within which all, with occasional exceptions, should be
compelled constantly to remain until such time as their general
improvement and good conduct may supersede the necessity of such
restrictions. In the mean time the government should cause them
to be supplied with stock, agricultural implements, and useful materials
for clothing; encourage and assist them in the erection of comfortable
dwellings, and secure to them the means and facilities of education,
intellectual, moral, and religious.[38]

To fulfill these objectives and put the program in operation,
the rest of the Whig program needed the approval of Congress.
Lea therefore strongly urged the legislators to approve agents for
New Mexico and Utah, to appropriate money to conclude a
treaty with the plains Indians, and to give the department complete jurisdicton over the Indians of Texas. Since the tribes of

New Mexico and Texas were still in a state of war, their reservations would have to be established by military force in cooperation with the Indian Office. In this conclusion President Fillmore, Secretary of War Charles M. Conrad, and Stuart all agreed. It was also clearly indicated that the government felt that civilian policy must dominate. Conrad, for example, noted that military force could be only a temporary expedient and that the civilian branch of the government must eventually handle the reservations. "It is obvious," he stated, "that some other means besides the terror of our arms must ultimately be employed to restrain the Indians."[39]

When Congress met again in December 1850, the Indian department resumed its attempt to have the service reorganized in such a manner as to implement the reservation idea. For a while it seemed as if Congress would not act, and as late as January the commissioner reported no activity in the congressional committees. But working together with Congressman Robert W. Johnson of Arkansas, Lea finally got his proposals before Congress. Johnson, it will be recalled, had long been the spokesman for frontier interests and had opposed attempts by his own party to reduce the Indian department in 1848. He now held the office of chairman of the House Committee on Indian Affairs. On February 20, 1851, Johnson introduced a group of amendments to the Indian appropriations bill. "The object of the series of amendments which I shall offer is to effect that organization of the Indian Department which the changed relation of our Government, her very considerable acquisition of territory, the increased number of tribes, and the amount of responsibility require."[40]

Johnson's amendments embodied most of the department's earlier proposals. The old system of superintendents would be done away with and replaced by full superintendencies for "the Indian tribes east of the Rocky Mountains, and north of New Mexico and Texas." The bill recommended the establishment of three independent superintendencies for the tribes west of the Mississippi, but not including the Mexican Cession. The salary of these officers would be set at $2,000. In lieu of the twenty-three agents and subagents then operating in the above territory, the

President would have the authority to appoint seventeen agents (eleven major agents at $1500 and six minor agents at $1000), and the office of subagent would be abolished. In New Mexico and Utah, the office of ex officio superintendent would remain a responsibility of the territorial governor. However, the president would be allowed to appoint four agents for New Mexico and one for Utah at an annual compensation of $1550. The federal trade and intercourse laws would also be extended over the two territories.[41]

House debate on the Johnson amendments presented the specter of Democrats defending the measures and a Whig opposing them. Willard P. Hall of Missouri and several other frontier Democrats agreed on all measures. The only real opposition came in a heated exchange between Edward W. McGaughey, a Whig from Indiana, and Johnson. McGaughey opposed the measures because they increased the expenses of government. He particularly disliked the increased salaries for superintendents and agents. When Johnson remarked that the bill actually reduced the number of officers in the old Indian country and higher salaries would provide more efficiency, the Indiana representative retorted that this might be true at the moment but soon the commissioner would want more agents and the whole affair was bound to snowball. Johnson replied simply and to the point. We must look forward, he said, not backward. "Who is so preposterous as to expect all the new territories and hundreds of new tribes, numerous and warlike, to be embraced under the old or any other system without increased expense and additional offices."[42] The House agreed with Johnson and approved the amendments. Senate concurrence came several days later.

On February 27, 1851, the Indian Appropriation Act became law, including all of Johnson's amendments for enlarging the Indian department.[43] Six long years after American expansion began and three years after the United States officially acquired the Mexican Cession, Congress finally approved an Indian department designed to meet existing conditions. Now the Indians could be collected on reservations and looked after by the federal government.

The Indian bureau wasted no time implementing the reorganization. Three full superintendencies—Southern, Central, and Northern—were created for the tribes east of the Rocky Mountains. The Southern superintendency replaced the old Western superintendency and was held responsible largely for the tribes living in Oklahoma. The Northern office was established to handle the Indians still residing in Wisconsin and Michigan. The Central superintendency succeeded the St. Louis superintendency and retained jurisdiction over the border tribes of the Missouri and the tribes along the Platte and Arkansas. David D. Mitchell, the St. Louis superintendent, assumed control of the Central office. The commissioner, in accordance with the provisions of the act, also appointed one agent for Utah and four for New Mexico, thus rounding out the department.[44]

During the same session the legislature also came through with an appropriation to enable the Indian department to negotiate the long desired treaty with the mountain and prairie tribes. With Atchison at the helm, Congress granted $100,000 to secure peace on the frontier and clear the native population from the trails westward. Lea immediately authorized Mitchell to go ahead with the treaty. His instructions leave no doubt the department hoped to force these tribes onto some sort of reserve. All the western tribes heretofore without official relations with the United States were to be signed. As "a portion of the tribes own or claim to own the country through which the inland routes pass to Oregon, California, Utah, and New Mexico," they must relinquish these lands for the passage of Americans. Furthermore, a fixed boundary for each tribe would henceforth be assigned and the "strongest inducements should be held out to the Indians to resort to agriculture & the raising of stock."[45]

The summer of 1851 accordingly brought to the Indian department the necessary implements for the commencement of a limited reservation system. By now also a definite reservation psychology can be noted in the thinking of government officials responsible for Indian affairs, and this basic attitude remained until all tribes were placed on reservations. Most aspects of the modern reservation system had therefore been studied and accepted by 1851. The government had proposed, for the first time, wholesale restrictions on the nomadic habits of the frontier tribes by concentrating them all on defined sanctuaries. As this move necessarily limited ancient tribal means of subsistence, the tribesmen were encouraged to adopt agriculture and other aspects of the white man's civilization, and these seemed best taught in a reservation atmosphere. Segregation on reserves also required an enlargement and reorganization of the Indian bureau. Before expansion, the existence of one large Indian barrier implied that the Indians could live together without much supervision. But acceptance of the idea of concentration brought added responsibilities and required more agents, farmers, and teachers to protect and civilize the tribes. The national government recognized this now, although perhaps not at the same time realizing the full extent of the responsibilities entailed in such an undertaking.

Yet the idea of reservations as it grew from 1846 to 1851 was premature. Although in every area of the Far West the reservation idea received general support, factors in each individual area dictated whether or not reservations would be attempted, whether or not they would be limited or extensive in scope, and whether or not they would prove successful. It will thus be necessary in the following chapters to study in some detail the situation of each of the four selected frontier areas from 1846 to 1851 to see why reservations were required and why local factors impeded their initial success.

4

Reservations or Removal:
Texas and the Government

❧ Texas provides an interesting example of the difficulties the
federal government found in applying its general policy to a particular geographical area. Indian affairs in Texas during the era
of Manifest Destiny tended to suffer from a number of problems
originating out of past events. An assortment of tribes resided on
the Texas plains. These included Comanche, Kiowa, Lipan
Apache, Waco, Caddo, Wichita, and others, many of them fierce
and warlike. Like other Indians in the Southwest, most of these
natives had had prior contact with Europeans: Spaniards, Mexicans, and Anglo-Americans. As a result, by the time Texas entered the Union in December 1845, Indian-white relations had
reached a point of constant tension. A problem of boundaries
and responsibilities added to the general confusion. Tribes freely
moved back and forth over lands claimed by both the United
States and Mexico. Clouding the situation even more, the relationship between the federal government and the aggressive,
states-rights-minded Texans regarding Indian affairs was not
settled by admission to the Union. Before any program to bring
peace to this troubled frontier could succeed, the federal government needed to establish its right to control Indian affairs in
Texas and to reassure both Texans and Indians of an effective
policy.

A formidable Indian population confronted the United States in Texas. By all odds the most dangerous were the southern Comanche, who inhabited the northern and western portions of the province.[1] These nomadic warriors formed a north-south frontier some 800 miles long between the Red River and the Rio Grande. As with most of the plains tribes, the Comanche's life consisted primarily of hunting and raiding. Long before the Americans arrived he became the best horseman on the prairies and like the Apache and Navajo in adjacent New Mexico, he found the Spanish settlements ripe for plunder. Spanish authority, as everywhere on the frontier, proved ineffective, and for nearly a century Comanche war parties terrorized the borderlands without fear of reprisal. By the early nineteenth century raiding formed an integral part of Comanche culture.

The numerous other tribes also contributed their share of the unrest. The Kiowa and Lipan, for example, though numbering no more than a few thousand, were generally regarded as superior warriors and often generated more fear than the Comanche.[2] Several of the other small tribes, most of whom occupied the same territory as the Comanche, proved equally dangerous. These tribes aggravated conditions by occasionally joining with their more numerous brethren in raiding the scattered outposts in Texas and Mexico. Thus when the American frontiersmen arrived to threaten their way of life, the Texas tribes were well equipped to defend their land and heritage.

The story of Indian affairs in Texas before annexation may be briefly told. Despite the efforts of Sam Houston and a few others to respect native rights, the expansion of Texans to the westward inevitably brought conflict. During the period of the Republic frontiersmen and Texas Rangers conducted murderous campaigns against the Comanche and other tribes. Such events led to full scale war by 1840. In the mid-1840's President Houston attempted to mitigate some of the difficulties by establishing a boundary line between the two civilizations, to be marked by a series of trading posts where the Indians might procure goods at a fair price.[3] However, the creation of an Indian barrier in Texas failed to produce the desired results. Only one trading post was established, Texans persisted in entering Indian territory, and warfare continued. While Houston's failure rested partly in his own idealism, it was also caused by the Texas theory of land ownership, which refused to recognize any Indian rights. Unlike the United States, which at least nominally conceded that the natives had some rights to the lands they possessed, the Republic assumed all land belonged to the state.[4] Thus the aggressive frontiersmen, no matter how much their government might attempt to keep the races apart, continued to enter lands they considered their own. This practice created even more difficulties when the United States assumed control in 1845.

Texas entered the Union under unusual circumstances, being allowed by the national government to retain her vacant lands.[5] Contemporary federal Indian policy operated under the assumption that its jurisdiction applied only to the territories. Presumably by the time an area attained statehood, most public lands would be settled, the Indians removed, and therefore, federal laws were not required. But Texas came directly into the Union as a state, possessing both her public lands and a major Indian problem. This situation immediately led to confusion—to what extent did regulations extend over the state? Commissioner Medill readily admitted the embarrassing situation in his 1846 annual report by stating that "the lands which they occupy, as well as most of the other rights they enjoy, are under the control and legislative authority of the State, and it is questionable whether the intercourse act, or other laws for the government and regulation of Indian affairs, can be extended to these people without interfering with the local jurisdiction of Texas."[6]

Texans welcomed the extension of federal authority so long as it furthered their ends. Many, in fact, had hoped the government would use its power to sweep all Indians from the state. They had strong ideas on how the Indians ought to be treated, seeing no reason for a lenient policy and no necessity of yielding to the federal government if it came to treating the Indians in a benevolent manner. Furthermore, Texans saw no reason to relinquish any of their lands to the Indians to help obtain peace. In April 1846 the first Texas state legislature defined its position on Indian affairs by resolving that it recognized no Indian title to any land and no right of the federal government to negotiate any treaty without the consent of the state.[7]

Because of the states-rights issue involved in such a claim, Congress hestitated to take any action contrary to the Texas claim. Yet it soon became clear that the federal government needed to step in. Border incidents continued. The Comanche habit of capturing women and children caused deep hatreds. Local newspapers spared no effort in playing up these incidents, and most citizens readily agreed with the editor of the Austin *Democrat* when he demanded that the government should claim the captives "with a strong hand, the sword should be made to avenge and liberate. It is useless to talk of treating with those barbarians, until they are first humbled by chastisement." Congress responded to these frontier sentiments by appropriating $15,000 to send two commissioners on a full-fledged expedition to conclude peace with the hostile tribes and secure release of all captives.[8]

The two commissoners, Pierce M. Butler and M. G. Lewis, set out early in 1846. In May, after considerable difficulty, they succeeded in bringing representatives of eleven tribes together on the Brazos River. By the time the council met a new objective was added to their work—word reaching the commissioners from General Taylor that war had commenced with Mexico, making it imperative that the Texas tribes be kept loyal to the United States. The resulting treaty of "Council Springs" attempted to solve all the problems of the past decade, but did so largely by exceeding the government's intent. To convince the tribes of American generosity and give them an incentive to cease their hostile activities, the ambitious commissioners promised a liberal supply of presents. Butler and Lewis then took it upon themselves to define the exact relationship between the Indians and the federal government. In fact, they told the assembled chiefs, the United States was now supreme, and they wrote provisions into the treaty placing the tribes under the protection of the national government and giving the United States the authority to establish agencies and trading houses and to regulate trade and intercourse. Pleased with the promise of presents and the fact they would no longer be under the jurisdiction of Texas, the tribes willingly pledged themselves to "perpetual amity and friendship."[9]

News of the treaty caused an uproar in Washington. Congress quickly questioned its legality. The Texas delegation under the leadership of Timothy Pillsbury protested that the provisions conceded control of Indian affairs to the United States. States-rights-minded Texans felt such an arrangement implied that the federal government retained some control over Texas lands. Since Texans fought for this land, Pillsbury declared, "she earned it with blood. . . . The history of Texas shows that she has redeemed the country from the savage; that she has a personal lien on its property."[10] Although the senators did not all agree with such sentiments, they decided the issue was too cloudy for any final decisions and refused to ratify the treaty.

What now? The Comanche agreed to peace primarily because of the promise of presents, and they soon tired of waiting. In October the acting governor of Texas, A. C. Horton, wrote to Polk that the Indians had once again returned to the warpath in the belief that the United States would not live up to the treaty stipulations. Horton asked that immediate steps be taken to lessen their fears lest more trouble ensue. Yet the president found himself in the uncomfortable position of being without the authority or means of fulfilling the treaty's provisions. All that could be done under the circumstances was to use the executive power to appoint a special agent to explain the delay and persuade the Indians to remain at peace until Congress acted.[11]

Robert S. Neighbors proved an admirable choice for special agent. Just thirty years old, he had served with distinction in a similar capacity under the Republic. In this age of mediocrity in public service, Neighbors stood apart as a man of great ability. He was imbued with much of Houston's ideology, knew and liked the Indians, and had no illusions about white men. Texans never understood his compassion. The Major, as he was called, was handed a nearly impossible task. He needed to pacify the tribes by explaining to them the foibles of Congress. He was backed by absolutely no power or authority other than his own diplomatic skills. Armed only with a message from Medill, a letter from Houston to the chiefs, and a great deal of intestinal fortitude, he set out in early 1847 to meet the prairie tribes. Fortunately, Neighbors was equal to the task and managed to convince the tribes to remain at peace on the condition that the promised presents would be distributed in the forthcoming spring.[12]

Meanwhile, Congress acted on the Council Springs treaty. Fear that inaction might result in renewed warfare created sufficient alarm to secure ratification. But the Senate was not prepared to challenge Texas control of Indian affairs or to define the exact relationship between the state and federal government. Accordingly, in the belief that the issue had little immediate impact and would soon be clarified, the articles defining the federal jurisdiction were stricken from the treaty.[13] In essence, then, ratification accomplished only an appropriation for presents, and the key issues were left unresolved.

This placed the Indian Office in a quandary. Apparently none of the laws regulating intercourse could be extended over Texas. The War Department believed so anyway, and Marcy acted on the assumption that federal Indian regulations did not apply. The department, therefore, decided nothing could be done without imposing on the legal rights of Texas. "If the department have no power to enforce its orders," Medill later noted, "it can render little service, and will require but few agents." Congress realized, however, that contact must be kept with the tribes. Hence they wrote into the Indian Intercourse Act of March 3, 1847, a provision extending the services of Neighbors for another year to keep up communication with the Indians.[14]

Medill's letter informing Major Neighbors of the appointment indicated the limitations under which the agent would be forced to operate. He was to keep in contact with the various bands and persuade them to remain peaceful and away from white settlements. But the agent had no real power to prevent white encroachment on the lands claimed by the Indians. Texas reigned supreme and none of the federal laws restricting entry into Indian lands applied. Therefore, when whites of an "improper

character, calculated to disturb the present peaceful relations between the Indians and the government," appeared on the frontier, Neighbors was directed to seek correction through the authorities of Texas.[15]

Thus empowered, Neighbors set out to maintain peace. He
soon found Texans the major obstacle to tranquility. On May 22,
1847, he held a council at the main Comanche village to explain
the actions of Congress. The chiefs were predictably saddened to
learn that the presents had not yet arrived. More important, they
protested that Article III of the treaty promising to keep the
whites out of their lands had been deleted. "For a long time,"
said one chief, "a great many people have been passing through
my country; they kill all the game, and burn the country, and
trouble me very much. The commissioners of our great father
promised to keep these people out of our country. I believe our
white brothers do not wish to run a line between us, because they
wish to settle in this country. I object to any more settlements."[16]
Here was potential trouble. The Comanche fully intended to protect their ancestral hunting grounds, and Neighbors had no power to keep whites out. A collision appeared likely if such conditions continued to prevail.

Events during the summer of 1847 confirmed Neighbors' predictions. Texas, claiming full sovereignty, attempted to profit
from its public land by granting speculators large tracts of land,
much of it in territory occupied by the Indians. The recipients
of these tracts sent out survey parties to prepare for the expected
settlers, and within a short time Texas was threatened with another Indian uprising. One influential outfit, the "German Emigration Company," with a contract to settle German colonists, received a grant of land along the Llano River northwest of San
Antonio on lands claimed by the Comanche. The company hired
Robert Hays, brother of Colonel John C. Hays of the Texas
Rangers, to conduct the survey. A band of Indians, reportedly
Comanche, came across the surveyors at work and killed four.
Word of the killings soon spread across the frontier. Colonel
Hays tried to get Neighbors to go to the Comanche camp and
demand the murderers be delivered up, implying that if he re-

ceived no satisfaction the Rangers would take matters into their own hands.[17]

Texans used the incident to demand a more vigorous policy toward the Indians. Most citizens wanted complete removal of the troublesome Indians. Newspapers throughout the state defended the right to enter Indian lands and denounced the humanitarian activities of Neighbors. The *Democratic Telegraph and Texas Register*, for instance, opposed any peace with the tribes and called for a war of extermination. In August, Neighbors described the impact of the public indignation over the murders and the inflammatory newspaper articles. "This has had," he wrote to Medill, "a powerful influence upon the frontier citizens whose immediate exposure has always bid them to an easy participation in any measure for their security likely to be sustained by the public thereby jeopardizing the safety of the whole frontier."[18]

Because the War Department could not maintain sufficient force on the Texas frontier during the Mexican War, Texans wanted the Rangers subsidized by the federal government and sent after the Indians. This proposal coincided with the desire to eliminate Mexican nationals from Texas soil. Mexican agents were generally believed to be among the tribes encouraging depredations and spreading stories that Texans intended to steal tribal lands and exterminate the Indians. Texans thus saw a chance of killing two birds with one stone—the Rangers promised to stop Indian depredations and limit the activities of Mexicans. During the summer the government yielded and five additional companies of volunteer Rangers were called to service and placed on the frontier.[19]

These forces did nothing to keep whites out of Indian country. By midsummer encroachment became so blatant that Neighbors went to Governor J. Pinckney Henderson to urge him to prevent any more surveyors from entering Indian lands. Henderson, however, rather apathetically told the agent that he had no authority to stop these activities. This disclosure prompted Neighbors to write Medill that: "I am now more fully convinced than ever that our friendly relations with them [Indians] cannot be maintained permanently" until the government finally assumed jurisdiction over the Texas Indians. A number of other concerned Texans expressed similar sentiments. David G. Burnet, former vice president of the Republic, wrote a series of letters to Indian officials suggesting that peace in Texas required the early intervention of the government. Unless this happened, predicted Burnet, the result could only be the "entire and absolute extermination" of the Indians.[20]

Still the federal government did nothing. And until state and national authorities reached agreement on the status of Texas Indians the Indian department hesitated to intervene. In response to Neighbors's request for definite instructions all Medill could do was recommend a careful use of diplomacy and continued consultations with Texas authorities. Furthermore, the commissioner made it clear that the agent could count on no more presents to calm the tribes.[21]

The Comanche carefully noted these developments. They had not yet received the presents promised in 1846. Their "Great Father" seemed to be deceiving them. "Why is it that we can not have these things promised us? . . . You tell us, you want peace, our great father is a good man. We want the blankets for our squaws and old men! You promised we should have them."[22] In this frame of mind the Comanche could not be expected to keep the peace while land-hungry Texans appropriated more Indian lands and the federal government procrastinated.

Fortunately, Neighbors received a timely shipment of the presents authorized by the Council Springs treaty. He used the occasion to call a great council at Torrey's Trading House on the Brazos for September 25, 1847. The council gave the agent an opportunity to assess the disposition of the Indians and to use his persuasion to keep peace. Upwards of 2,200 people from eleven tribes gathered for the ceremonies. Predictably the talks centered on the Texans. The chiefs reported that everywhere they went they received the same information: the Texans intended to kill all the Indians and take their lands. Especially annoying to the Comanche were the German settlers, who persisted in taking tri-

bal lands and telling the Indians that Rangers would soon come
to massacre them. Yet Neighbors remained optimistic: "Although
these reports keep our border tribes in constant excitement, I
have no fears of their leading to a general outbreak. I have been
able, thus far, to contend successfully with all such evil influences, and from the many pledges given my during the council,
I feel confident that they will have less weight in the future."[23]

Neighbors's surface optimism, however, was tempered by the
realization that if the Texans were not soon stopped the Indians
would take measures into their own hands. It was imperative,
therefore, to forestall any hostilities until Congress resolved its
own dilemma. Accordingly, in October Neighbors suggested sending a delegation of sixteen Comanche chiefs on a visit to Washington. As the Comanches were the most influential tribe in
Texas and could hold other bands in check, the visit promised to
keep the tribes quiet while the war chiefs were absent.[24]

The Washington bureaucracy could not be expected to act
with haste, so Neighbors simultaneously turned to local authorities for help. To prevent the recurring inroads of surveyors and
settlers, the agent suggested resurrecting Houston's old idea of an
Indian barrier, a line designated specifically to keep whites out.
This time Governor Henderson admitted that a problem existed,
and the state for the first time attempted to exercise authority over
its own citizens. Henderson declared that the Indian laws of the
Republic remained in force, and he established a temporary line
some thirty miles above the white settlements "above which no
white person should be allowed to go, unless for legal purposes."[25] The Indians were told to remain above the line, and
eight companies of Rangers were stationed along the boundary
with instructions to keep whites and Indians separated. Thus
along several hundred miles of frontier in northwestern Texas
the Indian barrier was revived.

Creating the line was one thing, putting it into effect another.
Like earlier attempts at separation in the United States, the venture failed because white men could not resist the lure of Indian lands. It was too much to expect Texans to obey regulations

they considered a violation of their rights. By the end of 1847 a number of citizens had again entered Indian territory, marked off homesteads, and threatened to "shoot the first Indian that came on the land."[26]

The sole federal agent, without physical force to support him, found diplomacy impossible in preventing white intrusions. Texas speculators persisted in violating the restrictions of their own government. In February 1848, a particularly dangerous situation arose when the "Texas Emigration and Land Company" proposed sending an armed force into the Indian country to survey a new colony. The line to be established ran due west from the Trinity River (south of Dallas) to the Brazos and then north to the Red River, passing through lands claimed by eight tribes and substantially violating Henderson's declaration. Company officials bluntly told Neighbors they would brook no interference on his part.[27]

Complicating matters even more were the activities of several Texas newspapers. For reasons of their own, the editors of these papers persisted in perpetuating the illusion that open warfare raged along the frontier. Rumors were printed as fact while editorials urged the Rangers to destroy the Indians and criticized federal officers. Some papers also claimed that the legislature possessed no right to establish any boundary line.[28] The climate of opinion thus hindered any attempt to bring peace. Undoubtedly much of the hostility exhibited in the press was simple hatred of Indians, but Major Neighbors also thought some of the hostility was the result of the activities of speculators who stood to gain by inciting an outbreak which might justify eliminating the Indians and opening all Texas lands.

Several of the Rangers stationed on the frontier agitated conditions by taking the side of the settlers. The Rangers, in fact, acted as if they deliberately wanted to provoke the Comanche into war. They pushed the barrier line several miles above the agreed location, refused to allow Indian hunting parties below the line, and declined to halt white settlement on Indian lands. When asked if these actions might not cause the Indians to retaliate, the Ranger colonel commanding on the frontier bluntly replied that if the Comanche dared any further attacks, he would order the entire Ranger force to punish the Indians.[29]

"A crisis has arrived," Neighbors wrote to Medill on March 2, 1848. Already reports of Indian unrest were beginning to filter in. When the agent had visited the Comanche villages in February, the chiefs told him they were having difficulty keeping their young men from retaliating against continued white activities.[30] Apparently Neighbors could do nothing to stop the impending war. Texans had made a farce out of the temporary line. "I deem it proper to notify the Department," he wrote after the council, "that the Indian country in Texas is *now* open to all persons who may choose to visit or settle therein." Under these conditions he felt he was wasting his time, and submitted that if the government did not step in and take the tribes under protection, his continued employment would be futile.

Although Neighbors's plea did not fall on deaf ears, the political situation in Washington tended to perpetuate governmental indecision. In April 1848 the Senate once again attempted to determine the exact relationship between the Texas tribes and the federal government. Thomas S. Rusk of Texas began the movement by presenting a resolution calling upon the government to take a firm hand by establishing "a chain of military posts between Red River and the Rio Grande, and the adoption of measures for preserving the friendly relations between citizens of the State and the Indian tribes."[31]

The Texas proposal clearly placed emphasis on the creation of a military barrier. Texas wanted U.S. dragoons to keep the Indians under control and remove them if possible. The Senate, however, apparently refused to consider this proposal unless provisions were also included to extend some civilian control over the tribesmen. Consequently, Rusk, on April 4, 1848, introduced a bill proposing to regulate trade and intercourse with the Texas Indians. The exact contents of the bill have not survived, but much of it can be pieced together. The Senate proposed the creation of a superintendency for Texas and perhaps as many as four agents to handle the duties now assigned to Neighbors. Trading houses would be established and "rules and regulations of trade and intercourse . . . *not inconsistent* with the relations existing between the State of Texas and the said tribes of Indians" were to be drawn up by the Indian Office.[32]

David R. Atchison, chairman of the Committee on Indian Affairs, submitted the bill to Medill for comments on April 13. The commissioner was pessimistic about the proposition. Fundamentally he saw no change in the situation; the federal government still remained subordinate to the state in Indian affairs. And if the department was powerless to enforce the laws and regulations, the entire question of agents seemed academic. So the bill's passage meant nothing as long as Texas laws remained in force, and Medill strongly hinted that more energetic action was required.[33]

The real question before Congress was one of giving the national government control over what Texans believed to be an internal matter. It involved much more than Indian relations, however. By mid-1848 the question of the Wilmot Proviso deeply concerned Texas. Two aspects of the debate caused Texas to resist federal attempts to extend its jurisdiction. First, the Texans hoped their public debt, which amounted to some ten million dollars, might be assumed by the federal government in any sectional compromise, and the state's public lands offered a bargaining point. Furthermore, Texas claimed much of New Mexico and actively opposed attempts to organize that area as a separate territory. Under such circumstances the extension of national control over the Texas Indians could conceivably imply that the United States possessed the right to disregard the Texas claim to New Mexico. As a result, Texas, while agreeing on the need for agents, refused to grant the national government any of the powers necessary to operate an effective policy. The state got its way when Congress, in June, refused to take any action on the Texas Indian bills, leaving the entire matter unresolved.[34]

This situation left the status of Neighbors up in the air. His appointment had expired in April, but Medill persuaded him to

stay on until Congress decided his fate.[35] Although the commissioner desired to continue the temporary appointment, Neighbors' concern for the Indians and his efforts to prevent hostilities
had created frontier opposition to his continuation in office.
Eliphas Spencer, a man whom Neighbors had repeatedly ejected
from Indian lands, drew up a petition demanding the agent's
recall. The petition, addressed to Polk and dated April 18, 1848,
claimed that Neighbors, "this unworthy agent of yours who the
settlers look upon as a greater eval [sic] and pest," encouraged
the Indians to kill whites. A number of newspapers and local
politicians also added their voices to the outcry. Fortunately, Congress, including the Texas delegation, recognized that only Neighbors stood between the Texans and an Indian war, and in August
the special agency was retained.[36]

Meanwhile, things worsened in Texas. The Rangers began
taking matters into their own hands. During March a company
of troopers, acting on the rumored murder of a settler, met a
party of Wichita Indians on the Llano River. The Indians fled
on sight, but the Rangers overtook the party, drove them into the
river, and slaughtered twenty-five of the helpless band. The tribe
retaliated by killing three surveyors. Another Ranger company
then set out to bury the dead and coming across a sixteen-year-old
Caddo boy, hode him down and riddled his body with rifle fire.
"Enough is known to everyone in the section of the country,"
Neighbors reported to Medill, "that the circumstances did not
warrant the result as the boy had given no offense whatever."
José María, the Caddo chief, attempted to keep the boy's relatives from taking revenge, but matters had reached a breaking
point.[37]

On June 12, 1848, a large group of tribesmen met with Neighbors to express their concern over conditions. In particular they
were distressed about the action of the Rangers. As a result, they
told the agent, they no longer considered the temporary line in
effect. They intended to hunt where they pleased from now on,
and if the troops resisted there would be war.[38] Neighbors, in reporting on this council, noted that the Wichita and Caddo were
already making preparations to attack the white settlements.

In the next months warfare began in earnest. Waco, Wichita, and Comanche fell on the outlying Ranger stations, stealing horses, destroying crops, and causing a general disturbance. The Texans, attempting to recover stolen property, struck out at any Indian they met. One company, for instance, fell upon a band of Lipan Apache who they mistakenly believed had stolen some horses, and killed or wounded a score of them. The Lipans immediately retaliated by raiding a government wagon train. By the end of August reports were coming in from the Red River to the Medina that war parties were attacking all whites.[39]

To further complicate the problem, the military situation began to fluctuate when the peace treaty with Mexico became effecive in July 1848. Although the United States assumed responsibility for stopping Indian incursions south of the border, the administration decided to reduce the armed forces to prewar levels. In Texas regular troops were to be stationed along the Rio Grande and the Indian frontier, thus removing the necessity of employing Rangers. But a storm of Texas protest arose over disbanding the Rangers, and this, coupled with the War Department's failure to provide enough regular troops, led Secretary Marcy to retain the Rangers.[40] Consequently, a number of Ranger companies remained on the frontier charged with the added duty of keeping the Indians out of Mexico.

The Rangers launched into their new duty with relish. It offered a new excuse for punishing the Indians. More hostilities consequently erupted when the troopers attempted to keep the tribes north of the border.

Neighbors found himself unable to make any suggestions to end the warfare when he met with the Comanche in October 1848. As he saw it, the difficulty rested squarely with the Ranger companies whose officers were only under the nominal control of the federal government and had the privilege of making war at discretion. "Under the present system the Treaty [1846] is forgotten and if a horse is stolen by an Indian there is no demand made through the agent for his recovery, but the first party of Indians that is fallen in with, is attacked and massacred." So it went. During the fall of 1848 Indians killed eighteen or twenty whites in the area west of San Antonio, and, as panic spread across the frontier, all the inhabitants were prepared to "shoot the first Indians they met with."[41]

The failure of the federal government to take a strong stand on Indian affairs in Texas after annexation had extremely unfortunate results. Unnecessary friction was created between the state and national government as the United States demonstrated its inability to solve the Indian dilemma. Texans expected the federal government to solve their Indian problems. When matters grew worse citizens became convinced that the policy of extermination best fitted the situation. This attitude invoked a determination to solve the matter themselves.[42] Perhaps the government policy of protecting the tribesmen and the Texas determination to remove all Indians from their soil could never have been reconciled, but governmental inaction ruled out any hope for a workable solution.

The government, moreover, found itself unable to live up to its pledges to the Indian. The Texas tribes showed remarkable restraint and trust in federal attempts peaceably to separate the two civilizations. But such attempts were foreordained to failure unless the nation asserted authority over the state of Texas. It did not, and as a result by the end of 1848 matters had reached the point of war, with the federal government somewhat between the two contending sides, trusted by neither and almost completely ineffective.

It was in this atmosphere that the Whigs took control of Indian affairs, and thus were handed the responsibility for settling problems in Texas. Unfortunately, several developments tended to aggrevate the situation. The end of the Mexican War and the discovery of gold in California created an urgent need for new routes through west Texas, and in constructing these routes, Texans discovered that much of the area was suitable for farming. Added pressure was subsequently placed on the Indians to give up their lands. Moreover, frontier defense no longer depended solely on the Rangers: the United States assumed responsibility for internal defense as well as the enforcement of the treaty of Guadalupe Hidalgo.[43] In performing these duties, the army generally tried to protect Indian rights, thereby increasing the already tense relations between state residents and federal authorities. Fnally, the Whig use of the spoils system took away the one man seemingly capable of keeping peace between white and Indian, Robert S. Neighbors.

Neighbors, however, expected to remain in office. Consequently, on March 9, 1849, three days after the new administration entered office, he made a bold proposal designed to solve the Indian difficulties. His proposal called for a reservation system in Texas, placing the Indians directly under federal jurisdiction and requiring a permanent separation of the races. Writing to Major General William J. Worth, U.S. military commander in Texas, the Indian agent first suggested that the Indian tribes be removed from territory which the Texans were likely to require in the near future and that reservations be established: "The general Government should acquire from the State a sufficiency of territory for the permanent location and settlement of the Indians; said land to be divided among the several bands and tribes according to their numbers, and the usual inducements offered them, to encourage settlement." To protect the tribes in their new homes the federal government must then provide agents and extend the trade and intercourse laws over the Texas Indians.[44]

General Worth fully agreed with the proposal. In fact, he not only approved of the reservation system but recognized that Neighbors was the key to its success. "Enough appears to satisfy my mind that an agent is indispensibly necessary to preserve quiet," Worth wrote to the commissioner of Indian affairs, and "that Major Neighbors is precisely the man for the place." Yet Secretary of the Interior Ewing persisted in handing the agent his walking papers, and replacing him with John Rollins. The appointment drew severe criticism from the dejected Neighbors, who felt that Rollins, a Whig and not from Texas, would receive no cooperation from Texans.[45]

The elderly Rollins confirmed some of Neighbors's apprehensions by remaining in Washington for some time and not arriving in Austin until mid-November.[46] Thus, with Neighbors's removal, no representative of the Indian department was present in Texas during a period that proved to be critical—the summer of 1849.

Antagonism between the independent tribes and Texans had finally reached the breaking point. Despite the warnings of federal officers, Texans continued to penetrate Indian lands. These aggressions, combined with the senseless massacres of several Indian bands by Texas Rangers, finally caused a general uprising. In the early spring war parties of Comanche, Lipan Apache, and others attacked the southern frontier, killing settlers, taking women and children captive, and destroying property. By summer the entire southern portion of the state lay desolated. At least 171 Americans were killed, twenty-five taken captive, and over a hundred thousand dollars worth of property stolen. Even the little village of Corpus Christi on the Gulf Coast lost thirty-nine citizens between January and August.[47]

Texans displayed intense hostility toward the national government over the uprising. Local inhabitants, overlooking their part in the affair, blamed the army for most of the difficulty.[48] Frontier editors criticized the war department for leaving Texas defenseless, and a number of petitions circulated among the residents stating that the military was ineffective and asking President Taylor for help from "these merciless marauders [who] have prosecuted their atrocities to our very doors." The army justified the situation as best it could. Secretary of War George W. Crawford blamed the ravages of cholera for undermining the effectiveness of his already undermanned forces and strongly implied the Congress was at fault for not authorizing an increase in the military establishment. At least one officer also wrote from Texas that the inhabitants generally exaggerated conditions "for the purpose of getting troops ordered to, or volunteers called out on the frontier districts of Texas, with all the expensive concomitants of such military operations."[49]

Yet excuses could not whitewash the critical nature of the situation. Major General George M. Brooke, assuming command of the Texas frontier in June following the death of General Worth, soon discovered his forces entirely inadequate and requested Governor George T. Wood to call out three more com-

panies of Rangers. During the summer the combined forces
carried out a series of campaigns and finally succeeded in pushing
the hostile tribes back into their country west of the old dividing
line. The Comanche, who suffered a rather severe setback,
quickly assured the government that they would abstain from
further hostilities.[50] Thus relative quiet temporarily returned to
Texas, but with none of the fundamental problems solved.

As far as the Indian department was concerned, the brief
flare-up confirmed the need for the federal government to assume
responsibility for the Indians. Commissioner Orlando Brown in
his annual report for 1849 proclaimed that until Congress made
some drastic changes, the department could not be held account-
able for any of the difficulties. Brown also set forth the administration's program for the establishment of peace, which represented practically a verbatim restatement of Neighbors's earlier
ideas for a reservation system:

A particular district or districts shall . . . [be] set apart for their
permanent residence, within which the general government will have
the same power to prevent intrusions, and to regulate trade and intercourse with them, as it has in regard to our other Indians on territory
of the United States, and . . . a suitable number and description of
agents shall . . . [be] authorized for them.[51]

However, until Texas agreed to relinquish some of its lands to
the federal government or until Congress asserted its powers to
regulate trade and intercourse, the Indian department found its
hands tied, and had to look to the military to carry out its program.

Secretary Crawford ordered Brooke to carry out administration
Indian policy. "A friendly intercourse," Crawford directed, "will
promote a state of kindly feeling and attachment. . . . To the extent of your authority you will redress their wrongs." Fortunately
Brooke wholeheartedly agreed with the objectives of the government. He was thoroughly familiar with the proposals of Major
Neighbors and agreed that a permanent separation of the races
was the only workable policy. After residing in Texas for but a
short time, the commander became convinced that the attitude of

the Texans presented the major cause of difficulty. In a letter to
the Adjutant General he wrote that Texas laws denying Indians
title to any land were responsible for the unrest; that the tribes
were "at an entire loss to know where are to be their boundaries,
and where to be permitted to hunt and cultivate." If left to
themselves, he predicted, Texans would take every last foot of
Indian land. This Brooke opposed: "As a humane and just
people, are we to deprive the aboriginal proprietors of their
whole country?"[52]

To the army, then, fell the task of protecting the Indians. The
best means to accomplish this goal seemed to be the reactivation
of the old idea of an Indian sanctuary marked by a series of
military posts. Such a line promised twofold benefits: the Texans
could be kept out of Indian territory and, by forcing the tribes
to keep on their own lands, the white settlements would also be
safeguarded. If this separation proved effective, it would provide
a de facto solution to the problem. Nominal reservations, defined
only by a chain of posts, would be established, and later, after
Texas and the government resolved their difficulties over state
sovereignty, the reservation system might be refined and agents
sent to begin the process of civilization.

Some Texans suggested a different proposal. They had never
recognized any Indian rights and did not intend to do so now.
It seemed best simply to remove all the Indians from the state.
The justification for such a maneuver first appeared in a letter
to the commissioner of Indian affairs, May 12, 1849, written by
H. G. Catlett, an Indian trader who claimed that his twelve
years' experience on the frontier gave him an insight into the
problem.[53] Catlett believed that only a few Indians were native
to Texas. Among these he listed the Lipan, Waco, Comanche,
and others whom he considered "not formidable enemies." The
rest were intruders and did not properly belong in Texas.
Though admitting that whites were at least partly responsible
for the difficulties, he rationalized white activities on the ground
that the Indians had no right to Texas lands.

Catlett believed that all transient Indians should be removed from the state and a military post established on the Red River from which mounted companies could constantly patrol the borders to keep them out. As for the native tribes, he thought they should be restricted to a small area of northwest Texas. Here, hemmed in by an increasing volume of white settlers, the Indians would soon move out of the state.

While removal seemed a perfect solution to many Texans, it remained unsatisfactory to Washington. Although officials of the Indian department agreed with the idea of removing foreign tribes, removing all of the Texas Indians seemed out of the question. Many of the tribes properly belonged in Texas, and their transportation north, where a number of displaced tribes already resided, would only serve to confuse the situation there.[54] Thus the administration, and particularly Secretary Ewing, rejected the Texas proposal and continued to follow a policy of establishing reservations for the native tribes within the boundaries of the state.

General Brooke carried out as much of this policy as possible in 1849. The line that Neighbors had tried to establish in 1847–48 was still marked by a scattered string of Ranger posts and trading stations running from northeast to southwest between the Rio Grande and Fort Worth. Brooke attempted to make this line stronger by constructing a series of strategically located forts, connecting them by roads. He also ordered the establishment of a line of secondary posts along the Mexican boundary to keep the Indians out of Mexican territory.[55]

It soon became obvious that maintaining a boundary line some 400 miles long was more than the army could handle. Brooke lacked sufficient troop strength to keep the Indians on their land or the legal authority to keep the Texans off it. Although some twenty-eight companies had been assigned to the frontier, the ranks of most companies were only half full. Texas put pressure on the army to call out more volunteers to fill the gaps, but this the commander rejected, believing it would only cause more trouble: "I have an objection to placing rangers in immediate contact with the Indians on the frontier, as I am fearful, from

their general and natural hostility to the Indians, that they would
be very apt to bring about what we wish to avoid—a general
war."[56]

In October, Brooke ordered Lieutenant W. H. C. Whiting of
the Corps of Engineers to survey the entire line. Whiting's report
confirmed the ineffectiveness of the line. He observed in particular that German settlers were pushing their way beyond the
barrier and there was no way of stopping them. This report,
which was soon published, also noted that the Indians' lands
were very fertile, and this served even more to convince the
Texans that the Indians must go. Undaunted, however, Brooke
continued to build his forts; the final line included Fort Lincoln
at Eagle Pass, Fort Martin Scott near Fredericksburg, Fort Croghan on the Colorado, Fort Graham on the Brazos, and Fort
Worth on the Trinity. "This line of posts is," Brooke wrote to
Winfield Scott on October 2, 1849, "as good as can be had for
some years to come, and is rather in advance of the settlements."[57]
Brooke proved to be no prophet.

So by early 1850 a lively contest between frontier citizens and
the national government was developing over the Indian policy,
and political controversies served to hinder the settlement of the
differences. This was a year of national compromise, but before
such an agreement could be reached, relations between the Whig
administration and Texans nearly ruptured. Texans believed
that most of New Mexico rightfully fell within their boundaries.
President Taylor rejected this claim and by 1850 was sponsoring
statehood for New Mexico, much to the disgust of Texas. Such
an atmosphere tended to make Texans extremely suspicious of
any attempt by the government to extend its jurisdiction, and
this specifically applied to Indian policy. Even moderate citizens
were not willing to agree to federal control of Indian affairs until
other matters were resolved.[58]

Nor were Texans mollified by the events occurring on the
frontier. Despite all efforts by General Brooke to make his barrier
line effective, raiding parties continued to slip down into the
settlements and plunder outlying stations. Citizens from some of
the affected counties appealed to the governor to take matters

into his own hands. Governor P. H. Bell, a moderate man who personally sympathized with the basic goals of federal Indian policy, found it nearly impossible to resist the increasing pressure of frontier inhabitants and other citizens seeking a drastic solution to the Indian problems. Writing to the Texas legislature on January 18, 1850, he observed that the residents were looking "in their present embarrassments and trouble, to the government of their State," a necessary action since aid had "been withheld by the government of the Union."[59] Indicating that the present state constitution was too vague in allocating executive powers to meet the current Indian problem, Bell recommended the passage of a law authorizing him to employ local forces to meet the emergency. Thus it seemed that public displeasure over the inability of the army to safeguard the frontier might force Texas authorities into sending out their own forces.

John Rollins, having now lived in Texas long enough to size up the situation, feared the consequences of any separate action by the state. In correspondence with Texas Congressman Volney Howard, the agent pleaded for restraint and urged the state to settle its differences with the national government before a general war erupted.[60] Most citizens seemed to want a confrontation with the Indians, and this desire was encouraged by local newspapers and persons who stood to make a profit. Should public pressure result in volunteers being called to deal with the Indian problem, it might end in disaster, as the militia was known to advocate extermination or forced removal. "These Indians," Rollins told Howard, "are not in a condition to be removed. They are too wild to understand, too independent to submit to it and such is their aversion to removal that they would defend to the last a country which they believed with some justice to belong exclusively to themselves."

By this time Rollins was thoroughly convinced that the government's idea of establishing reservations was the only solution to the dilemma. Texas retained more territory than she could possibly use in the foreseeable future. It would not harm the state to grant some of this land for reservations. During the succeeding years, he pointed out, the Indian tribes might be advanced in civilization and if the state finally needed the land, removal could take place "without the shedding of blood or further deliberate destruction of hundreds of beings whose greatest offence is being 'in the way.'"

Most Texans, however, resisted the idea of giving any of their lands to the Indians. Like other frontier populations, they believed they had suffered too much to have any compassion for the Indians. The Texas legislature reflected the feeling by passing resolutions requesting Congress to remove the Indians. Congressman Howard passed these demands on to the House of Representatives and simultaneously authored a series of resolutions asking for additional army regiments to protect the Texas frontier. Yet while the Texans demanded more protection by the government, they somewhat inconsistently refused to implement that protection by allowing the imposition of the trade and intercourse laws, laws which would help calm the tribes by preventing whites from entering the Indian country. The February 1850 session of the state legislature in fact rejected a specific proposal to authorize the United States to extend the laws.[61] Both personal and political reasons explain this dichotomy; some traders stood to lose substantial profits if federal regulations were strictly applied, and Texas politicians felt there must be an adjustment of political considerations with the United States before any other concessions were allowed.

The army remained the only means the federal government had to extend these laws. If General Brooke reversed the trend of events and stopped some of the depredations, perhaps the Texas legislature might be more willing to cooperate. Brooke became aware of this possibility in June when Governor Bell wrote that he favored the idea of reservations and extending the intercourse laws, but he could not help if the raids continued. The paramount responsibility of the executive, Bell told Brooke, was to his own citizens, and these obligations "do not permit me to extend to the Red man kindness, sympathy, or aid, when it costs one drop of the blood of our own people, or the sacrifice of peace."[62]

Unfortunately, Brooke found himself barely able to maintain the status quo. The tribes west of the barrier were out of hand. On May 28, 1850, Brooke wrote to Winfield Scott that the Indian raids were increasing both in number and strength.[63] Brooke also stressed the necessity of buttressing his line of posts with more troops, and he reiterated his belief that only reservations would provide a permanent solution. The reluctance of the government to provide him with the tools to achieve this goal he could only attribute to the dispute with Texas over the New Mexican boundary.

Encouraged by Governor Bell and his own desperate condition, Brooke decided to mount an offensive campaign in the hope of decisively defeating the renegade bands and restoring peace. Accordingly, orders were issued on June 4 for a general campaign to clear the Rio Grande Valley. Throughout the remainder of the summer all available regulars and several companies of Rangers roamed along the border attempting to bring the Indians to bay. Brooke's troops, however, spent most of their time in frustrating patrols without spotting any hostiles. Even when sighted, the Indians usually made a clean escape. Colonel William J. Hardee reported to his commander in September that the present mode of warfare was useless. The Indians simply had the advantage: "If in danger of being overtaken, the scatter, and, each pursuing a different route to some remote point, they effectually baffle the skill of the most experienced trailers."[64] Only fourteen Indians were reported killed in the entire campaign, and the whole affair had to be classified as a failure.

A number of Texas extremists opposed Brooke's campaign even though they had previously criticized the army for not being more aggressive. Part of this attitude stemmed from the attempt of the Taylor administration to bring about separate statehood for New Mexico; it seemed to some Texans that Brooke was really operating under orders from Washington to place his troops in a position to prevent Texas from pressing her claims.[65] A clash between Texans and American troops over this issue was not beyond the realm of possibility.

During August, the Texas legislature mirrored the split over Indian policy. On only two points could they agree; that the army needed to be reinforced and that all foreign tribes must be removed from the state. Resolutions demanding both of these measures were passed by both houses. But the issue of the native tribes was stalemated. An extremist position was represented by the presence of H. G. Catlett, who was lobbying for a resolution urging the army to move its line of posts far into the Indian country. Catlett justified this request by explaining that the present line was not effective and restricted the settlement of fertile lands. It is more likely, however, that Catlett saw a westward extension of the military barrier as the first step in removing all the tribes. General Brooke believed that Catlett intended to incite a general war and he recommended to the War Department that Catlett be permanently barred from the Indian country.[66] Whatever his motive, the trader had substantial support and succeeded in having his resolution passed in the House. The upper chamber rejected the proposal.

By this time the government had begun to realize it needed the cooperation of the Texas legislature if its Indian policy was to succeed. The death of Zachary Taylor in July removed one obstacle. Fillmore's administration played down the difficulties and attempted to use more subtle persuasion. The new president, in fact, personally tried to convince the Texans by asking them to assign "a small portion of her vast domain for the provisional occupancy of the small remnants of tribes within her borders, subject, of course, to her eventual ownership and eventual jurisdiction."[67] Commissioner Luke Lea backed up this moderate tone by suggested the appointment of a commission to confer with Texas authorities "for the purpose of effecting the conventional arrangements indispensable to a satisfactory adjustment of our Indian Affairs in the State." These overtures met with a favorable response from several Texans, including William M. Williams, chairman of the Texas House Committee on Indian Affairs. Williams called upon his state to adopt a new policy, one that would allow the Indian department to extend the intercourse laws and set apart some portion of state territory for a reservation.[68] But the Texas legislature failed to approve the proposal and affairs between the state and national government remained stalemated.

Meanwhile, agent Rollins decided to take matters into his own hands. The failure of the army to restore peace and the deadlock between the state and national authorities led him to believe Indian difficulties might best be resolved by a little personal diplomacy. Soon after assuming office he held several conferences with the Comanche and Lipan. The Indians intimated peace might be restored if they were guaranteed protection. In September, therefore, after the Texas legislature had declined to extend the intercourse laws, Rollins concluded that the time had come to act. Although without authority from his superiors or the state, he proceeded to make a treaty with the Indians. After some difficulty, Buffalo Hump, Shanaco, and several other Comanche chiefs were consulted. Readily admitting violations had occurred on both sides, the chiefs indicated they were tired of war and agreed to a general council on the San Saba where differences might be adjusted.[69]

Rollins proposed to rewrite the Butler and Lewis treaty of 1846 which, it will be recalled, failed to extend federal laws to the Texas Indians. Rollins had concluded that he possessed the power to extend the intercourse laws. This idea was based upon an opinion rendered by the acting attorney general of Texas, A. J. Hamilton, who concluded that under the United States Constitution the government had the power to regulate the Indian tribes.[70] Under this interpretation, which was not accepted by Texas or the Senate, Hamilton ruled that if the tribes were within the limits of the Union, no matter who held sovereignty of the soil, they fell under the control of the national government.

Rollins finally assembled some 600 Indians, mostly Comanche, on December 8, 1850. After explaining to the tribes the provisions of the 1846 treaty, he invited the various Indians to stop their warfare and return to peaceful pursuits. Two days later the assembled tribes affixed their signatures to the treaty, which was a virtual restatement of the Butler and Lewis document. Its most

important feature was an article assigning to the national government the right to extend its trade and intercourse laws over the
Texas Indians. As usual the tribesmen also agreed to remain at
peace and return all captives and stolen property.[71] Rollins believed he had now secured peace. The Indians seemed to him
more than willing for peace, and he had made them pledges that
the government would protect them from the whites.

Unknown to Rollins, Congress had in the meantime made
possible a more general adjustment of Indian difficulties. After
settling the sectional problems with the Compromise of 1850,
Congress had finally gotten around to Indian affairs. Though still
refusing to extend the trade and intercourse laws, it authorized
two more special agents for the state and appropriated $300,000
for a three-man commission to go among the Texas Indians,
gather statistics, and if necessary negotiate treaties.[72] Commissioner Lea immediately appointed John A. Rogers and Jesse
Stem agents, and Charles S. Todd, Robert S. Campbell, and
Oliver P. Temple commissioners. The Indian department intended to make the most of this opportunity. Todd, Campbell,
and Temple were instructed to look into all aspects of the Indian
problem and were given rather wide latitude to make their own
decisions.[73] It seems likely from the vague nature of their instructions that the department intended for them to lay the
foundations of a reservation system as well as halt incursions into
Mexico.

Lea's instructions to the new agents also suggest that the commissioner saw an opportunity to promote the idea of reservations.
Certainly he was preparing for this eventuality. On November
25, 1850, Lea wrote to the agents that the government still held
no jurisdiction over the tribes, but that they were to be especially
vigilant in preserving the peace, and in "preparing the way for
such a further disposition of the various tribes as may hereafter
appear practical and expedient."[74] Moreover, the agents received
instructions to give the Indians every possible encouragement to
confine themselves to particular districts of territory away from
white settlement, and to depend on agriculture for a living. To
help the Indians accept overtures of this nature, Rogers was

authorized to purchase $6,000 in presents to be distributed to the Texas tribes.

The arrival of Rollins' treaty in Washington furnished Lea with an additional opportunity to extend his control over the Texas Indians. Though recognizing that it conflicted with Texas sovereignty, he submitted the treaty to the secretary of the interior with the recommendation that it be presented to the Senate for ratification (it never was). Prior to this, General Brooke had ordered the army to live up to the spirit of the treaty (which meant keeping whites out) as a reciprocal move designed to show that the Americans accepted the Indians desire for peace.[75] These moves, all by men desirous of establishing a reservation system, indicate the hopes of perhaps concluding a fait accompli. Rollins' treaty extended the intercourse laws and if enforced, whether legal or otherwise, would provide a de facto solution to one of the problems. If the three commissioners arranged some type of reservation, the whole matter might be wrapped up.

Todd, Campbell, and Temple arrived in San Antonio in December and immediately began to gather information. They soon concluded that reservations provided the only alternative to extermination. As early as January, Campbell wrote to Lea that the condition of the Indians "demands the immediate action of the government."[76] Texans were continuing to survey and settle Indian lands with an apparent determination to take possession of all tribal lands. Under the constant pressure of white settlement and the loss of hunting grounds, "no alternative is left them but starvation or successful forays upon American and Mexican settlement." The only way to end these raids, Campbell continued, was to establish reservations. He suggested, however, that instead of waiting for Texas to donate the land, the United States should purchase sufficient territory from the state. Such a measure offered a cheaper and more effective alternative to maintaining a military barrier line, and it would put an end to the question of jurisdiction.

Several conversations with Governor Bell seemed to bring a promise of state help. By February 1851, the complete plan was ready; first the United States must secure the land, and then the

Indians should sign a treaty agreeing to settle down. To obtain
Indian approval, the commissioners proposed to make use of the
fact that not all Indians were respecting Rollins' treaty. Several
bands of Comanche continued to create trouble along the southern portion of the frontier. Brigadier General William S.
Harney, taking command after the death of Brooke, proposed mounting a
large expedition to move into the heart of Comanche country between the headwaters of the Colorado and Brazos and give the
recalcitrant bands a severe chastisement. Todd and company approved of the expedition and hoped to accompany it in order to
secure a treaty that would force upon the Comanche a fixed
boundary and make the tribesmen accept "the cultivation of the
Soil which it is hoped a more civilized condition may Superin-
duce."[77]

As logical as this plan might have appeared, it soon ran into
difficulty. Governor Bell began to have second thoughts. Although still agreeing that reservations were the only means of restoring permanent peace on the frontier and the removal would
result in renewed warfare, he believed he lacked the power to
sell state territory without the sanction of the legislature and
admitted "some delicacy" in recommending such an action. And
even if Texas agreed to sell some territory, it would in all likelihood be country unfit for habitation.[78] Undaunted by this dis-
agreeable intelligence, however, the commissioners continued to
make preparations for their treaty. In conference with Rollins,
and taking Bell's remarks into consideration, they began to mark
out the exact location of the proposed reservations. The old military barrier line was to be discarded and the Indians confined
to the northwest portion of the state, behind a line running in a
southwest direction from the Red River near present Wichita
Falls to the confluence of the Colorado and the Concho rivers,
and thence westward to the boundary of New Mexico.[79] This
move cleared the Indian population from the entire southern
portion of Texas and removed them from the proximity of the
international boundary.

Then suddenly, in April, the commission came to an abrupt
end. Lea reluctantly wrote the commissioners that Congress had

adjourned without appropriating any funds to continue their activities; they were also informed they no longer held the power to negotiate a treaty, one feature of the Indian Appropriation Act of 1851 being a proviso ending all special commissions. This economy measure denied Todd and company the power to conclude their treaty. They were given the alternative of returning immediately or existing on the frontier to gather statistics until their remaining funds were exhausted. Todd hurried to Washington to plead for a continuation of the mission, but after an exchange with the secretary of the interior, in which the matter was laid before the president and the cabinet, it was decided that the commissioners should return.[80] The three men closed their books and prepared to return home on June 16, 1851.

Once again the government had failed to impose its policy on Texas. Yet it would be a mistake to assume the commission had no impact. The commissioners' official report, dated August 23, 1851, gave renewed strength to the idea of reservations and outlined a more specific policy.[81] These recommendations served as the basis of the reservations that were finally established in 1854. Essentially, the commissioners rejected the Texas argument for removal on the grounds that Texas had sufficient territory for her needs without dispossessing the Indians, and that honor and humanity demanded that the Texas tribes be allowed to retain a portion of their ancestral homes. The old idea of a military barrier cutting through the full length of the state was discarded. All of south Texas must be cleared "and the separate territory proposed to be secured in Texas lies north of the route usually travelled to El Paso and New Mexico." Thus the area allocated to the tribesmen diminished even further.

The report of the Todd commission marks the final adoption by the government of a specific plan for the Texas Indians. All that remained was to overcome Texas opposition and convince them that the Indians deserved a land of their own. But this of course was no small problem.

After the commissioners returned home, the Indian department again decided to secure Texas cooperation, and though a new treaty was negotiated with some of the Comanche in October, no attempt was made to assign reservations.[82] Instead, intensive pressure was placed on the Texas legislature by the administration to convince them of the benefits of a reservation system. Both the Interior and War Departments pleaded convincingly that only Indian sanctuaries offered peace to the troubled frontier. Secretary of War Conrad, for example, in his annual report for 1851 implied that more troops would not solve the Indian problem. It was Texas and its land policy which were to blame, said Conrad. "It would seem, therefore, to be for the advantage of Texas herself, and of the United States, that these Indians should be left in undisturbed possession of a small portion of her vast territory.[83] Pressure for a reservation also intensified within the state legislature. Robert Neighbors, now serving in the lower chamber, led the fight. On December 16, 1851, in a long speech before his colleagues, Neighbors recommended the setting aside of a portion of state lands for the Indians as the most humane way to get the Indians to settle down and end the long years of border warfare.[84]

Yet Texas citizens cared little of humanity and persisted in antagonizing the tribesmen. By the end of 1851 white settlements were well beyond the military barrier line. Agent Jesse Stem observed the disastrous effect of the continued encroachment; all his efforts in persuading the tribes to build permanent villages, clear fields, and plant corn went for naught as the Texans moved in and forced the tribes to yield up their land without compensation. Under such circumstances there could be no peaceful intercourse with the natives.[85]

Certainly, then, by the end of 1851 the reservation idea had not proved workable in Texas. The tribes had not been pacified and Texans had not accepted the idea of a permanent Indian population within their borders. Yet by this time the advocates of Indian reservations had gained the upper hand. All those who hoped for a humanitarian solution to the dilemma of the Texas Indians in the six years following annexation—Neighbors, Brooke, Rollins, the Todd commission, Lea—agreed on the necessity of Indian sanctuaries within the state, and their ideas finally prevailed. On February 6, 1854, the Texas legislature finally relented and approved a reservation much like the one suggested by the Todd commission. The federal government also gained sole jurisdiction over the native population.[86] Two large reservations were accordingly organized, one on the main fork of the Brazos for the smaller tribes, the other on the Clear Fork of the Brazos for the Comanche.

The Texas reservations failed immediately, despite all the glowing predictions. There were too many inherent problems to make the experiment a success. Texas contributed too little land, not all the bands settled down, and whites continued to create difficulties. Occasional warfare continued, causing so much animosity that the reservations never had a chance. When the authorities tried to put the reservations into operation, local citizens took their hatred out on the peaceful tribes and the agents who protected them. As armed parties invaded the reservations and began a systematic slaughter of the tribesmen, the government finally relented, and in 1859 authorized the complete removal of all Texas tribes north of the Red River.[87]

Thus the Texans finally had their own way. But this did not end Indian troubles. Renegade bands continued to roam the Texas frontier and plunder the inhabitants. One can only conclude that if the Texans had accepted the idea of substantial Indian reservations within the state, as the government proposed between 1849 and 1851, and carried them into effect with a spirit of humanity and responsibility, the results might have been far superior.

5

Military and Civilian Policy:
New Mexico, 1846-52

✤ Indian affairs in New Mexico, in contrast to Texas, at first fell exclusively under military jurisdiction. Only after the area officially became a territory in 1850 did the civilian branch of the government enter the picture in any significant way. However, the Indian problems in Texas and New Mexico were similar in many ways. Both were new and rich lands, ripe for American exploitation, and occupied by a wide variety of Indian peoples. As a result, the United States also found itself confronted with a thorny Indian problem when it acquired New Mexico. New Mexican settlements needed protection from the hostile Navajo and Apache. The friendly Pueblo Indians had to be safeguarded both from enemy tribes and from the New Mexicans, who were not always circumspect in dealing with Indians. Finally, the long supply line, the Santa Fe road, had to be kept open. Solutions to these difficulties seemed simple to the new American rulers—secure a true and lasting peace with all the Indians. Unfortunately, it proved easier to devise a solution than to implement it.

Two distinct groups of Indians lived in New Mexico at the time of American occupation. First were the sedentary Pueblo Indians, people who had suffered nearly two hundred years of economic and religious exploitation, war, and disease at the hands of the Spanish and Mexican governments. These people had also en-

94

dured frequent raids by their more powerful Indian neighbors, the Navajo and Apache, who came in quest of slaves and sheep.[1] Consequently, the Pueblo settlements along the Rio Grande Valley had long since come to live in mistrust of both white and Indian. Little wonder, then, the Pueblo people were not overwhelmed with the arrival of American forces. The change in overlords seemed to promise little in the way of better treatment.

In contrast to the Pueblo Indians, New Mexico also contained several very powerful and aggressive tribes—Ute, Navajo, Apache, Comanche—all long at war with the Spanish settlements. Most important of the unrestrained tribes were the Navajo, numbering over 7,000, and inhabiting the vast canyon lands north and west of the populated areas of New Mexico. The Navajo had long raided the Spanish and Pueblo settlements for women, sheep, horses, and other booty. This led to perpetual guerilla warfare, with the New Mexicans doing their share to prolong hostilities by seizing on every opportunity to kill Navajo men and sell their women and children into slavery.[2] When the Americans moved into New Mexico, the Navajo were at the apex of their power and they were not impressed with the newcomers.

The Apache, perhaps a total of 6,000 in various bands, generally occupied areas east and south of Santa Fe. Their relationship with the New Mexicans approximated that of the Navajo. War was a constant part of life and by the 1830's the Apache had made it nearly impossible for Europeans to travel outside the larger settlements. So complete was Apache domination of some parts of the countryside that the entire economic life of New Mexico was disrupted. The Mexicans struck back brutally, in some cases perpetrating wholesale slaughter of the Apache. After such events, it was not surprising, as one observer wrote, "that the Apaches look upon all white men as their enemies, whether Mexican or American."[3]

The remaining tribes usually stayed on the outskirts of New Mexico proper although they occasionally raided settlements. Along the road from the United States to Santa Fe, particularly in the vicinity of the Arkansas river, lived portions of three tribes, Comanche, Cheyenne, and Arapaho (who are discussed more thoroughly elsewhere). While the latter two tribes were generally at peace, the Comanche had long been a threat to the Santa Fe trail. Since the Santa Fe road was the major route of communication with New Mexico, the United States government found it necessary to pacify these tribes in order to continue the occupation of New Mexico.

These were the problems to be faced by the Americans when the Mexican War brought New Mexico into the fold. One of President Polk's immediate objectives when the war broke out in May 1846 was the occupation of New Mexico and the Southwest, and to this end, he promptly dispatched an army of Missouri volunteers, under the command of General Stephen Watts Kearny.[4] Kearny knew that he would be forced to deal with the Indians and his reasoning told him he could easily resolve Indian troubles in the province. He assumed, as did most other Americans, that Indian difficulties in New Mexico existed due to the inefficiency (and even cowardice) of the Mexicans. The Americans felt superior to the Mexicans and were confident that the solution to all problems rested with the inauguration of an American government. They also assumed the Indians would immediately recognize the superiority and justice of the American government and rush to make peace. For a time events in New Mexico seemed to confirm the American belief. By the time the mistake had been recognized, the Indian situation had gotten out of hand.

The primary purpose of the army was to conquer the Mexican provinces of New Mexico and California. From the beginning, however, the Indians occupied considerable attention. Initial orders to Kearny noted "that many of our citizens engaged in trade with Santa Fe have vast amounts of property (perhaps a milion or two) in jeopardy, which it becomes the duty of the Government to protect." Though this order stressed protection from Mexican nationals as well as Indians, the War Department was concerned enough about the Indian situation to send another communication suggesting that Kearny take with him a supply of presents to help keep the Indians along the route quiet and loyal.[5]

Kearny formulated his policy toward the New Mexicans and the Indians on route. Convinced of his ability to halt Indian depredations, he hit upon the notion of offering protection to the territory and "ameliorating the condition of its inhabitants" as the best means of persuading Mexicans residents not to resist occupation. This idea matured as he came upon Las Vegas, the first major settlement in New Mexico. Here they found a fortified village with the inhabitants living in daily fear of Ute and Navajo raiders. Obviously a people forced to live under such circumstances would welcome a government which promised to bring the Indians under control. Kearny used this fact to his advantage in addressing the people of Las Vegas on August 15, 1846. After reporting that he came as a friend and admonishing the citizens not to resist, he noted the Indian situation: "From the Mexican government you have never received protection. The Apaches and the Navajos come down from the mountains and carry off your sheep, and even your women, whenever they please. My government will correct all this. It will keep off the Indians, protect you in your persons and property."[6]

The army then continued on toward Santa Fe, repeating similar assurances to every village along the way. They arrived in the capital on August 18, without firing a shot. This easy victory, and the fact that Mexican forces actually ran away from Kearny's troopers, served to convince the Americans that they were indeed correct in their assessment of the New Mexican government and people. This impression, in turn, led Kearny to make further commitments to the inhabitants. Still having no assurances the population intended to peacefully accept the occupation, he continued to stress his ability to offer protection from the Indians. Four days after his arrival, Kearny issued a proclamation once more pledging "to protect the persons and property of all quiet and peaceful inhabitants . . . against their enemies, the Eutaws, the Navajoes, and others."[7] Most New Mexicans, stunned by their defeat, seemed convinced the Americans could in fact live up to their promises, and they sat back to watch the results.

Kearny, to fulfil his promises, needed prompt action. He and his army would soon have to continue the march to California. In the meantime, all of the tribes had to be informed of the change in government and agree on some provision for halting the warfare. The Americans held the initial advantage due to the psychological effect of their swift victory—the Indians would hesitate in challenging this new power which had so easily defeated their old enemy.

The Pueblo tribes, not being at war with the Mexicans, rapidly came to an agreement. The loyalty of these people was critical to American success. They comprised a large segment of the New Mexican population, and their hostility could create a costly setback to plans for a peaceful transition to American rule. Fortunately Kearny's promises to return stolen property, his pledges of protection from the other tribes, and the impact of the Mexican defeat inclined the Pueblo to be receptive to American overtures. Delegations from the nearest Pueblo villages soon arrived to talk with the man who had so easily conquered their Mexican masters. However, not all the Pueblo were convinced of American good will. One young chief wanted to know if the Americans really intended to protect them. "The priests," he told Kearny, "had told him, that the Americans would plunder and kill them, and that such as they took prisoners they would brand on the face with a red-hot iron, and thus make them American citizens." The chief hinted that he might join with Mexican rebels to resist American occupaton if some assurances were not forthcoming. Kearny, impressed with this frank discussion, assured the delegations of his friendship and protection, and in return he received indications of friendship from the Pueblo. So convinced were the Americans of the success of the talks that Lieutenant William H. Emory quickly concluded that the Pueblo "are our fast friends now and forever."[8]

The real key to a successful Indian policy, however, rested in securing a peace with the so-called wild tribes. Assuming these people could be handled in the same manner as the Pueblo, Kearny decided to bring the tribes in for a conference, tell them of the American occupation, and require them to stop committing crimes. But the hostile tribes were not anxious to meet the Americans and the Apache brazenly plundered several Mexican ranches within the sight of American troops. Consequently, the army sent out detachments of troops to invite the Indians forcibly to the conference table. Kearny's dragoons chased the Apache and

Ute for several days before rounding up a few chiefs and bringing them back. Only Colonel Congreve Jackson, charged with
finding the Navajo, failed to bring in a delegation. Under the
presumption that these delegations represented their tribes,
Kearny admonished them to stop their raiding. He told the
Apache, for example, that they must stop all robberies. If they
agreed they would be protected, if not they would be destroyed.
At this point the Indians were still impressed with Kearny's bluff,
and one chief reportedly told the general that "I take your counsel because you are stronger than I."[9] To the Americans it seemed
as if both the Ute and Apache had agreed to respect the property
of the New Mexicans and the laws of the United States. Although
no Navajo came to Santa Fe it appeared only a matter of time before they too would come to terms.

During this first month of occupation, the Americans in New
Mexico, both civil and military, seemed confirmed in their opinions about the Indians. Everyone believed the Pueblo to be a
strong and brave people, decidedly grateful for the arrival of the
United States. The Pueblo, noted one correspondent, "are our
friends, and, indeed, in my opinion, the only people who heartily
wish for the continuation of the American government."[10] Toward the other tribes there existed an attitude of contempt. The
ease with which these tribes apparently had succumbed convinced
the Americans of the effectiveness of their methods. Susan Shelby
Magoffin, a contemporary observer of Santa Fe, wrote in her
diary that the Navajo would soon make peace, "which 'tis prob
able they will do thro' fear, as they deem the Gen. something almost superhuman since he has walked in so quietly and taken
possession." Soldiers echoed the same sentiments. The Indians,
noted one trooper, were readily brought to terms because they
were now dealing with Americans. Another said the Apache
would rather do anything than meet American troops in combat.[11] All seemed to believe a secure and lasting solution to the
Indian problem had been attained.

General Kearny, having secured peace in the territory, prepared to move on toward California. To keep an effective administration operating (although with somewhat dubious authority

since the territory had not been formally annexed) he appointed a territorial government headed by Charles Bent.[12] Three days later the American commander marched off toward the Pacific, leaving Colonel Doniphan's regiment behind to hold New Mexico until relieved by a regiment of fresh Missouri volunteers.

Kearny's peace collapsed even before he could leave the territory. As the army marched westward reports of Navajo depredations began to filter in. Then came word that Polvadera, a small village located only a few miles from the army, had been attacked. This disregard of the American presence forced Kearny to take stronger steps.[13] He found himself in a predicament, however. He had neither the time nor troops to engage in an extensive campaign against the Indians. Yet if he failed to carry out his promise to prevent raids, not only would the Indians lose respect for American power but the Mexicans might decide that rule by the United States offered no advantage.

Finally, on October 2, Kearny sent instructions for Colonel Alexander W. Doniphan to chastise the Navajo. His orders stated that since the Indians had not made peace as requested, it had become necessary to force them into better conduct. To help compensate for the lack of troops, Kearny issued orders permitting citizens from the Rio Abajo area to form "War Parties, to march into the country of their enemies, the Navajos, to recover their property, to make reprisals."[14] The only restrictions were that women and children must not be injured. Thus the Americans set a harmful precedent; the brutalities of these civilian armies created more problems than they ever solved.

Alexander Doniphan immediately prepared to carry out his orders. The colonel, a lawyer by profession who had joined the Missouri volunteers at the outbreak of war, seemed well equipped to carry out his task. The job would not be easy. He needed to convince the Navajo to bury their age-old hatred toward the Mexicans and stop the war. The situation itself was likely to confuse the Indians; they would have difficulty in understanding why the Americans made war upon the Mexicans while at the same time asking the Navajo to make peace.

Doniphan left for the Navajo country at the end of October. Even before entering the Indian territory, Colonel Jackson's detachment found several Indians who were willing to enter the Indian stronghold and arrange peace talks. The tribal headman refused to meet with the Americans in any of the Mexican villages and insisted that the white men come to them. Captain John W. Reid, hoping to find an agreeable meeting site, volunteered to lead a small company of men deep into the great Navajo nation. The exploits of this little band among hundreds of armed Indians further increased on both sides the belief that Anglo-Saxon frontiersmen were invincible:

The ease with which these few hardy and adventurous men appeared to obviate the difficulties, and surmount the obstacles which impeded their progress, and which seemed, until essayed, incredible of performance, afforded convincing argument that, in the affairs of men, to RESOLVE IS TO CONQUER; and that *men*, at least *AMERICANS*, can accomplish whatever is within the scope of possibility.[15]

The daring of the Missourians indeed impressed the Navajo. Reid's company was the first group of Americans to enter the Indian domain, and they did it with a boldness the Mexicans had never dared. Eventually, Reid came face to face with Narbona, now nearly seventy years old, whom the Americans believed to be the chief of all the Navajo. Narbona decided not to test these brash young men, and after some heated discussion with his own followers, sent word for his people to meet the soldiers. On November 21, the Indians gathered at Bear Spring where Colonel Doniphan waited. Negotiations began at once. The American officer explained that the United States now possessed New Mexica and all the inhabitants would be protected. But the United States also wanted peace with her "red brothers" and would offer them the same protection. If the Navajo refused American terms, however, they would be destroyed.

The Navajo were confused over American logic. One chief replied that the Americans had strange reasons indeed for war against the Indians: "We have waged war against the New Mexi-

cans for many years. . . . Our Cause was just. You have lately commenced a war against the same people. . . . You now turn upon
us for attempting to do what you have done yourselves. We cannot see why you have cause to quarrel with us for fighting the
New Mexicans on the west, while you do the same on the east."[16]
Doniphan, hard put to answer this argument, simply replied that
it was a custom to treat those who surrendered as friends.

Though still confused, the chiefs decided it best to sign a
treaty; if nothing else it would get the Americans out of their
country. Perhaps also some Navajo "ricos" hoped for federal protection of their flocks. The treaty, concluded on November 22,
dealt with all the problems Americans considered necessary for
a lasting peace. The Navajo agreed to stop warring with the
Mexicans, allowed free access into their country, and promised to
return all captives and stolen property.[17] Doniphan, in wording
the treaty, assumed the Navajo were ready to make important
concessions. All benefits went to the whites with only vague
promises of friendship to induce the Indians to keep the peace.
In its simplest form, Doniphan's treaty was based upon the myth
of American superiority. If this myth collapsed, there was little
to prevent the Indians from returning to their previous habits.

Indications that the Indians would not suddenly change their
ageold habits came as soon as Colonel Doniphan proposed taking
some of the Navajo chiefs with him to the Pueblo of Zuñi to conclude a treaty between the two tribes. Only a few Navajo could
be persuaded to attend the conference and they went in fear of
their lives. Once in Zuñi the antagonists fell to quarreling, and
the Americans soon found it one thing to get the Indians to agree
to peace in their own homes and quite another thing for them to
practice tolerance when face to face with their old enemies. Doniphan, however, intended to carry out his instructions, and the
two tribes were forced into a treaty of friendship and peace.[18]

The Missouri volunteers seemingly had accomplished their assignment. All of New Mexico was at peace. Doniphan, reporting
on the results of his expedition, stated that he visited every portion of the Navajo country and that over three-quarters of the
tribes had made the treaty. Surely they would not dare test the
awesome power of the United States. Yet not everyone seemed so

convinced, and one shrewd prophet wrote from Santa Fe the day after Doniphan returned that the Indians would not be brought to peace so easily—they would have to feel the power of American arms before a lasting peace could be secured.[19] Regardless of such adverse comment, the army was convinced its policy had proved successful. Colonel Doniphan marched off to new glories in Chihuahua, leaving Colonel Sterling Price, who had just arrived with a regiment of volunteers, to maintain the peace in New Mexico.

Meanwhile, Governor Bent, a man with considerable Indian experience, began to make recommendations to the Office of Indian Affairs for the permanent security of New Mexico. In a letter to William Medill, Bent estimated there were nearly 40,000 Indians now under American control in the territory. Agents and subagents would be needed immediately to control and pacify the Indians. In fact, he noted, it might even be wise to send a delegation from each tribe to Washington. A trip to the "States" could be beneficial since "they have no idea at this time of the power of the United States and have been so long in the habit of waging war and committing depredations against the Mexicans with impunity that they still show a disposition to continue the same kind of warfare now that the Territory is in the possession of the U.S." Bent also disagreed with the army's policy of using troops to negotiate treaties and then withdrawing to the villages. He felt that forts must be established in the Indian country. These posts—to be set up among the Ute and Navajo, at the crossing of the Arkansas, and on the Mexican border—would have to contain enough troops to punish any breach of the peace. Bent, consequently, when he heard about Doniphan's treaty, wrote that he had "but little ground to hope it will be permanent."[20]

Bent could only make recommendations. The Office of Indian Affairs had no power to send agents until New Mexico became part of the United States. Thus, for all practical purposes Indian affairs remained entirely under military jurisdiction. It required some time before Bent's ideas gained general recognition.

Colonel Sterling Price, a Missouri congressman who had resigned to fight the Mexicans, assumed command in New Mexico upon the departure of Doniphan.[21] Hardly had he settled down when indications began to appear that all was not well in the province. Some of the leading Mexican citizens, especially those deprived of power and prestige by American rule, were unhappy with the occupation. During December this faction began plotting to overthrow the American government and return the province to Mexico. Indian aid was essential to their plan, and using rumors that the Americans intended to confiscate Pueblo property, members of the clergy and others applied pressure to the local villages. To add encouragement, the insurrectionists stressed the great amount of booty to be obtained by a Mexican victory. The tactics worked well. By early January 1847, Governor Bent was receiving intelligence reports of general unrest in the Taos valley. Yet the Americans failed to heed the warning signs. When Colonel Price managed to break up one group of conspirtors he assumed the Mexicans had learned their lesson and he did nothing more.[22]

The Taos Revolt which erupted in January was political in motivation, not racial. The insurrectionists intended to kill all those in power, whether American, Mexican or Indian. They struck January 19, killing Governor Bent and a number of other officials in Taos. Colonel Price quickly rallied his troops and defeated the rebels in a pitched battle at the Indian pueblo. Price's official report on the action gives no indication of how many natives were involved, but it may be assumed that most of the one hundred and fifty casualties were Indian.[23] The affair had a significant impact on the Pueblo. They found themselves once more the victims of Mexican treachery; never again would they test American arms. The quick suppression of the revolt might have reassured the Americans had it not been for the obvious fact that something had gone wrong with their Indian policy.

The Taos Revolt marked the end of the bloodless conquest of New Mexico and the myth of American superiority. From the Indian point of view, American casualties in the insurrection had shown the troopers to be mortal and spread too thin to be very effective in checking the activities of the more powerful tribes. The Navajo, Apache, Ute, and Comanche began to realize that American power was little more than a bluff and nothing really prevented them from returning to their old way of life. They were aided in this belief by the activities of Mexicans who wanted to harass the United States government and keep New Mexico in turmoil.[24]

Indian affairs in New Mexico soon disintegrated. In February came word that "the Nabajoe Inds. have broken their treaty and recommenced depredations." On the east, Apache and Mexican raiding parties began falling upon the outlying settlements. They attacked army grazing detachments, killed a few soldiers, ran off the horses, and made good their escape. By May conditions were intolerable. The overtaxed government forces could do no more than send out token expeditions to pursue the raiding parties. These tactics hardly impressed the Indians. To make matters even worse, the Missouri volunteers actually fled from the enemy on several occasions. This display of American "superiority" only confirmed the Indian belief that they had little to fear from the army. Colonel Price noted the startling effect of such developments when he reported that failure to capture the guilty parties only caused the Indians to become more aggressive and bold.[25]

Even more disturbing to the Americans was the fact that the success of the Apache and Navajo encouraged other tribes to act. Most significant from the military viewpoint were the tribes located along the Santa Fe road. This route provided the only source of supplies for the military establishment in New Mexico. During the latter part of 1846 and 1847, military supplies, troops, mounts, and merchants plied the trail in increasing volume.[26] At this critical time, however, the government found it necessary to leave the trail unguarded. Soldiers were needed elsewhere, and all that stood between the travelers and disaster was Indian fear that the Americans had the power to chastise them. With such tempting bait and so few soldiers, it only took the events in New Mexico to set the Comanche and other tribes to work along the Arkansas.

During 1847 the St. Louis papers carried numerous reports of successful Indian attacks along the route. By July even the army was finding it impossible to traverse the trail and few supplies were getting through. In such an atmosphere complaints began to rise above the confusion. One returning volunteer noted in disgust that the Indians were "constantly committing their high handed measures, almost with impunity. . . . They begin to think, no doubt, Americans are afraid of them. It is high time the Government was taking some steps to protect her citizens and herself from these repeated outrages." "The Pawnees," noted another observer, "are playing the duce with the provision wagons. . . . [They have] killed men, burned several wagons . . . and I am glad of this because now, perhaps, Uncle Sam, the old fool, will punish these Indians who have so long committed outrages upon the traders with impunity."[27]

The federal government slowly reacted to these complaints. As early as April 1847, the Adjutant General's Office had requested a new regiment of Missouri volunteers, but only a few of these troops were designated for service on the Santa Fe route. During the summer, however, it became clear to the War Department that much more protection was needed to prevent the embarrassing losses. The crescendo of demands from frontier editors, politicians, and army officers, all of whom seemed to feel that more troops would solve the dilemma, finally forced department officials to yield and assign the entire new regiment to protect the route to New Mexico.[28] It was hoped that fresh troops could provide some measure of safety to travelers and regain some of the army's waning prestige.

The new battalion enlisted three infantry companies of Dutch and German emigrants after the Missourians refused to volunteer upon discovering they were going to be on garrison duty in Indian country rather than winning glory fighting Mexicans. Lieutenant Colonel William Gilpin, a man with considerable frontier experience, commanded the new battalion.[29] The regiment marched from Fort Leavenworth in late September. Two companies of dragoons proceeded to the vicinity of the Arkansas with orders to attack and disperse all hostile Indians. Gilpin and the German troops advanced to the crossing of the Arkansas and there built a post, called Fort Mann.[30] These two moves, the government believed, would assure the permanent security of the Santa Fe trail.

Omens of pending disaster plagued the expedition from the beginning. Most of the German troops spoke or understood little English. They quarreled with the Americans and disobeyed their officers. Even worse, they took all Indians to be hostile and it "required some vigilance and constant watching to prevent them from killing every Indian they met on the road." Soldiers of this nature seemed ill-suited to further efforts toward securing any kind of peace. No sooner had Fort Mann been occupied than serious trouble began. Colonel Gilpin, anxious to carry out his orders, immediately took the field leaving Captain William Pelzer, an emigrant, in command of the post. Soon thereafter a party of Pawnees arrived at the fort professing to be friends. Pelzer first invited the Indians into the fort, then becoming suspicious, attempted to take them captive. In the wild melee that followed several of the Indians were murdered in cold blood.[31]

The uncalled-for massacre at Fort Mann ruined American plans to pacify the Indians along the trail. Thomas Fitzpatrick reported to the Indian department that "such wanton and uncalled for attacks on Indians are highly reprehensible; and cannot result otherwise than in the utmost contempt, and still more hostility towards us." The army, too, was aware of the setback. Charges were eventually brought against Pelzer for conduct tending to subvert attempts to pacify the Indians. Colonel John Garland, who conducted the investigation, tried to salvage the situation by releasing the remaining prisoner with instruction to carry back to his tribe word that their "Great Father" had punished the guilty man.[32] Unfortunately the damage had been done.

Failure thus marked the first full year of occupation. The Indians had called the American bluff and had gotten away with it. Seemingly the Anglo-Saxon frontiersmen were powerless to prevent the Indians from doing as they pleased. Statistics give a partial indication of the situation. On the Santa Fe trail alone, some forty-seven men were reported killed, 330 wagons destroyed, and 6,550 head of stock plundered. In New Mexico proper losses, particularly property, were undoubtedly higher as the

Navajo and Apache had resumed raiding. In fact, by the end of the year only the occupied villages could feel secure—the Indians controlled the countryside as effectively as they had before Kearny arrived. Still the government believed in a simple solution. If Americans were just given complete control in New Mexico, President Polk told Congress in December 1847, "we could effectually prevent these tribes from committing such outrages."[33] The spirit of Manifest Destiny died hard.

Opinions on improving the situation were rife on the frontier. Many army officers still believed they could handle the Indians and waited with anticipation for the campaigning season of 1848. Colonel Price and some others also felt the Mexicans were behind much of the trouble, and believed that once the war ended the Indians would be relatively easy to handle. New Mexicans generally clamored for more troops and civilian war parties. The ever-present Fitzpatrick, afraid that Indians under his charge above the Arkansas would be influenced by the events in New Mexico, believed the trouble existed within the military organization. He disapproved of using infantry and artillery in a situation that obviously called for dragoons. His letters to the Indian Office continually stressed the necessity of chastising the Indians before they would respect the power of the United States.[34]

Several factors became obvious as the new year advanced: the government did not intend to do anything new, the citizens of New Mexico were becoming outraged by the continued troubles, and the Indians could use the situation to their advantage. The actions of Colonel Price led to a further deterioration of the American position. Price had been reluctant to deploy all his troops against the Indians because of persistent rumors of Mexican activities in Chihuahua. Early in February he acted on these rumors, taking nearly all the mounted force in the territory on a useless expedition to the Mexican province and leaving Colonel E. W. B. Newby in command of the few remaining troops. The military position of the United States reached a new low during this period and Indian raids increased proportionally. "The consequences of all this," Newby reported to Washington, have made themselves woefully manifest in numerous instances, and under circumstances exceedingly aggravating— It has only been some three weeks since, that a band of Navajo Indians actually came within twenty miles of this point [Santa Fe] and after committing several murders among the Mexican inhabitants, carried away some prisoners and drove off eight or ten hundred head of stock. More recently, the Appaches, in considerable numbers drove off with impunity, several hundred sheep from a rancho, only sixteen miles distant from Las Vegas; and but three days since a band of the Navajoes again actually came within one mile and a half of Albuquerque—almost in sight of the garrison, and after murdering four Mexicans, drove away four thousand sheep.[35]

Newby further explained that the American position in New Mexico was becoming extremely grave and producing adverse effects on the Mexican population. "Perhaps," he wrote to the adjutant general, "in no other province of Mexico, as yet conquered by our arms, have the people manifested a higher feeling of friendship . . . [and a disposition to] pass permanently under the protecting wing of our republic." But the declining American power undermined the feeling of friendship. Newby's lack of troops left him "utterly powerless" and "no matter how great his anxiety to accomplish what is certainly expected from him, he has no other chance than to sit still, while murder and robbery are being committed under the very eyes of his garrison and within a few miles of the Capitol of the territory."

Reports of raids upon the Mexican inhabitants continued to pour into army headquarters. Newby finally could take no more and decided to lead a small expedition into the Navajo country. At the last moment a few chiefs came out and agreed to a treaty. But Newby's treaty, like Doniphan's, was not based on force. Rather it asked the Navajo to exchange prisoners and affirmations of peace with the Mexicans in return for vague promises of American friendship.[36] For the Navajo, signing the treaty simply put off the Americans. The Colonel, however, seemed convinced that one troublesome tribe had been pacified and he marched back to Santa Fe, leaving the Indians more than ever convinced that the Americans were no real threat.

A number of people in the territory strongly criticized Newby's treaty. Major A. W. Reynolds, who had been on the expedition, publicly criticized his superior for not marching into the main part of the Indian country and forcing a stronger treaty on them. As it was, Reynolds noted, Newby had made an insufficient peace, "he halted upon the *banks of the Rubicon*, without ATTEMPT-ING to cross." Most inhabitants had no faith in Indian promises and agreed that a lasting peace would not be forthcoming until the tribe felt the "strong arm" of the military. One man asked that the government take strong measures and if the Indians failed to respond, that it lay waste to their country "and wage a war of destruction, until they are anxious for peace, and glad to abandon their depredations upon the people of this territory."[37]

On the Santa Fe road things were little better. Gilpin's battalion had troubles of their own. The commander had decided to winter his dragoons among the Cheyenne and Arapaho living along the upper Arkansas because of rumors that Comanche success had persuaded other tribes to join in attacking travelers. While among these tribes, Gilpin hit upon the idea of using the Indians themselves to establish peace. Convinced that they had been overawed by the presence of his troops, and hearing some of the Cheyenne chiefs talk of settling down, the Colonel concluded that an agricultural community could be established at the crossing of the Arkansas. Once the settlement became a fact, the Cheyenne and Arapaho, cherishing their property, would help keep the other Indians in line.[38]

Gilpin attempted to enlist the aid of the Indian bureau by asking Thomas Fitzpatrick, the agent charged with the tribes involved, to cooperate. "No policy," the agent wrote back, "could be more uncertain, or dangerous than to employ Indians in any shape or form in this country for the purpose of attempting to tranquelise [sic] it. Their well known faithlessness and treachery and whom no difference exists in regard to villany ought to be forever a bar against such proceedings."[39] Moreover, he noted, if the United States could not provide safety for travelers then it might as well abandon the newly acquired territory.

Fitzpatrick's refusal to agree with Gilpin created a strain between the two arms of the government and worked to hinder efforts to secure peace on the trail. Gilpin, outraged at Fitzpatrick's
response, refused further cooperation with the Indian department just at a time when cooperation was necessary. Whiskey
sellers were invading the trail and the army represented the only
police power in the area. Liquor had existed on the trail for some
time but the old-timers knew better than to supply it to the Indians. Some of the new traders, however, ignoring the safety of
everyone, saw a potentially profitable trade in alcohol. Early in
1848 Indian agents along the Missouri reported that armed
groups of traders intended taking large quantities of liquor with
them in defiance of the government. The agents strongly urged
Colonel Gilpin's cooperation in stopping the caravans. Fitzpatrick himself suggested to Gilpin the necessity of letting no violation of the law occur in this remote country as the situation could
soon get out of hand. Undoubtedly Gilpin did not wish to see liquor enter the Indian country either, but when it came to coop-
erating with Fitzpatrick he would not budge.[40] Using the excuse
that he lacked troops, the commander at Fort Mann turned down
requests for assistance, leaving the Indian department no means
of punishing the offenders.

Gilpin meanwhile undertook a campaign to clear the entire
trail of Indians. The command first moved along the lower portions of the route in an attempt to force a fight. In this he was
manifestly unsuccessful. During the summer another campaign
was conducted in the vicinity of Fort Mann, and a good number
of Comanche warriors were reported killed. Yet these skirmishes
meant little. Although Gilpin's officers claimed victory, it was obvious that they were not protecting the trail. No one, not even the
Indians, doubted the army's ability to defeat them in individual
combat, but the army could not be everywhere and the Comanche
were noted for attacking where the troops weren't. Colonel Gilpin, however, humbly reported to his superiors that his advances
had succeeded in bringing peace to the entire western portion of
the trail. "It will be perceived then in what manner so many

tribes of Indians, inhabiting an immense and various territory have been defeated by a single battalion."[41] Such reports lulled the War Department into believing the Indians could be pacified without any significant changes in policy.

During the latter part of 1848 there were a few significant happenings. The mid-year ratification of the treaty of Guadalupe Hidalgo ended the necessity of having so many men under arms. Volunteers were mustered out of service, and the army began to think about a peacetime military organization for New Mexico. The secretary of war, William L. Marcy, suggested that not more than three or four posts were necessary and 1,200 men would be more than adequate to garrison these posts. On the Santa Fe trail Gilpin's battalion was also ready to leave the service, and some questioned that they should be replaced at all. Marcy believed (based on Gilpin's reports) the Indians to be "defeated and dispersed," rendering a garrison at Fort Mann unnecessary and saving the government considerable expense. Protest against any withdrawal came from the frontier. Gilpin himself wrote that the battalion must be replaced immediately or the Indians would again take possession of the trail. Santa Fe traders pleaded with the government to protect their lives and property. And Fitzpatrick again warned the Indian commissioner of the consequences: "Let not the government suppose, for a moment, that those marauding tribes who have been successful so long without meeting any reverses will now desist, and abandon that way which they have found so profitable, without some great cause."[42] Marcy refused to listen, and as Gilpin's command returned to Fort Leavenworth to be mustered out, the Comanche took control of the trail once more.

The return of peacetime conditions also brought a new military governor to New Mexico. On October 11, 1848, Lieutenant Colonel John M. Washington, an experienced military man, replaced Sterling Price. Washington immediately reorganized his forces "to more effectually secure the principal settlements against Indian incursions," sending his regular troops to six posts along the Rio Grande valley. Army headquarters were established in Santa Fe. Albuquerque, Socorro, and El Paso all received garrisons of troops with companies being scattered among several other villages. The total effective military force probably stood at about a thousand at the beginning of 1849.[43] The new governor believed that only military force could make the hostile tribes accept American control. Once pacified, however, Washington, fully believing in the superiority of the white man's way, thought some type of reservation must be established:

the period has arrived when they must restrain themselves within prescribed limits and cultivate the earth for an honest livelyhood, or, be destroyed. This subject will become one of serious interest with the Government at home and should be settled without delay. The particular location and extent of these limits and the inducements held out for a change from their present roving habits to the pursuit of agriculture, from the savage state to that of civilization, are well worthy of attention.[44]

A few days after Washington's arrival in New Mexico the Democrats were swept from national office. Because of the confusions that resulted from the slavery issue, Congress had refused to decide the exact status of New Mexico. The territory, though now a part of the United States, remained under military control with no recognized civilian law. Under such circumstances the Office of Indian Affairs still did not consider New Mexico under its jurisdiction. Yet sole military responsibility for the tribes had obviously failed to bring peace and the government of Zachary Taylor refused to wait for congressional action before thinking about a civilian Indian policy for the territory.

The military was relieved of its sole jurisdicton over the Indians of New Mexico as soon as the Whig administration entered office. Secretary of the Interior Ewing moved the old Council Bluffs agency to Santa Fe and appointed James S. Calhoun agent. From South Carolina and a staunch Whig, Calhoun was a politician by profession.[45] The new agent apparently knew little about Indian affairs or New Mexico, yet he proved a man of great ability with a genuine concern for the Indians. His one difficulty might best be described as a personality flaw; he became "very intemperate" when his advice was not followed, making it difficult for others to work with him.

Before Calhoun could reach his new post hostilities reached a new peak. In the spring of 1849 the Ute and Apache fell upon wagon trains and villages, killing a number of citizens, and running off substantial amounts of stock. By March Colonel Washington, finding the troops under his command insufficient to prevent the widely scattered attacks, issued a call for five companies of volunteers. He justified these additional troops as necessary "to meet the emergency before a wide-spread scene of havoc and ruin shall have marked the progress of the hostile and marauding bands over the Territory of New Mexico."[46]

Washington's volunteers did little to enhance the military in New Mexico. They remained on the defensive. Troops stayed in towns and villages, taking the field only in response to Indian raids or depredations. Consequently, the army was never in the right place at the right time, and when the troopers tried to punish the guilty parties, they found themselves outdistanced by the better-mounted tribesmen. During the summer Colonel Washington found it necessary to write a flood of unfavorable reports, all confirming the sad state of affairs. On July 4, for example, he wrote that "a large party of Apache Indians entered the Valley of Abique and murdered a number of inhabitants, amounting to not less than ten." A month later he reported that "within the last three weeks several of the inhabitants have been murdered by them and a considerable quantity of their stock run off."[47]

New Mexicans had suffered three long years of American mismanagement and they were angry at everyone. Wild rumors that all of the tribes were forming a coalition to destroy the "unprotected" settlements served to intensify their rage. Governor Washington drew most of the criticism. One prominent citizen, William S. Messervy, took the liberty of complaining both to the secretary of war and the St. Louis papers that "we are now in actual war with four of the most powerful and numerous tribes on the continent, all living in close proximity to the territory and all making daily incursions into our settlements."[48] In such circumstances, Messervy demanded a new and more aggressive military commander.

New Mexicans were further upset with the federal government for not providing them with a civilian government. Although one faction wanted immediate statehood and another desired territorial status, they all protested military rule. Inhabitants suspected that the federal government had abandoned them. The consistent lack of sufficient military force seemed to confirm this contention. One outraged territorial stated that the problem was not with Colonel Washington but the War Department, "who have *abandoned* him or his gallant little force to an unequal conflict."[49] Most citizens wanted Congress to provide them with a regular government and more troops. Only then did they foresee a solution to the Indian problem.

Such criticism and the continuous Indian raids prompted Governor Washington to launch an offensive operation in August. He firmly believed he could accomplish what the military had failed to do in the past—"lay the foundation for a lasting peace."[50] Agent Calhoun, who arrived in Santa Fe about the first of the month, was invited to represent the Indian department.

The great Navajo campaign of 1849 has become famous in New Mexico because it penetrated the heart of Navajo country for the first time. Washington's command of 350 men departed from Santa Fe on August 15, 1849. Two weeks later the expedition met in council three Navajo chiefs, including Narbona, whom the Americans believed to be the principal chief. Washington and Calhoun both tried to impress upon the Navajo that the tribe was now under American jurisdiction and must obey all laws. That the agent was clearly thinking about establishing a reservation for the Navajo and keeping them there by force was indicated in Calhoun's speech to the gathering:

Tell them that, by this treaty, the government of the United States are to be recognized as having the right to establish military posts in their country whenever they may think it necessary, in order to [assure] the protection of them and their rights.

That the government of the United States claim the right to have their boundaries fixed and marked, so as to prevent any misunderstanding on this point between them and their neighbors.

Any chance of a successful treaty was destroyed when one of the Mexican volunteers spotted a horse that had been stolen by the Indians. Washington ordered the horse returned, and when the Mexican moved toward the horse's new owner, the entire band resisted. Colonel Washington then "gave the word to fire & the guard did so & at the first shot the indians broke & fled up a ravine to the N. . . . Narbona the head chief was shot 4 or 5 places & scalped."[51] The death of Narbona ended any hope of peace with the Navajo.

Washington proceeded on to the Canyon de Chelly where he found another band of Navajo. After a display of military force, two chiefs, Mariano Martinez and Chapeton, agreed to negotiate the treaty Washington failed to get from Narbona. As usual the Americans assumed the signature bound the entire tribe. The treaty guaranteed everything the government desired: the tribe recognized they were now under American jurisdiction, that they would remain forever at peace, that all captives would be returned, and that the federal government might now determine the boundary of Navajo lands.[52] The army then returned to Santa Fe.

"This expedition has been effected, and, as I think, with important results," Lieutenant James H. Simpson wrote to Colonel J. J. Abert upon his return to Santa Fe.[53] Needless to say, the young lieutenant's predictions were overoptimistic. Again the Americans had drawn up a treaty that met their conception of peace without offering any visible advantages to the tribe other than the promise of American friendship; and from what the Navajo had just witnessed, American friendship was something less than desirable. The most significant feature of the treaty, therefore, was the Navajo consent to the establishment of a reservation and military post, an agreement the United States eventually forced all the Navajo to adhere to, even though it had been agreed to by only a small portion of the tribe.

The immediate relationship between the two antagonists was not altered by the treaty. No sooner had Washington returned to Santa Fe than the Navajo resumed raiding. New Mexicans, wanting something more vigorous, were furious with the entire expedition. One letter to the St. Louis *Daily Republican* stated that "Col. Washington, with a large force, was in the heart of the Navajo country, while citizens almost within sight of Santa Fe were compelled to sit upon their mules, and behold the enemy, superior in force, drive off their horses and cattle." Another letter denounced the government of Colonel Washington as well as the treaty: "Col. W. killed six Navajos, and returned deluded with the idea he had conquered them."[54]

At this juncture, Calhoun began a detailed study of the Indian problem in New Mexico. Past experience indicated to him that reservations were the answer. Writing to the Indian commissoner in October 1849, he noted that only the full display of military force would end the depredations. Calhoun saw little incentive for the hostile tribesmen to remain at peace until they were convinced that the Americans possessed the power to conquer and punish them.[55] Civilization could begin as soon as the tribes decided on peace. This ultimate goal might best be accomplished by concentrating the tribes in small villages modeled after the Pueblo towns. Such measures, he confidently predicted, would "restrict intercourse with them, and instruct them, and compel them to cultivate the soil."

Within a few months Calhoun worked out a more specific reservation proposal. Four tracts of land, not within a hundred miles of each other, would be selected for the home of the Navajo, Apache, Comanche, and Ute. Here they would be forced to remain. It would be necessary to supply the Indians until they could become self-sufficient. Admittedly, this was an expensive proposition, but Calhoun laid the matter on the line: "To establish order in this territory you must either submit to these heavy expenditures, or exterminate the mass of these Indians."[56]

Military force remained the key to any successful plan. But Calhoun realized that the army needed to change its policy of operating out of the Mexican villages. Posts were required in the Indian country to keep the tribes on their respective lands. Not surprisingly, Calhoun's recommendations coincided with the desires of many army officers and New Mexican citizens. Upon the conclusion of the Navajo expedition, Colonel Washington himself recommended to the adjutant general that the only way to secure a firm and durable peace with the Navajo was to plant a military post in their country. New Mexicans also felt that forts must be established. Thus when the territorials met in September 1849 to select Hugh N. Smith to lobby in Congress for a civil government, they issued instructions "that he shall urge the establishment of a fort in the heart of the Navijo [sic] country, to protect the people against incursions and robberies of this formidable and marauding tribe."[57]

Calhoun also vigorously demanded agents for the various other tribes. As matters then stood he was the only person in the territory to handle the civilization effort. Nearly every one of his numerous letters to the Indian department contained a plea for help. "The presence of Agents," he wrote in October 1849, "in various places in the Indian country, is indispensibly necessary—their presence is demanded by every principle of humanity—by every generous obligation of kindness—of protection, and good government throughout this vast territory."[58] Such sentiments received a sympathetic reception in the Indian department. Both the secretary of the interior and the commissioner desired to send more agents to New Mexico, but as long as the status of New Mexico remained uncertain and the question of slavery in the Mexican Cession occupied the nation's attention, Congress persistently refused to provide the required legislation (Chapter 3). The department could only write letters of encouragement. Calhoun continued to work for his objective alone.

At this time Calhoun became particularly interested in the fate of the Pueblo peoples who were spread throughout New Mexico. The South Carolinian, like most Americans, considered the Pueblo a special case, more fit in many ways for citizenship than the Mexicans. The Pueblo were everything the Americans considered admirable in an Indian. They lived in well-constructed cities, cultivated their fields, and kept large herds of horses and sheep. Calhoun believed that they must become citizens and participate in local affairs. It was a foregone conclusion that the Mexicans would receive the franchise when Congress established a civil government. In such circumstances, Calhoun thought, common justice dictated the inclusion of the Pueblo; *"they are from their general intelligence, and probity as much entitled to select their agents,* as the mass of New Mexico."[59] Yet citizenship for the Pueblo was a delicate question in the territory. Their wealth, property, and prosperity were attractive to whites and Mexicans who stood to gain by restricting their civil rights.

Calhoun impressed upon the Indian Office the necessity of providing the Pueblo with agents. These men, he believed, could teach the tribesmen more about agriculture, enhance their prosperity, and keep white opportunists away. To effect this objective, the trade and intercourse laws had to be extended to the Pueblo. He further suggested that the tribesmen be used to help bring the hostile tribes under control. "Allow me to organize a force from the Pueblo Indians, with the means to subsist them, and to pay them, and my life for it, in less than six months I will so tame the Navajos and Utahs that you will scarcely hear of them again."[60] The proposal to arm the Indians brought Calhoun into direct opposition to the army who considered the entire matter dangerous. However, as long as the military seemed unable to protect the frontier, the agent persisted in his demands.

The appointment of Colonel John Munroe to replace Washington as the military governor of New Mexico increased the possibility of friction between the military and civilians. The new commander arrived on October 22, 1849, and immediately assumed his duties. Munroe, once described as "the best mathematician in the army, as well as the ugliest looking man," was an artillery officer of Scottish heritage.[61] He was immediately resented by New Mexicans because he served as a daily reminder that the territory had not been granted a civil government. As strongheaded as Calhoun, he soon became immersed in a dispute over Indian policy.

In October 1849, a storm erupted over Indian affairs in the territory. At the center of matters was the massacre of John M. White and several others. White, a prominent Santa Fe citizen, had been attacked by Jicarilla Apaches along the Santa Fe trail. The murders themselves were enough to arouse the ire of New Mexicans, but even more disturbing was the fact that Mrs. White

and her young daughter were captured. The affair received great
publicity in the territory and set off an immediate search for the
women. Troopers eventually found the body of Mrs. White, but
the daughter never was recovered.[62]

The White massacre became the rallying point for criticism of
the government's handling of Indian affairs. The St. Louis *Daily
Missouri Republican* bristled with letters denouncing both the
army and the national government. Most complained that the
Indians were able to commit their depredations and murders
with impunity. One letter, printed on December 19, 1849, made
a mockery of the entire army effort since 1846. The author noted
that Munroe, instead of taking the offensive, simply repeated
tired old promises to make treaties with the hostile tribes while
threatening the Indians with dreadful consequences if the peace
we broken:

I fancy that I now see the *awful terror* of the chiefs as they listen to
the Governor's "consequences." Why sirs, the Navajos have *listened*
to the threat of "consequences" until they but have *to laugh at it*.
These same "consequences" have been held over them by Gen. Karny
[*sic*], Col. Doniphan, Col. Price, Col. Newby, . . . and our late
"Tecumseh Killer," Colonel Washington, but not one of them has
yet experienced what the *reality* of this bugaboo "consequences"
are.[63]

New Mexicans used Indian troubles as still another argument
for their own civil government. The state of Indian affairs was a
constant topic of interest at meetings demanding statehood.
Travel anywhere outside the cities, orators all too truthfully
noted, was impossible unless citizens went armed for battle. A
number of individuals proposed that New Mexicans take matters
into their own hands. If the overextended army would not or
could not provide safety, the inhabitants felt ready to do the job.
One local resident said that things were better under "the
imbecile" Mexican rule because at least citizens were allowed to
conduct campaigns against their enemy. Since the army would
not protect him, he now asked that private citizens be allowed to
attack the tribes and keep all plunder. This, he claimed, would
"do more to bring the Navajos to terms of lasting peace than a

thousand such futile campaigns as this last ridiculous one of Col. Washington."[64]

Such citizen armies would be little more than vigilante groups and neither Calhoun nor Munroe looked on them with favor. Warfare of such a vindictive nature would ruin all attempts at pacifying the hostile tribes by turning the legitimate grievances of citizens into a scalp hunt. Moreover, opening Indian country to white penetration promised to increase an already flourishing illegal trade in whiskey and guns.[65]

The year 1850 brought no relief to New Mexico. Continued deterioration of the military position was clearly evident. Apache, Navajo, and Ute raiders kept up a steady stream of attacks. As long as the troops remained stationed in villages, the Indians maintained the advantage of surprise and better mounts. Major Enoch Steen, for example, was forced to watch the Apache carry out a raid within view of his post at Doña Ana without being able to prevent it (the Indians fled before the dragoons could mount and take the field). "When Indians become so bold that they came in broad daylight within a mile of an U.S. Garrison where Dragoons are stationed and drive off stock and murder defenceless herders," the disheartened Major wrote to Monroe, "I think it then becomes necessary to chastise them."[66] Similar reports flooded the commander's desk in the early part of 1850.

Colonel Munroe's hands were virtually tied until the War Department changed its policy. More troops were needed and they must be mounted. The large body of infantry stationed in the territory might be acceptable for garrison duty, but they were worse than useless for field service against mounted hostiles. The department, however, was in no condition to aid the Colonel. Costs of maintaining troops on the frontier had proven extremely high. Congress, as usual, failed to provide for such a contingency, and General Winfield Scott therefore reluctantly rejected Munroe's request.[67] Matters grew even worse when in the middle of March the department proposed withdrawing some of its forces in New Mexico before replacements had arrived. Fortunately, Munroe prevailed upon the department to retain the troopers until the new men could arrive.[68]

In addition to strictly army matters, Munroe had civilian problems. During the early summer the drive to obtain statehood for New Mexico intensified, and in May Munroe was forced, reluctantly, to authorize the election of a convention to prepare a state constitution.[69] As might be expected, Indian affairs figured in the debates that followed. The Pueblo in particular were becoming increasingly apprehensive about the formation of a state government before the U.S. intercourse laws were extended to New Mexico. Without federal protection, a local white government might be inclined to deprive the Pueblo of the civil and property rights granted to them under the Mexican government and maintained by American military rule. Some citizens had encouraged these fears for a number of months before Munroe approved of the convention. According to Calhoun, who favored statehood, such activities were perpetuated by certain "designing Americans" opposed to any form of government in which they might lose power. For whatever reason, the Pueblo were worried and actively complained to Calhoun about the possibility of "aggressions, encroachments upon their lands, and unjust interference with their laws and customs, and the general administration of justice." Several chiefs urged the agent to intercede on their behalf by requesting the president to extend the trade and intercourse laws over them, and one group even asked Calhoun to come and live in their village so that they might benefit from his personal intervention.[70] Calhoun, of course, could do nothing more than offer reassurance. Congress still had given him no authority to act.

The statehood faction finished their constitution despite Pueblo unrest and lack of encouragement from Congress and called for voter approval on June 20, 1850. The Indians became quite agitated as the election approached. A violent contest erupted as those desiring territorial status worked to defeat the constitution. The arguments of both sides seemingly confirmed the Pueblo belief that they would be deprived of their rights if the constitution passed. To add to the difficulty, Governor Munroe issued a well-meaning but misinterpreted proclamation on June 6 advising the Indians to remain out of New Mexican affairs. This seemed to convince the chiefs that they were about to be abandoned by the government. When the territorials approved the constitution all their fears seemed on the verge of fulfilment.[71]

The actions of New Mexicans after the election gave the Indians little comfort. Citizens generally believed the adoption of a constitution gave them the right to operate a civilian government and they proceeded to elect a legislature and governor. As long as Congress refused to legalize the status of the territory, however, New Mexicans had no authority to exercise civilian control. Thus Munroe continued to pursue the duties of governor, much to the anger of New Mexicans. The Pueblo were still uneasy, and so on June 25, 1850, the governor, in cooperation with Calhoun, wrote another letter to the chiefs stating that they had not been abandoned by the government and were in the same position of safety as before the election. Even this did little. The statehood enthusiasts continued to excite Indian fears. Civilian Lieutenant Governor Manuel Alvarez and Munroe argued violently over civilian affairs in the territory, and the newly elected legislature commenced meeting in spite of Munroe's protests. Although the constitution of 1850 did not expressly exclude the Pueblo Indians as citizens, the legislature soon indicated that they would grant participation in government only under an impossible system of taxation.[72] So Pueblo apprehensions were not eased. Later in the year, however, Congress denied statehood to New Mexico, and a few months later the trade and intercourse laws were extended over the territory. This appeased the Pueblo for a while.

Meanwhile, Secretary of War George Crawford had ordered Colonel George A. McCall, Third United States Infantry, to investigate the confusing conditions in New Mexico. McCall's first report, dated July 15, 1850, took pains to stress the necessity of placating the Pueblo Indians lest they turn against the Americans.[73] Most of the report, however, revolved around the military situation in the territory. McCall was convinced that the economic prosperity of New Mexico was being destroyed by the unchecked depredations of the hostile Indians. Citizens could not carry on the normal economic life of the province—mining, agriculture, and stock raising—because of the danger from Indian attack. "It would," McCall wrote to Crawford, "from certain indications appear that the future prosperity of the state, . . . will in a great measure depend upon the impression now to be made on these Indians."

The inability of the United States to repress the Navajo and Apache occupied much of the inspector's attention. His solution was for the government to inaugurate the decisive action long demanded by New Mexicans. He particularly recommended the establishment of a fort in the midst of the Navajo nation. "Their thievish propensities could then be controled [sic], and they might in a short time by judicious management be induced to give up their roving habits and settle themselves in permanent towns in the vicinity of their fields." If this measure proved a success, predicted the colonel, the Navajo should soon be as loyal and docile as the Pueblo. McCall saw more difficulty with the Apache and other tribes but he believed that essentially the same solution would succeed. The Indians would have to be placed on reservations, fed, taught, and civilized.

McCall's report is significant not because it stated new ideas, but because of its adoption by the War Department. Returning to Washington, the colonel issued a follow-up report that guided decisive changes in the military situation in the territory. He suggested three forts "in the heart of the Indian country." These posts would have to be strong enough to impress the Indians and "to punish them in their strongholds for the offences they commit beyond their own boundaries."[74]

Not unexpectedly, then, changes in the New Mexican Indian situation occurred in 1851. As will be remembered, the Compromise of 1850 brought territorial status to New Mexico at the end of the year. The Whig administration appointed James Calhoun governor, and as such he also assumed the office of ex officio superintendent of Indian affairs. Moreover, the Indian appropriation bill passed by Congress on February 27, 1851, extended the trade and intercourse acts to the territory and authorized four full agents to work under the superintendent. For the first time,

Calhoun felt he possessed the means necessary for the reforms he had long advocated.

At the same time, the army, under Colonel Edward V. Sumner, began to implement the changes suggested by McCall. Sumner had been named to replace Munroe as military commander of New Mexico in February and, upon receiving his orders, had indicated to the adjutant general his intention of making major changes. Of particular importance was his remark that "I should wish to withdraw the troops from the towns, where they become worthless, and station them . . . on the frontier."[75]

It was some time before Sumner arrived in New Mexico, and Governor Calhoun felt compelled to take more immediate moves to placate the population. He revised his earlier position on civilian armies and on March 18, 1851, he issued a proclamation to the people of the territory recommending the formation of "Volunteer Corps" for the protection of families, homes, and property. He permitted these groups to take the offensive, with all confiscated Indian property to be divided among the participants. The next day the same privileges were extended to the Pueblo Indians.[76] Calhoun apparently believed this was the only effective way to subdue the hostile tribes and restore peace. It also made the governor more popular with the people. But the military had other ideas. Retiring Colonel Munroe was very much afraid of such expeditions and strongly suggested to his superiors that citizens were exaggerating the situation in an attempt to call out the militia for the purpose of plunder.[77] Thus no help came from the military, who, incidentally, controlled most of the arms and ammunition in the territory.

New Mexicans were more than willing to form the suggested militia companies, but not to use their own funds to protect themselves; and Governor Calhoun soon discovered he lacked the means to provide arms and supplies. All he could do under the circumstances was appeal to the president and the secretary of the interior "for ammunitions of war of every kind," which of course he did not receive.[78] Much to Calhoun's chagrin, the war parties were thus left in a state of suspended animation. Indian attacks continued. Reports indicate that a serious incident occurred on the average of once a week. In April, Calhoun and Munroe tried the old expedient of concluding a treaty, this time with several eastern bands of the Apache. The Indians promised to stay at peace on lands assigned them and they agreed to the establishment of a military post in their midst. But the treaty was never ratified by Congress and, for that matter, was not respected by either side. In less than a month Governor Calhoun was reporting to the commissioner that conditions were again intolerable. Moreover, he expressed a concern for his political career and stated that the continual deterioration of the Indian situation "may endanger the good repute, which, I trust, I have heretofore sustained."[79]

The Pueblo dilemma also continued to plague the Governor. These people soon discovered that denial of statehood solved none of their problems: whites persisted in trying to appropriate their lands and restrict their rights. The chiefs again turned to Calhoun for aid. In May and June delegations from the various villages came almost daily to Calhoun's office protesting invasions of their lands and expressing their concern that the white government would not respect their old rights and privileges. The Governor tended to believe that the Pueblo were being agitated by those opposed to his administration in an attempt to embarrass him. Though sympathetic to their pleas, he apparently decided it politically wise to wash his hands of the delicate matter by dumping it into the territorial legislature. In his first message to the legislature on June 2, 1851, he raised the question of the status of the Pueblo people. Admitting that no easy solution to the problem existed, he refused to recommend their continued participation in political affairs. Instead, he told the assembly, there could be three solutions: "it is inevitable, that they must be slaves (dependents), equals, or an early removal to a better location for them and our own people must occur."[80] The decision was left to the delegates.

Such words, coming from the highest civilian officer in the territory, hardly pleased the tribal leaders. Undoubtedly Calhoun believed his decision was agreeable to the future of the Pueblo, and he repeatedly stressed that the governmnt would not abandon them. But some observers, including several prominent New Mexicans, thought otherwise. One citizen, commenting on Calhoun's speech, believed it "exceedingly impolitic," and "should these people gather from the Governor's message, that the policy of the government will be to drive them from their lands, spirit would be aroused among them which could be quelled but with their destruction." This commentator wondered how the tribe could be excluded from citizenship when the treaty of Guadalupe Hidalgo expressly bound the United States to grant all political rights to Mexican citizens in the territory (and the Pueblo Indians had been Mexican citizens). Governor Calhoun, however, determined to leave the matter in other hands. He believed the expected arrival of the new agents, some of whom would be appointed to the Pueblo villages, made the issue academic by preventing "evil disposed persons" from bothering the Indians.[81] Here matters rested for over a half century. The Pueblo people were not granted citizenship in the Territory of New Mexico. And, although the government agents did help protect them in some cases, the fears expressed by the chiefs in 1851 were borne out. Left to the mercy of a white-dominated legislature, the Pueblo saw their lands invaded by white squatters until much of the best land was gone. It was not until the 1920's that this process was slowed.[82]

In July 1851 the situation of the government improved. On July 19, Colonel Sumner reached Santa Fe, and a week later the four new Indian agents arrived. Sumner's orders were explicit. Secretary of War Conrad was now convinced that only a constant display of military force could restore peace. His official orders to Sumner, dated April 1, 1851, directed the new commander to make expeditions against the Navajo, Apache, and Ute and "inflict upon them a severe chastisement."[83] Troops were also to be removed from the towns and placed in the Indian country, according to the expressed desires of Sumner.

Calhoun was delighted. The establishment of posts among the hostile tribes seemed to be a perfect opportunity to start fulfilling the government's goal of civilizing the tribes. As soon as Sumner manned the forts, agents could be assigned to the tribes; John Grenier for the Ute, Edward Wingfield for the Navajo, and Abraham Wooley for the Comanche and Apache along the Sante Fe road. This arrangement, he hoped, would assure the most effective division of responsibility—the army to enforce observation of existing treaties and the agents to instruct the tribes in agriculture, the first step to civilization.[84]

Colonel Sumner did not hesitate in fulfilling his instructions. The day he arrived in Santa Fe orders were issued moving army headquarters to Fort Union, a post to be constructed on the Santa Fe trail near Moro. By July 23, soldiers were on the site.[85] From there the commander immediately initiated mounted patrols along the western portion of the trail; these generally proved successful in reducing Indian attacks on the main road to New Mexico.

More important, on August 19, Colonel Sumner departed for the heart of the Navajo country with four companies of dragoons, one company of artillery, and two companies of infantry. "It is my intention," he wrote to the adjutant general, "to establish a post of 5 companies in the heart of their country." He named the new post Fort Defiance. Calhoun's hopes for the expedition were temporarily threatened when Sumner refused to take agent Wingfield along, causing the governor to jump to the conclusion that the army would not cooperate with his plans. But Colonel Sumner felt that forts came first, and the army proceeded into Navajo country without Wingfield. Much to the regret of Sumner, no significant portion of the tribe was encountered, although the troopers fired on the Indians whenever possible. The important event, however, was the placement of Fort Defiance at the Cañon Bonito (on the present Arizona-New Mexico border). Major Backus, the post commander, was admonished to "treat them [the Navajo] with the utmost vigor, till they showed a desire to be at peace, and would pledge themselves to abstain from all depredations."[86]

Upon returning from the Navajo country, Sumner proceeded to withdraw the remaining troops from the towns and establish them in frontier posts designed to keep the Indians in check.

Accordingly, troops were removed from Las Vegas, Rayado, Albuquerque, Cibolleta, Socorro, Doña Ana, San Euzario, and El Paso. In addition to being stationed at forts Union and Defiance, these soldiers were also stationed at two other new posts, Fort Fillmore, located on the Rio Grande near El Paso, and Fort Conrad near Valverde south of Santa Fe. Army troops were for the first time stationed among the Indians. Most New Mexicans highly approved of the new commander and his employment of the troops. One wrote, for example, that "Col. S. is perhaps the only American who has come in contact with a Navajo for the last four years, without making a treaty. He is said to have told the Indians that he has come to fight, and not make treaties. If this be true, it is the best language ever used to a Navajo Indian."[87]

Construction of army posts in the midst of the hostile tribes initiated a permanent military policy for New Mexico. The civilian aspects soon followed. At the very time that Sumner was constructing his forts, the national government embarked upon a course intended to begin civilizing and educating the tribes now that they could, seemingly, be controlled. Commissioner Lea noted this policy in his annual report for 1851 by stressing that "liberal appropriations of money" as well as the use of agents must be the guiding principle for handling the Indians of New Mexico. Secretary of War Conrad agreed, stating that "policy and humanity both require that we should employ some other means of putting a stop to their depredations than the terror of our arms; we should try the effect of conciliatory measures."[88]

The government acted rapidly in implementing these sentiments. On January 22, 1852, a Navajo agency was created and Spencer M. Baird appointed agent. The new agency was located at Fort Defiance. A month later Congress approved the Southern Apache agency "with jurisdiction over the Mimbreno, Coyotero, and temporarily, the Mescalero Apache."[89] In the spring of 1852 the new agents began distributing seed and farm utensils, the first step in getting the Indian peoples to become agriculturalists. Congress again supported the move by appropriating a total of $85,000 for the purpose of continuing the experiment of keeping the tribes restricted on areas of land and teaching them to become self-supporting.

After the establishment of the forts and the assignment of agents to the tribes, an apparent change of attitude occurred among the Indians. Perhaps the determination of the United States to restrict Indian raids caused a certain amount of reflection. Whatever the reason, relative calm fell over Indians relations in New Mexico. Calhoun noticed it in February 1852 when he wrote to Commissioner Lea that the Navajo, eastern Apache, and Ute were quiet. The inactivity of the Navajo caused the governor to comment to Sumner a few weeks later that the peace was a direct result of Fort Defiance.[90] So peaceful did things become with the Navajo that by the end of 1852 agent Baird could state that he "did not think there are the slightest of apprehension of an outbreak, on the part of these Indians."[91] The Navajo had apparently decided to return to their canyon lands and leave the New Mexicans alone. There were still sporadic depredations, particularly by some bands of the Apache, but in early 1852 these seemed minor to the men in charge of Indian policy. The future looked bright.

The expectations of lasting peace in New Mexico were premature. The tribes had not been militarily defeated; and they were not ready to shed their way of life and settle down to agriculture on lands assigned them by whites. Yet the lull in hostilities at the end of 1851 marks the adoption of a basic policy toward the Indians of New Mexico. After six years of confusion and indecision, a policy of separating the tribes on restricted lands, supported by military posts in their country, had been established. There can be no denying that the "Indian problem" was not solved by the adoption of a reservation policy in New Mexico. In the following years an enormous amount of blood was shed. But all of this fighting was basically for one purpose; to force the tribes to accept the plans for their future that Calhoun had outlined in the years after the Mexican War. In the end this is what happened.

6

Across the Emigrant's Path:
The Border Tribes

❦   The country along the banks of the Lower Missouri River presented the nation with an entirely different situation from that in Texas and New Mexico. Here lived the so-called border tribes. This loose description encompassed a variety of groups, some partly assimilated and under the protection of the government, others still relatively free from the white man's influence. Because of their location these people probably suffered more than any other Indian group from American expansion in the 1840's. They sat directly in the path of Manifest Destiny. Americans, heading for the Pacific, passed through their lands, destroying crops and game and upsetting the precarious balance between the Indian and his environment. If this were not enough, these tribes also found that their rolling valleys were beginning to attract the landhungry settlers who had filled the lands just to the east. As whites moved in on Indian lands they brought with them the usual cultural baggage; liquor, disease, dispossession.

Pressure from the whites tells only part of the story, however. Many of the border tribes were simultaneously engaged in a running war with the powerful tribes farther out on the plains. Some of the trouble stemmed from traditional animosities, but the intensity of such conflicts increased as the white invasion destroyed the natural resources. Hereditary difficulties were slowly merging into wars of extermination.

All these factors combined to threaten the very survival of the border tribes, and the government found itself in the middle, trying to protect the tribes and at the same time meet the needs of is energetic citizens.

The border tribes were composed of two distinct groups. Most of the tribes located west of the Missouri were native to the region. Those on the eastern bank had been placed there by the government during the removals of the 1830's. By far the most powerful of all these tribes were the Pawnee, who lived farthest out on the plains. Although generally considered a plains tribe, they lived in permanent villages along the Platte River in the vicinity of Grand Island and Loup Fork in central Nebraska. Much of their time, however, was devoted to hunting and raiding on the prairies to the west and south, and they were often found as far out as the crossing of the Arkansas on the Santa Fe Road. Pawnee life patterns began to change in the 1830's as the Oglala and Brulé Sioux overran the best hunting grounds and began forcing the tribe off the central plains. Traditional intertribal hostilities increased at the same time, with the Pawnee often taking a beating. Eventually some elements of the tribe turned to the United States for protection. On October 9, 1833, several bands negotiated a treaty promising to settle down in an area north of the Platte in return for the government's pledge to provide for their education and civilization. Presbyterian missionaries also came to help the tribe, and by 1839 part of the tribe had settled along the Loup River with the government providing the promised farmers, blacksmiths, and teachers.[1]

The Indian Office, thoroughly convinced that agriculture would lead to the uplifting and civilization of the tribesmen, stressed manual labor schools and encouraged the Pawnee to pursue a farming life. Such a program might have achieved some success had it not been for the Sioux. Their raiding parties continually swept in from the west and north searching for scalps and loot. They sacked the hapless villages of their old enemies,

murdered women and children, destroyed crops and ran off live-
stock. The government, with few soldiers on the frontier, found
itself unable to offer any protection. By the mid-1840's the Pawnee were desperate. "They were," wrote agent Thomas Fitzpatrick,

completely invested by enemies so much so that they are in danger of
losing their scalps as soon as they put their heads outside their mud
hovels; and it seems to me that their feasting on buffalo, are nearly at
an end. The Platte River, the headwaters of the Kansas, and even
south west to the Arkansas were formerly the great hunting grounds
of the Pawnies; but now those of the Sioux, Cheyennes, and Arapahoes,
who are all gradually nearing the Pawnies, with a full determination
of wiping them out.[2]

Between the Pawnee and the advancing white frontier in Missouri and Iowa lived the remainder of the border tribes. To place
these tribes in some perspective one can start with the point
where the Platte enters the Missouri in present Nebraska. In this
vicinity lived the Oto, Missouri, and Omaha, all native tribes.
"The Otos and Missouris," said agent John Miller in 1848, "are
now one tribe & live on either side of the Great Platte and not far
from its mouth. . . . The Omahas inhabit the country west and
north of the Platte, bordering the Missouri River which exposes
them more directly to the marauding parties of Sioux."[3] On the
east bank of the Missouri around Council Bluffs in western Iowa
were a number of transplanted tribes—Potawatomi, Ottawa,
Chippewa, Winnebago, and some of the Sac and Fox who were
then in the process of moving from their previous homes in Iowa.
Taken together these tribes made up the main portion of the old
Indian barrier penetrated by Americans.

All these tribes faced common problems in spite of their di-
verse backgrounds. They were few in number and in a state of
near destitution, constantly being raided by the plains tribes, and
occupying lands desired by white settlers. Moreover, all of these
tribes possessed treaties with the United States and most received
annuities, thereby making them attractive to traders and whiskey
sellers.

Typical is the experience of the Sac and Fox. This tribe originally lived east of the Mississippi, but American expansion brought on sentiment for removal and finally led to Black Hawk's War in 1832. These events forced the Sac and Fox from Illinois and Wisconsin to Iowa. Eventually some of them were placed on small reserves where they were told they would be allowed to remain forever. But life was unpleasant; they fell in with traders and liquor peddlers, began feuding with other border tribes, and finally started engaging the Sioux in deadly combat. In addition, it soon became evident that their Iowa lands were coveted by white farmers. Pressure rapidly built for the tribe to move farther west, and in 1836 they began the piecemeal process of relinquishing their lands, a process which lasted until 1842 when they finally sold the last of their homes in Iowa and agreed to move to Kansas.[4] The other transplanted tribes had a similar history, although they managed to retain small portions of their land in western Iowa. However, by 1846 Iowa was preparing for statehood and citizens demanded that all Indians be removed. The government soon agreed.

The Oto and Omaha, living across the Missouri in unorganized territory, faced a less immediate threat from white settlers. Yet they too had many problems. Numbering altogether about 2,500, they were completely overwhelmed by the neighboring Sioux.[5] Their hunting parties, competing for the rapidly disappearing buffalo, frequently collided with the tribes of the central and northern plains, with casualties in some instances amounting to over a hundred. Close proximity to the whites also left its mark. "Although these two tribes have been contiguous to, and had intercourse with the whites [wrote agent John Miller], they unfortunately appear only to have learned their vices. The Omahas . . . have given, in the last twelve months, some 30 horses for whiskey, not getting more for a pony than from two to four gallons, and that well watered." Reverend Edward McKinney, Presbyterian missionary to these tribes, observed from his own ethnocentric viewpoint that "the condition—both social and moral—of the Ottoes and Omahas is truly deplorable. Their ignorance of the principles of true religion and morals is extreme;

and hence there is little that bears resemblance to law and order among them. Their entire destitution . . . leaves them almost always both naked and hungry."[6]

The vulnerability of the border tribes presented the government with numerous problems. To Thomas H. Harvey fell the primary responsibility for resolving these difficulties. Harvey had served as a Democrat in the Missouri legislature between 1838 and 1842 and developed a reputation as a "good legislator, a fluent speaker and one of the most popular men that ever lived in Saline county." In 1843 Senator Benton backed Harvey as a replacement for the then Indian superintendent at St. Louis, David Dawson Mitchell, who had fallen out with trading interests. President Tyler responded favorably to Benton's request, and on October 3, 1843, Harvey assumed a post which gave him responsibility for all tribes west of the Mississippi and north of Arkansas.[7] The superintendent soon distinguished himself as a champion of the Indian, which inevitably brought him into conflict with traders. Yet while he was opposed to unjust treatment of Indian peoples, he, like most Indian officials, was not out of tune with white concerns. He favored a reduction of land areas and insisted the tribesmen obey the dictates of the federal government and recognize the right of American passage through their country. Under Harvey's command were the agents and subagents who dealt with the individual tribes. Several of these men, particularly John Miller at Council Bluffs and Gideon C. Matlock on the Upper Missouri, exhibited sincere concern for the fate of the tribes and worked hard to assure their survival.[8]

The difficulties of the border tribes really began to come to a head in 1846. By far the most dangerous situation arose with the intensification of intertribal warfare during the summer and fall as the Sioux renewed their efforts to conquer territory and obliterate the smaller tribes. Their targets, as they had been for some years, were the Pawnee villages on the Loup Fork where the government teachers and Presbyterian missionaries were attempting to foster agriculture. Sweeping in off the plains, Sioux raiding parties made several visitations to the villages in June, destroying everything in sight, shooting up family dwellings, trampling the crops, and threatening the missionaries. The fear-stricken John Dunbar, head of the mission, quickly turned to the government for help. However, with the Mexican War just underway and troops being withdrawn from the frontier, his appeal went unanswered. Under such circumstances Dunbar reached the logical conclusion "that myself and my family were unsafe residing in the Pawnee country and unless something should be done, in some way, to render us more secure, it would be my duty ere long to leave. . . . We have been waiting and hoping our Government would do something, but have hitherto waited in vain. As our country is now involved in war, I fear it will not look after the red men very carefully."[9] With these words, the government farmers, the school teacher, and Dunbar himself packed up, abandoned the main portion of the tribe, and moved to Bellevue (across the Missouri from Council Bluffs) where they tried to carry on a school for Pawnee children.

Left unprotected, the Pawnee quickly forgot about becoming farmers and struck out on their own. Hoping to evade their enemies they moved south of the Platte to join some renegade portions of the tribe that had consistently refused to participate in the civilizing experiment. This move precipitated a direct confrontation with the United States government; the tribe settled in the area where the Oregon Trail crossed the Nebraska grasslands between Independence and Grand Island. Here some of the tribesmen, faced with starvation, having a culture where raiding played an important role, and looking upon the white as the source of their misfortune, began molesting emigrant trains. The War Department, in one of its more unenlightened decisions, branded the Pawnees outlaws because they had violated the treaty of 1833. As long as the tribe stayed north of the Platte, stated Secretary of War Marcy, they were considered peaceful, but, in a piece of questionable logic, "those who remain south of the river are treacherous and evil disposed." Commissioner Medill also demanded that the tribe be returned to their old lands, but at least to him it was a matter of humanity as well as clearing a nuisance from the Oregon road. "It is," he said, "important that the Pawnees remaining south of the Platte should be removed

north of that river according to the stipulations of the treaty, in
order that the great objectives of the treaty, their education &
improvement in agriculture may be carried out."[10] Despite such
sentiment, nothing was done to protect the Pawnee, and they remained where they were.

Other tribes were also menaced by the Sioux during this
period. The Omaha and Oto probably took proportionally greater
casualties. In December of 1846, after a number of small encounters, a particularly strong war party of Yancton Sioux
caught the Omaha villages unguarded:

instead of a battle between warriors, it was a cold-blooded butchery
of women and children, in the absence of all the warriors of the
village. On the night of the 12th and 13th . . . a war party of the
Yancton Sioux Indians defeated and destroyed *fourteen* lodges of the
Omaha tribe of Indians. . . . The men and warriors of the Omaha
had left camp to hunt; and the Sioux, soon after they attacked the
camp, discovered that they only had women and children to contend
with. The slaughter was terrible. *Seventy-three* were killed, and nine-
teen mortally wounded.[11]

Although spectacular and drawing more notice than usual, this
incident was not isolated. The Sioux continued to probe the de-
fences of the border tribes and in the early months of 1847 several
more attacks were launched, with equally devastating results.

As if the Sioux were not enough, the Missouri tribes also faced
an increasing threat from white Americans. Migration to the
Pacific had become continuous by 1845, when some 3,200 weary
travelers crossed the heart of Indian country. Few of these individuals were well-informed about the Indian population and
probably none had any respect for Indian culture. Francis Parkman, who visited some of these people in 1846, described them
as being "for the most part, . . . the rudest and most ignorant of
the frontier population; they knew absolutely nothing about the
country or its inhabitants." Fear of the Indians afflicted all voy-
agers. "We had been told," noted Heinrich Lienhard in his diary,
"that somewhere along the Little Blue there was a large camp of
Pawnees whose hostility toward the whites was generally feared.
. . . Everybody kept his rifle loaded and ready." Frontier news-

papers added to emigrant fears by printing exaggerated and inflammatory stories about Indian troubles. One paper noted, for instance, that "the Grand Pawnees are very hostile to the whites, and have attacked many of our trains plundering them and murdering the wagoners. The principal Chief threatens to resist all efforts on the part of the whites to recover their property. A short time since the Pawnees fitted out an expedition, ostensibly against the Jatans [Comanche], but really to plunder the emigrant trains." Other accounts vividly described thefts of property, cattle, and the occasional murder of an emigrant. "Their mode of procedure," said one, "is to drive off from camp a number of cattle during the night, with the expectation that small companies will go out for them in the morning. If so, and they encounter the Indians, they are robbed, and if necessary shot."[12]

Although most incidents on the trail were more of a nuisance than a threat, they led to immediate calls for government protection. "We think," wrote the St. Louis *Reveille*, "it is high time the attention of the Government was called to the matter, and that they should take some other measures with the Indians than making them presents and smoking with them the peace pipe."[13] By 1847 the War Department keenly felt the pressure of such complaints. Most officers took the protests at face value and placed full blame on the hapless Indians. "They are vain in their powers," stated Secretary of War Marcy in calling for the punishment of the Pawnee, "and hence they think they can commit depredations and outrages upon our citizens with impunity."[14]

Though such charges were manifestly unjust, they are quite understandable, given the viewpoint of most whites. Americans persistently refused to recognize that the tribes were often driven to such activities. Emigrants, cognizant only of their own well-being as they marched west, destroyed most of the natural resources that came within reach. They fouled the water, used up the wood, ruined pastures, and drove off game animals. The most significant loss was certainly the buffalo. In 1846 Superintendent Harvey noted that already bison were disappearing; "all experience proves that game rapidly disappears before the fire-arms of

the white. . . . He kills for the sake of killing."[15] Under such circumstances, it is not surprising that the tribes looked upon the
white as a source of their misfortune and that they tried to seek
a means of retribution.

Some tribesmen attempted to ask the "Great Father" for help.
On more than one occasion proposals were offered asking the
government to compensate the Indian people for the use of their
territory. They also requested that emigrants be resricted by
law and military force be used to limit the destruction of natural
resourccs.[16] While many officials recognized the legitimacy of
these complaints, they made no serious efforts to change the
situation.

A new type of white emigrant appeared in 1846, when the
exodus of the Latter Day Saints from Illinois to Salt Lake
quickly doubled the number of whites in Indian country.[17] Being wary of other emigrants, many of whom were the hated
Missourians, the Mormons chose to stay north of the established
trails, thus penetrating previously unspoiled lands belonging to
the Omaha and Oto. The military-type organization of their mass
migration necessitated way stations where the large group could
spend the winter and be resupplied. They finally chose the area
around Council Bluffs for their headquarters. This movement
brought them into immediate collision with the Indian Office.
Under ordinary circumstances any large body of people intend-
ing to remain in the Indian country would have been resisted.
The fact that the emigrants were Mormon complicated the situation even more.

Most people on the frontier, including many Indian agents,
knew little of the Mormons or their purpose. There existed a
general fear that they would decide to remain in the area or perhaps stir up the Indians against other whites. Such fears were
intensified by a strong prejudice against the religion of these
people. Those concerned with Indian affairs believed the Saints
would lay waste to Indian lands, cheat and bring liquor to the
red men, and cause more unrest among the tribes.[18]

Various reports and rumors filtered into the Indian Office as
the Mormon advance guard moved into the Indian territory

during the summer of 1846. Early parties traversed the Indian domain as far as Grand Island looking for suitable encampments. Non-Morman observers, such as Rev. John Dunbar, reported a possibility that the Saints were hostile to the government, planned to incite the Indians against it, and intended to remain.[19] It soon appeared that these predictions might be fulfilled. By early winter Mormon parties occupied the abandoned Pawnee mission on Loup Fork and had established settlements among the Omaha, Ponca, and Potawatomi. In each instance they started farms, set up mills, and constructed permanent buildings in defiance of federal regulations. By December, the Saints reported some 15,000 of the faithful living in the Indian country.[20] They were dead set on remaining until church leaders discovered the new Zion.

One more problem, that of the advancing line of farming settlements, served to compound the difficulties of the border tribes. Several groups yet inhabited the western portions of Missouri and Iowa. Until 1846 the Indian barrier philosophy had ruled official thinking; so the tribes, while remaining on the frontier, were moved only slightly away from the path of expanding settlement. Now, however, white demands for possession of all organized territory forced a new round of treaties. In June 1846, under pressure from the Indian Office, the Chippewa, Ottawa, and Potawatomi sold some six million acres in Iowa and Missouri and agreed to move to the unorganized Kansas country within two years.

These sale agreements contained a typical example of the administration's unfortunate attempt to couple the civilization program with economy of government. The Indian Office inserted into the treaties a provision that as the seemingly inevitable decrease in tribal population continued, annuity payments should decrease proportionately. The benefits promised to be twofold. Obviously the government could reduce expenses. However, Commissioner Medill also saw it as fostering a more rapid Indian conversion to civilization. With a philosophy that said a person could advance only through hard work, he believed that Indians not earning money by manual labor would never learn "industry and frugality" and simply waste it on alcohol and other temporary wants.[21]

On October 13, 1846, the Winnebago tribe also agreed to give up their "valuable lands" in Iowa, although they could not agree with the government on a location for their new homes. The Indian Office wanted all the tribes away from the expanding frontier and therefore assigned the Winnebago a location on the Upper Mississippi. Again the Indian commissioner believed this move would benefit the tribe by concentrating them in one spot where they could be protected from white "influences now operating to bring down upon them misery and degredation."[22] Unfortunately, Medill failed to appreciate the fact that such a move would place the Winnebago between the northern Sioux and the other border Indians. Not surprisingly, the Winnebago demonstrated little inclination to live next to the Sioux, and they decided to remain in Iowa until receiving a better offer. This action placed them in a state of limbo, having agreed to move, but knowing not where.

State residents were little disposed to let the tribes take their time moving. As soon as the treaties were signed, harassment and intimidation began. Reports that the tribesmen were drunk or stealing were used to justify such activity. The lack of troops on the frontier gave residents additional reason to hurry the tribes along. John M. Kelley, speaking for the citizens of Holt and Atchison counties in Missouri, offered the secretary of war a typical expression of local sentiment when he wrote, early in 1847, that: "We of this county and Atchison County have numerous Indians on three sides of us, sufficient to devastate and destroy our Counties & its citizens in a few hours if so disposed." Admitting that no acts of violence had occurred, Kelley insisted that the danger remained and he told the secretary that the blame for a massacre would be his. This type of argument certainly encouraged the government to hasten removal, and most of the tribesmen remaining in Iowa and Missouri were hustled off to their new homes well in advance of the deadlines.[23]

The removal of these tribes temporarily solved one problem, but it still left several tribes west of the Missouri. Believing that these people would remain in their homelands for several years yet, Thomas Harvey began evolving a plan to provide them protection and assure better relations. The first task involved con-

vincing the Pawnee to return to their villages north of the
Platte. To promote a favorable atmosphere, Harvey, in February
1847, hired a former St. Louis judge by the name of Alexander
McElroy to return to the Pawnee farms on the Loup and resume
operations. The judge and several helpers rode out to the abandoned mission as soon as the weather permitted. They found the
place destroyed by a Mormon party that had wintered on the
site. By hard work McElroy put the farms in order once more
and persuaded three bands of reluctant Pawnees to return. But
no sooner had the tribesmen settled down than, on May 21, 1847,
a large Sioux raiding party hit the village, killing twenty-three.
McElroy tried to keep things going, but Sioux warriors returned
several more times during the summer. They "destroyed literally
everything with the exception of the buildings, one wagon, 2
carts and bar iron," by the time they finished. The raiders did
such a good job that they even filled the mission well with
hammers and spades, destroyed all the corn, and smashed the
grindstones and ploughs.[24] Under such circumstances, it was
impossible to continue operations and Harvey was forced to
abandon the mission again.

The disgusted Pawnee once again returned to the rest of their
kin south of the Platte and were soon reported stealing from emigrant trains. Fear of government reprisal seemed the lesser of
two evils when compared with raids by the Sioux. War Department officials, of course, continued to ignore circumstances and
demanded that all the Pawnee return to the north. Marcy, writing to Medill in June, suggested that if the tribe would not move
voluntarily, they must be persuaded by the army: "destroy their
villages south of the Platte; drive them north of that river, compel
them to give up the plundered property they have in their possession, and take and hold some of their principal men as
hostages." Indian agent Thomas Fitzpatrick, who had no love
for the Pawnee, had already proposed the same solution:

I question very much whether the Panies [Pawnee] will ever allow the
government to benefit them much until they give them a severe
chastisement, which must be done sooner or later, the advice at first
may appear harsh, and inhuman, but you may rest assured it is the

only means by which to reform, and bring them to a sense of their duty not only to themselves but to the government.[25]

Thus came a call for troops; not to protect the Pawnee from their enemies, but to force obedience to an obsolete treaty. This eventually led to a clash between those civilian officials who wanted to protect the tribe and the army, which was more interested in clearing the Oregon Trail.

Any hope of protecting the border Indians from the Sioux required the presence of military force. Harvey agreed with this and so did some frontier newspapers. "It is necessary," commented the St. Louis *Daily Union* "that the Government should keep sufficient force in the Indian country to repress such outrages." Even the administration's own paper, the Washington *Daily Union*, occasionally called for governmental action "to prevent such wholesale massacres of these children of the forest."[26] Harvey and Agent John Miller also kept up continuous pressure for the government to offer more protection to the border tribes. Eventually the Indian Office agreed. In October 1847, Commissioner Medill stated that "something should be done for the punishment of the Sioux, and for the permanent protection of the weak tribes they injure and oppress." In accordance with these views, Medill suggested to the secretary of war that a military post be established near the mouth of the Platte to protect the local tribes.[27]

The idea of military establishments in the area was not entirely new. As early as 1840 Congress had considered the construction of forts along the Oregon Trail for the protection of traders and emigrants. The proposal, however, became entangled in the Oregon dispute with England, and for several years American statesmen, fearing to antagonize the British, blocked any permanent military activities on the plains. Expansionists finally passed the bill in 1846 by divorcing it from the Oregon issue and emphasizing the immediate needs of emigrants. This bill, signed on May 13, 1846, authorized the formation of an "Oregon Battalion" of mounted Missouri volunteers to establish military posts on the route.[28]

The Mexican War changed military priorities, delaying the battalion.[29] When recruiting finally did begin in the summer of 1847 the government faced a problem it had heretofore ignored —was the army to protect the emigrants or the suffering tribes? The answer would determine the location of the posts and garrison duties.

Army authorities held a uniform view; establish the forts directly on the trail at points where the emigrants might receive the greatest protection. Acting on the assumption that military thinking would prevail, Adjutant General Roger Jones issued instructions to the as yet unnamed commander of the battalion that it would be his duty to protect "the persons and property of all citizens of the United States lawfully within the territories of the Indian tribes."[30] Although the officer was admonished to keep peace between the tribes, the remainder of his orders instructed him to destroy the Pawnee villages south of the Platte and forcibly drive the tribe north.

Frontier observers generally approved of these tactics. Even Thomas Fitzpatrick recommended placing the first post near the head of Grand Island on the Platte because it would be directly on the trail and therefore render maximum security of the emigrants. Probably most frontiersmen agreed with the St. Louis *Daily Union* when it said the Oregon Battalion should be hastened foreward with instructions to "repress these Indian outrages and punish the offenders."[31]

Establishment of a single post at Grand Island, however, offered little protection to the border tribes. The very suggestion irritated Thomas Harvey, who protested to Medill, in November, that any fort at Grand Island would be too far out to afford protection to the Pawnee. Even a post south of the Oto and Omaha Nations (located somewhere between Fort Leavenworth and Grand Island), while it might render some help to those tribes, still could not prevent sneak attacks or aid the Pawnee. "I am of the opinion," said Harvey, "that a garrison on the north side of the Missouri River, in the Sioux country, would afford protection to the North West Settlements of Iowa & acting in concert with a garrison on Grand Island, would effectively re-

strain war parties of the Sioux against the Pawnees, Ottoes &
Omahas." John Miller, the agent at Council Bluffs and a genuine
friend of the Indians, wrote to the secretary of war urging a re-
consideration of priorities. He flatly stated that if the government intended to force the Pawnee north of the Platte, a fort
must be established for their protection; "it will be worse if
possible than murder to drive the Pawnees across the Platte unless they are protected." Harvey was also horrified at the army's
intention to chastise the Pawnee indiscriminately. "There are
many good people among the Pawnees," he told Medill. "It is
not in accordance with the humanity of our government that the
innocent should suffer with the guilty."[32]

The War Department paid little attention to such statements
and proceeded with its own plans. Under the command of
Lieutenant Colonel Ludwell E. Powell, the Oregon Battalion set
out for Grand Island late in 1847, traveling up the Oregon Trail
some 300 miles to the junction of Table Creek and the Missouri.
Here Powell halted for the winter and established his first post.
The idea of a fort at Table Creek, "christened with the name of
protection," seemed insane to John Miller, who asked "protection
for what? Not the Indians." The army did make one feeble attempt to protect the local tribes by sending out a party of 300
men to find the Sioux, but the soldiers returned without sighting
an Indian.[33] Thus the army failed to reach the Platte in 1847,
and neither the Indians nor emigrants received substantial protection.

The only success the Indian Office attained in protecting the
border tribes during 1847 came in the effort to move the Mormons from Indian lands. Even here results were limited. Brigham
Young and his followers continued illegal settlement of Indian
lands west of the Missouri. "Winter Quarters of the High Camp
of Israel" were officially located on Omaha lands during the
winter of 1846–47. Realizing the illegal status of their camps,
Mormon leaders appealed to Superintendent Harvey to understand their circumstances and grant permission to remain until
all the Saints had passed through. Harvey refused. The group had
already been granted permission to travel through Indian lands,

now they wanted to stay for an undetermined period. Writing to Alpheas Cutler, President of the High Council, the somewhat bitter superintendent stated "that no white persons are permitted to settle on the lands of the Inds. *without authority of the Government.* Your party being Mormons does not constitute the objection but the fact of your being there without authority of the government."[34] But the Mormons, already among the Indians, presented the St. Louis office with a very touchy situation; forcing the refugees to move might result in bloodshed, allowing them to remain would surely further decimate the local tribes.

Cutler, Brigham Young, and other Mormon leaders decided to go over Harvey's head, believing he had acted out of prejudice, and appeal directly to Washington. They found an invaluable aid and lobbyist in Thomas L. Kane, the son of a political friend of Polk.[35] By going directly to the secretary of war and the president, Kane finally obtained permission in late 1846 for the Saints to reside temporarily on the lands recently purchased from the Potawatomi in Iowa. Beyond this the government refused to go, since it might infuriate frontiersmen who had not forced the Indians out of Iowa to have their places taken by a bunch of polygamistic religious fanatics. "Continuance for any very considerable length of time near Council Bluffs," Medill told Harvey, "would interfere with the removal of the Indians—an object of so much interest to the people of that region of country; delay the survey and sales of the lands in question, and thus, in all probability, bring about difficulty between Iowa, now about to come into the Union as a state, and the General Government."[36]

Permission to remain on the Potawatomi purchase solved only part of the problem. Most of the Saints preferred to stay at Winter Quarters, located across the Missouri. In January 1847, Mormon leaders attempted to obtain authorization to remain among the Omaha. Thomas Kane, arguing the case in Washington, employed a rather unique strategy. First, referring to some temporary encampments along the Oregon Trail, he implied that the government was persecuting the Saints by denying them the privilege of wintering on Indian lands when other whites had done the same. Then, producing a treaty signed by several

Omaha chiefs granting the Mormons tribal permission to remain among them, he argued that the tribe actually benefitted by having the presence of armed white men to protect them from the Sioux. This service was deemed sufficient compensation for any loss of wood or game.[37] Actually, this latter claim contained a certain amount of truth, since the Mormon presence tended to keep the Sioux at a distance, a fact of which the Omaha took quick advantage.

There were, however, some adverse aspects of the Mormon encampment which Kane failed to mention. "It is a great pity," noted observer Samuel Allis, "that they were ever permitted to stop here on Indian land, they are cutting timber fast, the Indians are also killing the Mormon's cattle almost by the hundreds which is making them bad." Agent John Miller flatly told Brigham Young that the best service they could render the Omahas would be to leave as soon as possible and stop the great destruction of timber and game, "which to the Indians is a severe loss." The Saints also brought a disease with them called the "black canker" which rapidly spread among the Indians, taking a heavy toll.[38]

During the spring of 1847 the Indian Office kept a suspicious eye on the Mormons to be sure they moved on. But the Saints displayed no signs of departing; a large number of houses were being constructed, fields laid out, and a large area planted with various grains and other staples. Church headquarters, moreover, remained in the same place.

Government officials openly expressed alarm at these developments. Apparently the Mormons could be induced to leave only by force. In April the High Council confirmed that they intended to remain. In a letter to Secretary Marcy, Kane again requested that the Mormons be allowed to retain their settlements in the Indian country. He noted that only a portion of the refugees had yet started west and during the next few years perhaps as many as 30,000 more would be heading for Utah: "During the course of their emigration, necessarily tardy from their poverty as well as their numbers, they will occupy various stations as the winter quarters of detachments and for growing crops which must form their subsistence. Beginning at Council Bluffs, the first of these stations will be in Omaha Country." To strengthen his case, Kane also wrote Medill stressing Morman charity to the Indians and intimating that they were remaining "professedly for the sake of the Omahas who bless them as their benefactors."[39]

The Indian department hardly agreed. Medill felt the Mormons were taking advantage of "temporary" privileges to build a permanent settlement. On April 24, 1847, the commissioner decided to oppose any continuance of Mormon settlement. His reasons were simple and to the point. The Saints had been given permission to reside briefly on the Potawatomi purchase, but for all practical purposes were living in the Omaha country, where they violated the original agreement. Hence, seeing no reason to make a special exception for the Mormons, he demanded they leave because they were illegal trespassers in Indian country.[40]

Refused permission to remain, the Saints then wanted to know if "it is the intention of the War Department to remove them by force from the Omaha Country?" Medill gave no definite answer, relying on uncertainty to hurry them along. Soon they gave in. Continued government opposition and the likelihood of a bloody incident finally induced Brigham Young to give up his colony on Omaha lands. Early in 1848 those still living at Winter Quarters were ordered either to pull back across the Missouri or to press on for Salt Lake.[41] Thus the government finally succeeded in moving one group of whites out of Indian territory.

Success with the Mormons was more than offset by failure to check the illegal operations of Indian traders. Trading practices had been an ever present concern of the Indian department since 1846 when Commissioner Medill began his attempt to reform the business of supplying Indian wants. Two types of traders operated in the region of the Lower Missouri; small bands of unlicensed persons illegally invading the Indian lands with goods and liquor, and giant companies operating legally among the Indians but often smuggling in alcohol and defrauding the natives. Agent Thomas P. Moore, describing the operations of these men in 1846, presents an excellent view of the continuing problem:

The agent is charged with the duty of resisting and punishing infractions of the intercourse law, whether committed by a large and powerful trading company, or by a band of unlicensed traders. The first have the power, from their extensive intercourse with the Indians, and the number of their employees, to counteract every move adverse to their schemes, and to render his stay in the country impossible by denying him shelter or aid of any kind; while the second travel in small bands, prepared to resist the execution of the law.[42]

Small traders presented many difficulties, although they stood a better chance of conviction if apprehended. The border Indians resided in such a vast area that unscrupulous individuals had relatively free access. These "vagabond white men" traversed the Indian country, living off the natives. They resisted all efforts to control their activities and often found their customers willing to hide them. Even more difficult to stop were the whiskey-sellers in states bordering Indian country who encouraged the Indians to cross state lines, avoiding the intercourse laws which applied only to Indian country.[43]

Big trading outfits presented a greater problem. These traders, remnants of the great Rocky Mountain fur companies, were now engaged in securing buffalo robes from the Indians and supplying them with various trade goods. The largest trading house at this time was Pierre Chouteau, Jr., and Company, an old name in the history of the fur trade and the successor to Astor's bankrupt American Fur Company. Several major competitors made the rivalry intense and bitter, most companies engaging in a variety of illegal activities to increase their profits. W. G. & G. W. Ewing were perhaps the most notorious, and of the numerous fraud cases in the files of the Office of Indian Affairs, their name is conspicuous for its repeated appearance. They frequently used shoddy practices to acquire Indian annuity funds. Occasionally such practices would come to light and the government would revoke a license. However, little ever came of such sanctions and traders like the Ewings remained active in the Indian country, if necessary hiring other men to trade with the tribes, bribing agents to overlook certain activities, and even threatening to set the Indians against the government.[44]

No better example of the power and influence of the companies can be found than in the unsuccessful attempt of Superintendent Harvey to prosecute Pierre Chouteau, Jr. for selling liquor to the tribes along the Missouri. Events in the case date back to 1846, when the St. Louis office received information from a dissatisfied rival that Chouteau's company had been smuggling liquor into the Indian country. A hearing, held on March 5, 1846, produced considerable testimony to substantiate the charges, and Harvey, in line with the government's position on alcohol, ordered Chouteau barred from Indian lands and his license to trade revoked.[45]

Revocation of the trading license, if carried into effect, threatened to ruin the company. Chouteau immediately appealed the decision, questioning the reliability of the witnesses and putting pressure, through Thomas Hart Benton, on the secretary of war, who responded by postponing the revocation and calling for another hearing. Chouteau agreed to a speedy hearing in return for the postponement, but quickly threw every possible obstacle into the way of a trial. Thomas T. Gantt, U.S. Attorney for Missouri, who prosecuted the case, correctly believed the delay was directly related to company hopes of persuading witnesses not to testify. For the next two years, while the government procrastinated, Harvey and Gantt sat by helplessly as most of the material witnesses were hired by Chouteau and sent to remote parts of the Indian country where they could not easily be returned for the trial. The company, of course, made no effort to return the witnesses although it did ask for several continuances because the men were gone.[46]

By 1848 both Harvey and Gantt were adamant that the department quit stalling and declare Chouteau in default. Medill, although under great pressure from Benton, finally ordered the original decision to stand—but only after Chouteau had another hearing, scheduled this time for April 1849. During the intervening time Gantt attempted to gather enough evidence to secure a conviction. He first tried to persuade the remaining witnesses— among them the famous old mountain man Etienne Provost—to testify, knowing they had enough knowledge to destroy the company. Most of these men knew better than to defy the company, however, and indicated they were planning to be elsewhere at the time of the trial. Despite such discouraging developments, Gantt still believed he could win the case, yet having a few people who had been abused by Chouteau and were eager to testify.[47]

Apparently Chouteau and his attorney thought the government had a case. They therefore proposed a compromise; that they admit their guilt prior to 1846, forfeit the bonds for the period 1843–46, and further action would be dropped. Gantt and Harvey were asked to agree to these arrangements, and under pressure from their superiors, both relented. Gantt recommended a penalty of $7,500 and costs; Harvey $5,000 and costs. Even here the company was not satisfied and asked for the smaller fine. "The object of the Government was not to enrich the Treasury, but to break up an inhuman traffic; and permit us to assure you that as far as our knowledge extends this object has been fully accomplished." As a result Commissioner Medill ordered Gantt to drop the case and accept a judgment of $5,000.[48]

The most significant aspect of this case is the ability of Chouteau to resist governmental action. Witnesses could be bribed, delays obtained from Washington, and finally a compromise arranged, which for the small sum of $5,000 left the company's right to trade in the Indian country undisturbed. In fact, the license of the company remained valid throughout the entire proceedings and while the long debate wore on, the company operated as usual. Furthermore, little seemed accomplished by the entire affair; though everyone from Medill to Chouteau publicly stated that the introduction of liquor into the Indian country had ended, it was quite clear that the company had bested the government and would return to normal operations as soon as the unroar died down.

Failure to check effectively the activities of traders, combined with continuous emigration and repeated intertribal warfare, presented a dismal picture along the Lower Missouri. Even the Oregon Battalion, which finally arrived at Grand Island (Fort Kearny) in 1848, did nothing for the tribes in the vicinity. Colonel Powell, to be sure, made more promises to chastise the Sioux, but most observers recognized he could do little. "I have been lately informed," wrote Thomas Fitzpatrick, "that Col. Powell promises the Indians protection against their enemies, but for my part I doubt much the capability of the Col. to protect himself, should he undertake such a project."[49]

It thus became increasingly evident the border tribes were not likely to survive in their present environment. Superintendent Harvey certainly recognized this fact. For some time he had advocated the purchase of routes through Indian country. As it became abundantly clear to him that the government did not possess the power to protect the tribes from either the white or the Sioux, he began organizing a plan to assure their survival. The logical solution seemed some sort of a reservation. In October 1848, he wrote of the situation:

The immense traveling of emigrant companies over the prairies, and the consequent increased destruction of buffalo, has excited the anxiety of several of the western tribes for some years past. . . . The country occupied by the buffalo is gradually and rapidly being circumscribed, which shows their great diminution. The time cannot be distant, when they will be insufficient to subsist the numerous tribes that now depend upon them for food.

In line with this prediction, Harvey suggested securing a tract of land in the vicinity of the Missouri River where all the tribes without sufficient agricultural lands might come, be protected from the emigrants, and be taught the fundamentals of an agrarian life.[50]

Such a proposal, idealistic though it was, might have had a chance of success had it been acceptable to the administration. However, strong pressure was being brought to bear for clearing all tribes from the old Indian country and thus removal must accompany any reservation. At the moment Harvey made his suggestions, Medill, reacting to demands for the organization of Nebraska and for a route for a Pacific railroad, came forth with his proposed colonies. To Medill, colonies or reservations away from all routes of communication offered a more satisfactory solution for both white and Indian. The government would be able to keep close watch on the tribes and restrict the trade in alcohol only if all the tribes were concentrated.[51]

In his 1848 report, Commissioner Medill, responding to Harvey's gloomy predictions for the border tribes and his own developing beliefs that reservations were the only viable alternative, committed the Indian Office to a program of reservations for the border tribes.

The policy already begun and relied on to accomplish objects so momentous and so desirable to every Christian and philanthropist is, as rapidly as it can safely and judiciously be done, to colonize our Indian tribes beyond the reach, for some years, of our white population; confining each within a small district of country, so that, as the game decreases and becomes scarce, the adults will gradually be compelled to resort to agriculture and other kinds of labor to obtain subsistence, in which aid may be afforded and facilities furnished them out of the means obtained by the sale of their former possessions. To establish, at the same time, a judicious and well devised system of manual labor schools for the education of the youth of both sexes in letters.

Yet even the idea of colonies presented some problems for which Medill had no solution. Weaker tribes could no doubt be induced to move elsewhere, but what of the Pawnee? They were so antagonistic to other tribes that it seemed impossible to place them in colonies. Under these circumstances Medill predicted that this tribe must either be forced west by the tide of settlement or be destroyed by the Sioux.[52]

Neither Harvey nor Medill had a chance to develop their plans for the border tribes before the Democrats were removed from office in 1849. Both men had, however, brought an awareness to the Indian Office that the small tribes along the Lower Missouri were in danger on several fronts. The apparent solution, that of removal and reservations, had been adopted. The Whigs agreed to carry it out.

When the Whig administration came to power several events immediately affected policy among the border Indians. Under the new secretary of the interior, Thomas Ewing, the spoils system swept away many of the better public servants. Thomas Harvey was removed from the St. Louis Superintendency at the behest of the traders who had determined to oust him for his opposition to their interests. Former superintendent and fur trader David ˉDawson Mitchell returned to office. Although Mitchell had run afoul of the companies in the past, he seemed a better choice to the traders than Harvey.[53] Mitchell proved to be an able public servant and persisted in operating independently of the companies. Unfortunately, some of Ewing's other appointments proved less suitable. John Miller, who had been extremely active in advocating protection for the small tribes, was removed from his Council Bluffs office, which was reduced to a subagency, and replaced by John E. Barrow, a small-time politican favorable to the trading companies.

Mitchell quickly discovered that the border tribes needed attion. Intertribal warfare and poverty continued to take its terrible toll. The Pawnee as usual seemed to suffer most. By 1849 the condition of this once powerful tribe was truly pathetic. The cholera epidemic of that year swept the tribe with devastating effect. Subagent Barrow estimated in June that nearly twelve hundred Pawnee had fallen victim of the disease, he himself having visited villages with dead scattered about, their "bodies partly devoured by wolves and other animals." Scarcity of buffalo proved equally disastrous. "Our old friends, the Pawnees," noted one observer, "have had a hard time of it during the past winter. When they returned from their hunting grounds, their trail could be followed by the dead bodies of those who starved to death. Children, young men, and women have shared this fate."[54]

Tribal enemies took advantage of the situation. During the summer of 1849, Sioux war parties again fell upon the defenseless tribe, enough "scalps changing owners" to drive the Pawnee villages some eighty miles closer to the Missouri frontier. Other border tribes also carried out occasional raids. In May the Sac and Fox from the Osage Agency slipped away from their watchful agent and murdered a party of Pawnee. Even the usually peaceful Oto made an excursion in September and succeeded in killing eleven people. Barrow, charged with responsibility for the Pawnee, asked that the tribe be removed for its own protection:

"Unless the lands of this people are soon purchased by our government, and they are removed to a country where game is more
abundant, and which does not lie in the midst of their enemies,
this once powerful tribe, in a very few years must become an
extinct race."[55]

Frontier settlers also kept the border in turmoil. Several of the
bands that had been forced out of Iowa and Missouri—particularly the Sac and Fox and the Potawatomi—decides to return to
their former homes. Rumors rapidly spread across the settlements
that the returning Indians were ravaging the frontier. On Sep-
tembe 22, 1849, in response to complaints by frontier residents,
Major Samuel Woods, 6th Infantry, officially investigated the
situation. He discovered three or four hundred Indians quietly
encamped on their old lands in central Iowa. White residents in
the area demanded immediate removal despite Woods' confirmation that the Indians were peaceably inclined and had done little
damage. In fact, the residents of the small town of Marengo "collected to the number of 20 or 25, armed themselves, & forcibly
broke up the Indian encampment & drove the Indians off." Major
Woods interceded and asked the citizens to enumerate their complaints. He received a typical statement of frontier prejudice:

The grounds of complaint, are that they destroy large quantities of
timber in the winter, by cutting it for their ponies to browse on &
taking the bark from it to make their lodges—that they destroy the
Surveyor's landmarks, thereby creating confusion—that they kill all the
game—that they will steal—that they cause inquietude to the families
of Settlers when the males are absent—that they prevent the Settlement
of the country by alarming those coming in not accustomed to Indians
—that there is actual danger to isolated Settlers, when the Indians are
under the influence of liquor . . . that if they are left alone much
longer they will contend for a right to the country & perhaps cause
many more to join them from the Missouri River.

Woods' commander, Lieutenant Colonel Loomis, refused to send
a military expedition and suggested that the matter really fell
within the jurisdiction of the Indian department.[56]

The case of the Winnebago provides another example of this
same situation. By terms of the treaty of 1846 the tribe agreed to

move from Iowa. However, a portion of the people refused the
lands assigned them on the Upper Mississippi and remained in
the state, while those who made the move found the new land unsatisfactory and in early 1850 began migrating back to "their old
haunts." This presented the department with a dilemma. As in
other cases, white settlers angrily demanded the tribesmen be removed. The question was whether they should be returned to a
country they obviously detested or be located on a more suitable
land. Thomas Ewing suggested to Commissioner Brown on January 21, 1850, that the Winnebago might be located on the Kansas
River, a *"Country of good Soil,"* and, more important, away from
the routes of communication.[57]

The plight of the Winnebago became a political issue when
some opposition congressmen and newspapers latched onto the
affair in an attempt to embarrass the administration. A number
of charges were leveled, the main one being that the department
had tricked the tribe out of their homes and knowingly assigned
them land unfit for habitation. Brown responded to these charges
by stating that "no improper influences or persuasion" were used
on the tribe but then went on to describe their new country in
such glowing terms that he dare not let them migrate elsewhere
lest someone challenge his credibility. The commissioner thus insisted that the Winnebago return to the Upper Mississippi and he
hired a private contractor to move the tribe again. Although this
provoked a great deal of criticism, the department persisted and
the Winnebago once again found themselves returned to the
north.[58] Here they were not happy and some slipped back into
Iowa once again.

Even the tribes in unorganized territory across the Missouri ran
afoul of white settlers. Omaha and Oto tribesmen habitually
crossed the river to visit the white settlements and by so doing,
became targets for white repression. The Mormon community of
Kanesville, Iowa, where there once had been a degree of sympathy, now had no use for Indians. Ironically, the *Frontier
Guardian*, a paper edited by Orson Hyde, suggested that the Oto
and Omaha were nothing but beggars and thieves. "We recom-

mend a company be formed forthwith," stated the paper, "armed with good hickorys, and with stronger if necessary, and follow up the red jackets till they will be sick of stealing horses." John Gooch, one of the leading citizens of Kanesville, elaborated on these sentiments when he wrote to the secretary of the interior that "we have bore with these Indians as long as forbearance is a virtue."[59] He asked for dragoons or sufficient money from the government to raise and arm local forces to keep the Indians away.

Under such circumstances there was heavy pressure on the government to do something about the border Indian population. Superintendent Mitchell well knew, and Subagent Barrow confirmed, that the Omaha, Oto, and Pawnee were in a particularly bad way and that continual difficulties were going to cause "many of their bad men to commit acts of atrocity" upon emigrants and settlers.[60] Consequently Mitchell began to elaborate on some ideas that had been maturing for some time. He doubted the practicality or desirability of the department's idea for separate colonies or reservations for the border tribes. Realistically approached, Mitchell knew that continued separation of these tribes would leave the fundamental problem unresolved. Instead he suggested "an intermixture with the Anglo-Saxon race is the only means by which the Indians of this continent can be *partially* civilized." Although the old Indian country would have to be ended and Nebraska must eventually be organized to meet the needs of white expansion, it did not appear necessary to remove all the Indians from the territory. What Mitchell proposed, then, was an early form of severalty, where each family would be given a plot of land without the right of transfer for fifty years. This seemed to resolve the dilemma of the border tribes by bringing them civilization and protection without the cost or suffering of a forced removal. "It is fair," he said,

to presume that, after the lapse of fifty years, the Indian owners of the soil would be able to protect their pecuniary interests, having the example of the whites, by whom they would be surrounded and intermixed, before them. To these Indians I would grant the privileges of citizenship, as I know from personal observation, that they are far more capable of exercising them than a large portion of the *citizens* of New Mexico. After assigning to each family the requisite quantity of land, a large surplus would remain, which should be purchased by the government at something like a fair price, and thrown open to the pioneers of the country. . . .[61]

Like the later Dawes Severalty Act, which incorporated many of the same ideas, the plan may have been unrealistic in the long run and it certainly cleared more land for whites. Yet it never had much chance of success, for the administration had by now generally committed itself to reservations and removal, and only in a few selected areas would Mitchell's proposals receive fleeting attention.

The force demanding removal of the small tribes continued to operate through 1851. With the negotiation of the treaty of Fort Laramie that year (Chapter 7) clearing the Sioux and other tribes away from the Oregon Trail, all that remained necessary to create a giant corridor to the Pacific was to extinguish Indian land titles along the border. Using principles set down by Medill in 1848 for colonies north and south, the Indian Office and Congress succeeded in carrying out the final act of the drama with a series of treaties in 1853 and 1854 whereby the border Indians relinquished some thirteen million acres of land. By 1854 the remnants of the Missouri border tribes had been moved out of their homes to reservations elsewhere or left on small portions of their former lands. "These treaties," says one authority, "ceded to the government all the territory in the eastern part of the present states of Kansas and Nebraska except some large tracts in the Kansas River Valley." In line with Mitchell's earlier recommendations, the Indian Office did hope that some of the tribes would be given allotments of land in severalty. Accordingly Commissioner George W. Manypenny had written into some of the treaties provisions for eventual allotments.[62] But the system was never given a chance. The government's philosophy on reservations, as it worked out during these years, generally conceded that one area was as good as another. Thus in a few more years their homes were desired by expanding whites and they had to go again. So the reservations and colonies which were intended to provide such benefits for the Indian only aided the white man. All that was accomplished was committing the border tribes to smaller and smaller reservations. As it turned out, their suffering had only begun.

7

End of the Indian Barrier:
The Central Plains

❧ The establishment of the Upper Platte Agency in June 1846, and the appointment of former fur trader Thomas Fitzpatrick as agent, inaugurated official relations between the United States and the powerful and warlike tribes of the central plains. According to the Senate's definition, the newly created agency encompassed "the tribes of Indians residing upon the waters of the Upper Platte and Arkansas," thereby embracing most of the central plains between the Santa Fe road and the Oregon Trail.[1] Here lived the so-called "typical Plains Indian"—Cheyenne, Arapaho, Sioux—all of them powerful, potentially hostile, and able at this date to close the transcontinental routes at any time.

No major treaty existed between these tribes and the United States and they held only a rudimentary conception of the powers of the federal government. Many of the same forces threatening the border tribes also acted on the tribes of the central plains, but the situation here was altered by the power and strength of the tribes. The Indians in Fitzpatrick's charge remained in their native state, little damaged by any prolonged contact with whites, and were numerous enough to cause serious difficulty. As Fitzpatrick himself said of his agency: "On the above mentioned rivers, & the district of country which they drain, resorts principally the Indian tribes which we have at present most to dread."[2]

The problem of the national government, therefore, was to keep these tribes peaceful, away from the emigrants, and to prevent them from raiding other tribes and causing general unrest on the frontier.

Not until 1846 did the United States open official relations with these tribes, although Americans had long been known to them. Traders and trappers came among the natives of the central plains in pursuit of beaver and other fur-bearing animals. They left their imprint on the Indians. The mountain man did not materially alter the Indian culture, but he was responsible for introducing alcohol and other vices. To an extent, whites were even responsible for changing the balance of native power on the central plains. It was the intense competition of the fur trade that led the Rocky Mountain Fur Company in 1834 to move the Oglala Sioux away from their homes on the Upper Missouri and establish them in the Upper Platte Valley in the vicinity of Fort Laramie. "There were Sioux on the Platte now," as Bernard De Voto so aptly put it, "and they would never abandon it. And this destroyed the structure of international [tribal] relationships, producing a turbulence which was to last till the tribes were no longer capable of making war." The Oglala found the Platte Valley a paradise and, although it entailed a struggle with other tribes for possession, additional bands of Sioux soon migrated to the same area. By 1846 perhaps 7,000 well-armed Brulé and Oglala lived along the Platte, directly in the path of expanding Americans.[3]

With a Sioux monopoly on the Laramie Plain, the Cheyenne and Arapaho took up residence on the Arkansas. Here, in the vicinity of Bent's Fort, they traded pelts and buffalo robes, and obtained the products of civilized society. Although relatively few in number (Agent Fitzpatrick estimated the population to be no more than 2,500 Cheyenne and 2,800 Arapaho), they ranged over a vast extent of territory and were superior warriors.[4] Residence on the Arkansas, however, brought a problem over which the Indians had little control. Close proximity to the New Mexican settlements gave them easy access to "Taos Lightning." Bent and his traders were also known to supply whiskey when it suited their purposes, and under such circumstances it is not surprising these tribes became addicted to liquor. They were, wrote one observer, "very fond of whiskey, and will sell their horses, blankets, and everything else for a drink of it."[5]

The era of the mountain men and traders quickly ended and soon there came a new kind of white man, one ignorant of the Indian culture, indifferent to its fate, and determined to take what he wanted. The emigrants, like locust, destroyed all within reach. No reconciliation between these two groups was possible until one side or the other changed. As early as 1842 the Sioux expressed concern over the rise of emigration across their lands, and they even attempted, unsuccessfully, to prevent future travel. But the pioneers continued to come. The perpetual increase of whites on the trail to Oregon intensified the Indian feeling of unease. In 1845, John Charles Fremont, heading for California via South Pass, told of the unrest among the Sioux and their bitterness toward the emigrant parties they believed were driving the buffalo away.[6] This portended trouble. The tribes were being provoked, and only a few overt incidents might start an Indian war.

The excitement of the Indians, the fears expressed by travelers, and the possibility of the United States acquiring Oregon in the near future, forced the government in the years prior to 1846 to dispatch a number of military expeditions to impress the plains tribes with the power of the nation, persuading them to remain peaceful. During the thirties and early forties, several excursions marched into Cheyenne country, but they failed to have any effect.[7] Though the army might seem momentarily imposing, its appearance in Indian country on the average of once every five years did little to convince the Indians they needed to fear the United States.

It was not until 1845 that the western Sioux first saw American dragoons. In that year some 250 men of the First Dragoons, commanded by Stephen W. Kearny, marched westward along the Platte to exhibit to the native tribes the spectacle of American power. Parkman records that the Sioux were "lost in astonishment" when the straight lines of mounted warriors and their firebreathing howitzers made an appearance at Fort Laramie. Yet Kearny's expedition had no more lasting effect than earlier attempts along the Arkansas. The foray was clearly designed to overawe the natives and prevent attacks on whites; when Colonel Kearny spoke to the tribes gathered at Fort Laramie, few doubted the white man's ability to annihilate all who resisted. But the troopers soon rode back to Fort Leavenworth, and when renegade Indians later killed some trappers and received no punishment, the attitude changed from terror to "the height of insolence."[8]

Yet for all the potential danger, the tribes of the Upper Platte and Arkansas were at peace with the United States in 1846. The government hoped the appointment of Fitzpatrick would keep things that way. Nearing fifty, his hair turning grey, Tom Fitzpatrick was a living legend. He came west with the fur trade and made his mark with the likes of Jedediah Smith and Jim Bridger. After the fur trade declined, the energetic trapper remained on the frontier, leading early emigrant parties to Oregon and serving as a guide for Fremont and Kearny. Perhaps no other man then living had more knowledge of the Indians. Little wonder his choice as agent seemed perfect; he was literate, hardnosed, and a realist. The people of the frontier agreed with the selection. One St. Louis paper characterized Fitzpatrick as a man with more ability to control the Indians than the army.[9]

The outspoken Fitzpatrick did not assume his duties immediately. At the time of his appointment, August 3, 1846, he was serving as a guide for Colonel Kearny as the Army of the West marched toward New Mexico. It was not until the end of 1846 that he began official relations with the tribes of his agency.

Before Fitzpatrick assumed his duties the Indian situation on the central plains worsened. Although the emigration of 1846 was only half that of the preceding year, both whites and Indians exhibited increased anxiety. Whites passing across Indian lands—far from considering themselves intruders—persisted in appropriating native resources. All travelers to the Pacific killed bison and other game. Unusual indeed was the emigrant who could resist indulging in the thrill of a buffalo hunt, and diarists on the trail give us only a small glimpse of the wanton destruction.

Hunting provided both provisions and amusement on the dull trip across the plains. Edwin Bryant, for example, called the hunts he witnessed "a most exciting sport," while John Craig recorded the "Sport we had in running them on horse back over theas [sic] vast plains."[10]

The amount of game destroyed by the whites is impossible to estimate, but the effects of such activities were soon noticed. Wild game along the Platte disappeared. Father Pierre DeSmet, the renowned Jesuit missionary, noted in 1846 that with each passing year the buffalo range grew smaller, bringing the tribes in an already crowded area into closer contact with each other. Soon, he predicted, there would be wars of extermination until the Indians "become themselves extinct over the last buffalo-steak."[11] The only remedy for the situation as DeSmet saw it was for the government to take prompt and effective action to protect the indigenous tribes.

More important, the Indians themselves were aware of what was happening to their game. As early as 1842 Rufus B. Sage recorded Indian concern over the losses. The Americans, one Sioux chief told Sage, take the Indian's property, kill their game, drink their water, use their wood, travel their lands—all without any remuneration to the proprietors.[12] As more whites invaded their country the tribes of the Platte continued to express their displeasure, and in 1846 the situation deteriorated to the point that the Oglala and Brulé were compelled to complain about the emigrants directly to their "Great Father the President of the United States."

For several years past the Emigrants going over the Mountains from the United States, have been the cause that Buffaloe have in great measure left our hunting grounds, thereby causing us to go into the Country of Our Enemies to hunt, exposing our lives daily for the necessary subsistence of our wives and Children and getting killed on several occasions. We have all along treated the Emigrants in the most friendly manner, giving them free passage through our hunting grounds. . . .

We are poor and beg you to take our Situation into Consideration, it has been Customary when our white friends make a road through the Red man's country to remunerate them for the injury caused thereby.[13]

Superintendent Thomas Harvey at St. Louis (who was responsible for the tribes of the central plains as well as the border tribes) seconded the Indian claims. In forwarding the Sioux petition to Commissioner Medill he stressed the critical nature of the problem and recommended that the department do something to calm the tribes before a general war erupted. Were the buffalo simply allowed to vanish, the results would be wars of extermination among the various tribes, and "under such a state of things the whites passing through their country will not be safe." Therefore, suggested Harvey, it would be "decidedly good policy" to provide some compensation.[14]

But the Indian department showed little interest at this juncture. Medill's reply to the Sioux petition indicated the sterility of government thinking during this period of natural abundance. "It is the nature of the Buffalo & all other kinds of game," he wrote, "to recede before the approach of civilization, and the injury complained of, is but one of those inconveniences to which every people are subjected by the changing & constantly progressive spirit of the age."[15] The commissioner thus rejected the request for compensation, while steadfastly assuring "the willingness of the Government at all times to lend a willing ear to their just complaints." Only later, when the threat of Sioux dissatisfaction became more pronounced, did the government listen to these complaints.

Meanwhile, some of the Sioux took matters into their own hands by attempting to tax the emigrants. Groups of tribesmen occasionally descended upon wagon trains asking presents in return for passage through their lands, presents which most emigrants felt a certain reluctance to decline. Travelers who had to put up with this sort of annoyance soon began demanding that the government eliminate the evil. Letters from emigrants filled frontier newspapers, many expressing angry sentiments similar to one which appeared in the St. Louis *Reveille* on August 10, 1846:

The advance company of emigrants, which were for Oregon, under charge, I believe, of a Mr. Brown, comprising forty wagons, were *stopped in the road*, on arrival at Laramie by the Sioux, and not *permitted to pass until tribute had been paid*. The Sioux say they must have tobacco, &c., for the privilege of travelling through their country. . . . This may cause trouble, and Government should attend to it at once.[16]

Thomas P. Moore, the agent for the Upper Missouri (technically in charge of the Platte Indians until Fitzpatrick arrived), suggested sending some of the chiefs on a tour of the United States as a means of keeping peace. Such an excursion, he thought, might conceivably conciliate the Indians; if not at least it would "impress these wild and dangerous sons of the forest with the power of their government to protect or chastise." Yet even this feeble attempt failed. Medill wrote back that while the idea was a good one, there were (as usual) no funds to pay for such a junket.[17] The commissioner promised to present the matter to the next session of Congress, but it had little chance of passage. The situation on the plains had yet to reach alarming proportions—the only time Congress seemed willing to part with funds.

December 1846 saw Agent Fitzpatrick preparing to assume his new duties. He recognized the need for taking some kind of action to protect the emigrants and to keep the Indians quiet. Like most frontiersmen he conceived of the solution in military terms. Fitzpatrick, disagreeing with Kearny's earlier proposals for continuous patrols along the western trails, strongly backed the congressional decision to establish a fixed line of forts along the Oregon Trail. In one of his first reports the new agent recommended permanent forts on the route as the only way to maintain peace. First, there must be a post at the head of Grand Island to keep the Pawnee away from travelers. Such a post, however, could only be effective if it operated in conjunction with a post in the Sioux territory. "My opinion is that a post at, or in the vicinity of Laramie is much wanted, it would be nearly in the center of the buffalo range, where all the most formidable Indian tribes are fast approaching, and near where there will eventually (as the game decreases) be a great struggle for the ascendency."[18] At least three hundred troops, he believed, would be necessary to man the post and keep the Indians under control.

A few days later Fitzpatrick elaborated on his ideas for handling the Indians in a discussion with Thomas Harvey at St. Louis. The idea of holding a general council with all the wild tribes had occupied Harvey's attention for some time. Believing that a humane solution to the Indian problems was possible, the St. Louis superintendent hoped all the tribes might be brought together to work out intertribal difficulties and make an arrangement for the passage of emigrants. He asked Fitzpatrick for his opinion of the scheme. The old Indian-fighter, agreeing that peace among the tribes was a most desirable object, expected little from a council at that time. Experience with the Indians over the past quarter century convinced him the tribes would not respect American desires until they had been punished. He therefore suggested that before any council convened, some of the more troublesome bands be arbitrarily chastised. "Such a course I am convinced would have a very salutory effect, and be the cause of accomplishing more good to the Indians of the Rocky Mountains, than all the treaties and councils that could be invented."[19] Fitzpatrick justified these measures, drastic as they seemed, as the first step in civilizing the nomadic tribes. Once convinced of the power of the United States, the red men would be forced to stop annoying emigrants and warring with each other and settle down to a more acceptable agricultural way of life. His long association with Indians had not led to any respect for their culture.

At the very time Fitzpatrick and Harvey were discussing solutions to the Indian problem, intertribal warfare broke out anew on the plains. As will be recalled, the Sioux began a campaign to eradicate the border tribes during the winter of 1846–47. The uproar caused by the resulting slaughter, which the press and the Whigs spread across the country, brought a reaction from the Indian Office. Medill quickly asked Harvey for his opinion on sending an expedition against the Sioux "to require the punishment of those concerned in the murders of the Omahas & for the purpose of overawing them & giving to understand that they must keep at peace and refrain from injuring or molesting their brethren."[20]

The problem with Medill's approach was that he had little conception of the power of the Sioux or the impact such a punitive expedition would have on them. Superintendent Harvey, however, immediately saw the flaw and advised against any attempted punishment. These people, he knew, were extremely mobile, hard to find, and an effective job would require a larger force than the government could afford to send. The penalty for failure could be disaster, breeding even more contempt for the power of the United States and making the "Sioux speak of the Soldiers as squaws." He thought it would be better to accelerate the building of military posts on the Oregon Trail, thus securing the permanent presence of the army. In this way the government might concentrate on preventing new intertribal difficulties rather than worry about punishing old ones. If enough troops could not be spared while the war with Mexico continued, then perhaps the border tribes should even be permitted to form a government-sponsored militia to defend themselves.[21]

Harvey continued to flood the Indian Office with policy suggestions. Though recognizing the necessity of having sufficient military forces on the plains, he in no way wanted to exterminate the tribes. He felt a sincere concern about the people under his care and continued to suggest diplomacy as the best means of stopping the bloodshed and halting the plunder of emigrants. "The simple bringing of the tribes together that have been at variance," he wrote to Medill on February 5, 1847, "would have a tendency to make them better disposed to each other; we all must admit as a general rule the advantage of personal intercourse in removing prejudices."[22] Although Harvey himself underestimated the extent of intertribal animosities, he at least recognized that indiscriminate punishment would accomplish little.

The stream of advice from the two most qualified Indian experts served to guide the government in formulating a policy for the central plains. By early 1847 the Indian Office adopted a program for keeping peace based on the ideas of Fitzpatrick and Harvey. This program, however, contained a definite set of priorities: first the military situation would be stabilized by the construction of forts along the Platte; only then would diplomacy be attempted.

Residents of the frontier considered their policy uncertain and far too weak. People were packing the trails by 1847. More than 5,000 came for Oregon and California that summer in addition to the several thousand Mormons heading toward Salt Lake. Though no serious calamity befell the emigrants, the mere presence of so many "savages" along the trail created a wave of alarm on the frontier. During the summer of 1847 the citizens of Missouri, under the leadership of the St. Louis *Daily Union*, began to demand prompt action to safeguard the frontier. Forts and councils were to little use to these people; they wanted the army to take the offensive, and soon. When the *Union* received news that the Oregon Battalion was being formed, the editor was full of advice on how it should be deployed.

The Oregon Battalion, which will leave Fort Leavenworth in a few weeks, should be instructed to repress these Indians outrages and punish the offenders. . . . From recent indications, the Battalion will have ample employment for a time in quieting the Indians and protecting the government trains, the traders and emigrants. . . . Indeed, in the present position of affairs, the new battalion may be most profitably employed in looking after the Indians, and another be advantageously raised to go on with the establishment of government posts on the Oregon route.[23]

Despite the fact that the Sioux had done little more than annoy a few groups of emigrants, rumors and wildly exaggerated accounts of depredations caused considerable pressure, like that displayed in the above editorial, on the government to punish the Indians regardless of the consequences. Yet the administration held back, assuring the nation all would soon be well. Medill issued statements through the Washington *Union*, spokesman for his party, stating that ample protection was on the way and blaming frontier newspapers for exaggerating conditions in the hope of forcing the government to call out more troops.

Promises could not compensate for official inaction. As the year progressed it became obvious that the Oregon Battalion was getting nowhere. Army plans called for the establishment of two posts in 1847, one at the head of Grand Island and the other near Fort Laramie. As we have seen (Chapter 6), neither of these objectives were accomplished and this launched a new barrage of criticism. The Independence (Mo.) *Expositor* created a fictitious "Growing Indian War" and blamed it on the levity and indifference of Polk and his advisors. Hostilities had become perpetual, the paper assured its readers, and now that the Indians had been permitted to taste the "blood and plunder" of whites, it would be next to impossible to quiet them. In calling for a minimum of two thousand troops on the frontier, the editor lashed out that "Wisdom, the warnings of the past, the existing dangers, the blood that has flowed and is daily flowing cry against the *levity* which delay the remedy that shall punish and check the evils existing and to come."[24] It mattered not that the tribes on the plains were still generally at peace with the whites. Frontier citizens believed otherwise.

The situation was little better among the Cheyenne and Arapaho along the Arkansas. Fitzpatrick's first tour of his agency took him to Bent's Fort where he found things anything but quiet. The Mexican War had spurred a number of southwestern tribes—primarily Comanche, Kiowa, and Apache—to plunder the Santa Fe road. They did a superb job of creating havoc, as we have observed in relation to military supplies headed for New Mexico. The success of these tribes created a fear that the tribes assigned to Fitzpatrick, heretofore peaceful, might be drawn into the fray. Already a few Cheyenne warriors and a greater number of Arapaho had been reported with the Comanche. This situation presented a threat; if the Cheyenne and Arapaho engaged in open hostilities with the United States, the Santa Fe road might be entirely shut down and hostilities would spread northward. So concerned was Superintendent Harvey that he issued a circular in July 1847 asking his agents to be vigilant in persuading the tribes to remain loyal to the United States during the conflict with Mexico.[25]

In August, Fitzpatrick held a council with the Cheyenne at Bent's Fort, attempting to keep the tribe quiet. He experienced difficulty from the beginning. The government misplaced the presents Fitzpatrick had intended to distribute, and when the chiefs discovered that their Great Father had sent no gifts, they expressed great dissatisfaction with the American manner of doing business. Still, the smooth-talking agent managed to get a hearing, largely by promising more presents next year. Once he had the tribesmen gathered, he carefully explained that their Great Father was very upset about the depredations on the Santa Fe road and warned that soldiers would soon come to punish all those who dared attack the Americans. The Cheyenne leaders replied, as they usually did on such occasions, that they had always been friends with the whites and would do them no harm. Such statements did little to reassure Fitzpatrick. After the conference he wrote Harvey that the Cheyenne would keep their promises only if convinced that the government had the power to punish them.[26]

Fitzpatrick was by no means an Indian-hater and he did not want them destroyed. His report for 1847, written from Bent's Fort in September, indicates a strong sympathy for the Indian. He, like most of his ethnocentric contemporaries, advocated an agricultural life for the "wild" tribes as the only way of saving them from extinction. This transition would require a great deal of time and effort and, he wrote, "I fear that effort will be too great for them unless they are encouraged and assisted." Yet Fitzpatrick considered himself a realist when it came to the Indian nature and he was certain that only strong military pressure could maintain peace until the government actually began civilizing and educating the tribes. During the fall of 1847 an army battalion (Colonel Gilpin's Missouri Volunteers) was on the Santa Fe road but its utter failure to chastise the Comanche only gave Fitzpatrick more cause for worry. This demonstration of American impotence, he believed, would have an impact on the tribes of his agency. The Cheyenne, in fact, bluntly told him that they had no intention of halting their warfare with the Pawnee until the army proved more effective. All Fitzpatrick could do under such circumstances was recommend once more that the Americans send out a more effective military force to demonstrate their ability to punish the Indians. When his first full year ended, he could report no progress whatsoever in his agency: "It is evident that our Indian Affairs in this country . . . are in a very bad state; nothing having yet transpired to check their ardour and hostile movements, and [they are] becoming still more insolent and imboldened every day."[27]

During the winter of 1847–48 the Indian Office assessed conditions on the central plains. The outlook was indeed discouraging. Nothing positive had been accomplished since 1846 to calm either whites or Indians. Along the Platte the Sioux continued to cut up the border tribes at will. Moreover, the Sioux were beginning to display increased agitation over the white invasion of their hunting grounds and it was questionable how long they would remain quiet without some measures to pacify them. Then, too, the frontier population continued to express alarm over the failure of the government to keep peace and provide them protection. To the south, the Cheyenne and Arapaho remained generally at peace with the whites but with open Indian war raging in New Mexico and along the Santa Fe trail, their friendship seemed precarious in the extreme. Clearly more positive measures were needed to keep the frontier population quiet and to solve the Indian unrest.

Yet 1848 proved worse than the preceding year. While conditions among the Indians remained relatively stable, the government position weakened. With spring came the annual trek of whites headed for the Pacific. There were more Mormons this year, perhaps as many as 4,000, plus a smaller number of gentiles. As white travel increased along the Platte so did the number of encounters with the Indians. Although reports of actual collisions that summer are scarce, Fitzpatrick remembered "no one year, since the first immigration passed up the Platte river, that they suffered more than they have the present one."[28]

Intertribal warfare also continued unabated. Sioux bands along the Platte as well as the Santee and Yancton bands of the Missouri repeatedly struck the border Indians. Records of the Indian Office show that at least fifty Pawnee and twenty-six Oto fell before the Sioux in 1848. Undoubtedly the toll was higher as everywhere on the plains travelers observed Sioux war parties moving

on the border tribes. Superintendent Harvey was thoroughly convinced the continuing Sioux raids were a product of the increased
destruction of buffalo. "It cannot be disguised," he wrote to
Medill on October 4, 1848, "that the destruction of the buffalo
by the whites is far greater than by the Indians." He predicted
total disaster if this situation was allowed to continue much
longer: "the half starved bands will follow the buffalo into the
lands of other tribes; the one pursuing their only support of life,
the other protecting it against them, and it must necessarily lead
to strife."[29]

Trade in alcohol, which increased among the tribes of the
central plains during the Mexican War, added to the problem.
Stills in Iowa and Missouri operated at full strength to meet the
demand. Agent Gideon C. Matlock on the Upper Missouri reported one gathering of "dishonest and disaffected" white men
"twenty miles from the State Line of Iowa; upon which line
there are not a few settling with no ostensible object in view but
to sell whiskey to the Sioux Indians and whitemen in the Indian
Country." Fitzpatrick, too, observed the increasing liquor trade
among the tribes of his agency but saw little chance of halting it
so long as every "little frontier village of the Missouri" persisted
in violating the intercourse laws. Smuggling of alcohol was particularly noticeable among the Cheyenne and Arapaho. Mexican
patriots, trying to urge the Indians into open conflict with the
United States, imported a good supply of liquor from Mexico.
Santa Fe traders also began to take whiskey to the Indians along
the trail. During the season of 1848 bands of unscrupulous
traders began to force their way into the trade. And whiskey
promised quick profits. Solomon P. Sublette, working out of the
Osage Agency, tried to suppress these traders but found himself
overwhelmed. In reporting the incident to Harvey he noted that
the traders were fully prepared to resist by armed force any attempt to stop them and he called for the military to take
corrective action.[30]

Yet the government found itself unable to correct these conditions. Commissioner Medill, despite his deep interest in eliminating the liquor trade, was at a loss to discover the proper course

of action. Finally, in July, at the suggestion of Senator Benton, he ordered Fitzpatrick to Washington to advise the Indian Office.[31]

Arriving at the nation's capitol in August, the outspoken agent immediately launched a scathing attack on policy to anyone who would listen. Most of his remarks were directed toward the failure of the military. Again he recommended that the best possible protection for citizens of the United States traveling west, either to the Pacific or New Mexico, was the establishment of permanent posts on each road. More troops were not needed, but those present should be mounted and extremely mobile and they ought to be commanded by capable men who knew Indians. "It is want of this knowledge," he stated, "that had been the cause for the past few years of the total failure of all the expeditions made against the Indians; and which failures have a great tendency to make the Indians much more hostile, bold & daring than they were before any attempts were made to chastise them."[32] These recommendations were based on the belief that the Indians were completely unaware of the ability of the government to punish them, an ability which Fitzpatrick clearly believed the United States possessed if only it put its mind to it. Only an aggressive policy promised peace, but thus far the army had been solely defensive, reacting rather than taking the initiative.

Fitzpatrick's advice was not heeded in the east. The federal government, having just concluded the Mexican War and still remembering the expensive and scandalous Black Hawk and Seminole Wars, did not intend to become engaged in a controversial Indian campaign. Chastising the tribes of the central plains necessitated a greater effort than the administration was willing to expend. The army, moreover, in direct opposition to Fitzpatrick's assessment of the situation, repeatedly assured the government that all was well. So confident was Secretary of War Marcy that he disbanded the only detachment of troops on the Santa Fe road as soon as the war ended.[33]

Essentially the same thing happened on the Oregon Trail. The Oregon Battalion, although it began construction of Fort Kearny in 1848, made no attempt to establish a fort in the Sioux country.

The most significant problem here was desertion. Missouri volunteers would fight but not work. One officer of the battalion reported that since word of peace with Mexico had arrived, individuals, squads, platoons, and even whole companies had picked up and headed back. By September only Colonel Powell, a few officers, and eighteen men remained of the Oregon Battalion. "It might appear strange that we should leave before being regularly relieved," noted one soldier, "but our contract with the Government terminated with the termination of the War."[34]

Fitzpatrick and many others on the frontier were disheartened by the military pullback and mistakenly concluded that the inability of the government to provide what they considered adequate protection for whites was based upon a misguided sense of humanity. Whatever may be said of Washington officials, however, they never exhibited a reluctance to chastise troublesome Indians; their inaction stemmed more from the dictates of politics and economy. The frontier population, not being privy to the wiles of official thinking, continued to demand that the federal government act immediately. Even Fitzpatrick, though sympathetic to the plight of the Indians with whom he had lived most of his life, never forgot his sense of priorities. In concluding his general report for 1848 he spoke for the frontier viewpoint on Indian policy:

I am aware that great violations of justice have been committed on both sides; but the Indians, of whom I now speak, (the wild tribes of the prairies,) have always kept far ahead of the white man in the perpetration of rascality; and I believe it is only in order to keep peace, and hold his own with the Indians, that the white man is often obliged to resort to many mean practices. With this the poor emigrants have nothing to do; all they want is a free and unmolested passage through to their destination; and in my opinion, they ought to have it, *cost what it may*.[35]

With the conclusion of Polk's administration in early 1849, Fitzpatrick reflected on what had transpired in his agency since 1846. He was not optimistic about the future. He believed the Upper Platte Agency was the most important of all the Indian agencies because the natives of this territory were "the most numerous, the most formidable— The most warlike, the best armed, the best mounted savages of any similar extent of country on the face of the Globe." Across this same country passed all the great routes to the west and he predicted the confrontation of races would continue to cause trouble unless the government began to take the measures he had advocated all along.[36] Little did the old Indian fighter realize how accurate his predictions were. The California gold rush, with its mass of emigrants, was just a few months away and the period prior to 1849 actually proved only the calm before the storm. A policy of getting the tribes out of the way would quickly become more imperative.

It would be well, at this point, to note that persons wholly concerned with the fate of the Indian, though rare, were not entirely absent from the debate over Indian policy on the plains. Of course men of the Indian service, from Fitzpatrick to Harvey to Medill, were concerned with the welfare of the red man, but they paid equal attention to white interests. Father Pierre DeSmet expresses more than anyone else at this time a sincere concern for the fate of the people of the plains. Between 1846 and 1848 the Jesuit missionary and explorer traveled throughout the upper plains. What he saw brought him a great sense of sorrow.[37] He believed the incessant tribal wars and the loss of game were the major factors working for the destruction of these tribes. The Reverend Father hoped some means might be found to prevent these conditions from reaching their ultimate destination, the extermination of all the tribes. His solution implied the need for some type of reservation.

I have heard it frequently remarked by persons, supposed to be well informed on the subject [he wrote to Superintendent Harvey], that these Indians are utterly insusceptible to improvements either in religion or civilization. With this opinion I can not agree. Let liquor, the bane and destroyer of the Indians—the greatest curse the whitemen ever intailed upon the savage—let this be kept from them—let zealous missionaries, who have at heart *only* the welfare of the Indians, not their own private interests and aggrandizement— men filled with the spirit of God and of the true christian charity towards their Indian Brethren, let these be placed among them, and I venture to say that a change for the better will soon take place.

DeSmet saw, as did almost everybody on the frontier, that the buffalo culture could not long survive. He also agreed with the government that the tribes would have to adopt an agricultural way of life—but the transition could not occur immediately, and in the meantime the Indians must be protected, not destroyed. As long as the buffalo continued to roam there seemed little reason to expect any great success in the large-scale introduction of agriculture. A gradual program, however, might work:

Experience has shown that though unaccustomed to such patient, steady labor as argriculture requires, that a people can be induced to work a small field at first, which they will yearly enlarge, and as abundance increases around them, . . . the Indians, West of the Mountains, will become insensibly more attracted to the spot—their wandering propensities and along with them their incessant wars, will gradually disappear—and domestic cattle, hogs[,] poultry being introduced, they would by degrees forget and no longer need the Buffalo.

Father DeSmet therefore wanted the same result as the government, but he asked authorities to consider a policy which would not rely on troops to bring the tribes into submission. To his mind the government should lend timely assistance in saving the prairie tribes: "This would be a most honorable and Charitable work, and would, in my opinion, result in great saving to government—ten good missionaries, I think, would do more towards keeping peace and good will among the aborigines, than several companies of dragoons."

Whether this view was indeed realistic is, of course, subject to question, but the significant fact is that a completely peaceful solution received no practical consideration at that time. Superintendent Harvey, to be sure, seconded DeSmet's views and admitted "such a course would have a most salutary effect in curbing and holding in check the untamed spirits of these wild Indians."[38] The Indian Office even wrote encouraging letters to DeSmet stressing the government's desire to bring civilization to the wild tribes. But the die had been cast. Frontiersmen wanted the army, not humanitarian experiments, and their pressure assured that whatever policy the government followed, the protection of the frontier would not be entrusted to missionaries. Even the idea of starting the plains tribes on an agricultural life as a means of taming them would not be attempted for three years.

On the central plains, then, as elsewhere on the frontier, the government did little towards solving the Indian problems facing the nation prior to 1849. In fact no general policy had been worked out. Harvey suggested a general council to clear a road and nothing happened; Fitzpatrick suggested military posts on the Oregon and Santa Fe roads and nothing happened; frontier citizens and emigrants demanded they be protected and nothing happened; and finally, the Indians asked compensation for the destruction of their lands and were refused. It was obvious that a new and consistent policy, from every viewpoint, was needed. Polk's lackluster Indian policy may very well have been a factor in causing so many frontiersmen to reject the traditional Democratic party and vote for Zachary Taylor in the election of 1848. There is no doubt they expected him to do something about the Indian problem.

By far the most dramatic force urging the Taylor administration to accelerate the rather vague plans drafted by the Polk administration for removal and concentration of the tribes between the Platte and the Arkansas was the discovery of gold in California. During the succeeding years thousands of emigrants— over twenty thousand in 1849 alone—traveled the trails leading west, completely overwhelming the Indians in their path. The gold rush brought, as W. J. Ghent observes, a new element to the frontier: "There were still, and would continue to be, home-seekers in vast numbers; but there also came adventurers, restless wanderers, gamblers, gunmen, thieves, loose women, and all the misfits of a maladjusted world."[39] The possibility of conflict between the two races, which had been relatively minor, suddenly assumed greater proportions. Not only did these people destroy the land they crossed, but they brought disease and alcohol to ravage the defenseless tribesmen.

It was to these problems that the Taylor administration turned its attention. From the beginning, Secretary of the Interior Thomas Ewing believed the Indian department was inadequate to meet its responsibilities and he tried to provide more field officers for the vast plains. He clearly saw that the demands of the expanding frontier were passing the existing agencies and new ones were needed to "properly and effectively manager our Indian affairs." Yet because of the sectional controversy Congress did not immediately authorize new agencies. On April 12, 1849, Ewing did, however, manage to provide a modicum of added protection for the plains by converting the Upper Missouri office to a sub-agency and transferring the agent (John Wilson) to Salt Lake.[40] It was hoped he could prevent the Snake and Bannock tribes in the vicinity of Fort Bridger from molesting the emigrants. At the same time, David Dawson Mitchell replaced Thomas Harvey in the most important administrative post on the plains, the St. Louis Superintendency.

The first serious movement on the part of the Whig administration to deal with the Indian situation on the plains, however, came not from the Indian Office but the army. Taylor was well aware of the pledges made in 1846 to garrison the Oregon Trail and of the fact that only Fort Kearny had been constructed. Thus ten days after the Whigs took office, Taylor's secretary of war, George W. Crawford, issued orders for the army to finish the uncompleted work. A large expedition, consisting primarily of mounted volunteers, was directed to march from Fort Leavenworth to Oregon. Led by Colonel William W. Loring, the expedition was to reinforce Fort Kearny with a detachment of dragoons and infantry, then establish a station "at or near *Fort Laramie*," and finally select a third post in the vicinity of Fort Hall on the Snake River. The Loring expedition marched westward from Fort Leavenworth on May 10, 1849, and fulfilled its mission in relatively short order, purchasing both forts Laramie and Hall, converting them into military posts, and leaving garrisons.[41]

Major Osborne Cross, the official chronicler of the expedition, devoted a considerable portion of his journal to the problems facing the tribes along the trail, although he had little sympathy for the Indian. On several occasions small parties of Indians entered the army encampment complaining about the destruction of wood and game by the passing emigrants and asking for some small compensation. The Major thought the request "too absurd to think of for a moment" and expressed the opinion that the Indians only desired a "fine frolic." Despite such opinions, which may have blinded him to some deeper problems, Cross could not help but note the growing reduction of the buffalo caused by the 1849 emigration. By the time the expedition reached Fort Kearny in May some 10,000 gold seekers had already trampled through the Indian country. Cross observed that only a few years earlier game of all kinds were frequently seen grazing in the Platte valley:

But such has been the effect produced on them by the immense emigration this spring, that it has driven the game far beyond the bluffs; and the buffalo seldom return to the river except when forced to do so for the want of water, and then in small numbers. . . . I have no doubt, if the emigration continues a few years more, as large as it is this year, not one will be found along the borders of the Platte, or near Ft. Kearny, where they have been known to approach the out buildings.[42]

Cross did not realize he was describing the beginnings of the serious ecological destruction of the plains. What had been predicted by Harvey and DeSmet was now becoming fact. The Platte Valley was fast becoming an uninhabitable area for the Indians. Their protests indicate that they were more aware of the implications than progress-oriented whites.

Whites also brought with them a more immediate form of destruction—cholera. Early in 1849 the killer disease began to spread throughout the eastern states, and it finally came west with the gold-seekers. Steamboats brought the disease to St. Louis and other staging areas in early spring, where perhaps 20,000 people were packed together awaiting traveling weather. Soon it spread to the plains tribes. "The cholera," wrote one 49'er in May, "has made its appearance among several of the Indian tribes on the opposite side of the river [Platte], and a large number have died. It is said to be raging to an alarming extent among some of the tribes." Although it is impossible to determine how many tribes were affected, the disease struck the Indians of the Upper Platte particularly hard. As usual the death spread in advance of observers. Captain Howard Stansbury, surveying a new route to Salt Lake, came up the Platte in July and found almost every Sioux village full of dead or dying. The Indians knew whom to blame. "They attribute it to the whites," said one emigrant, "and they say they brought it amongst them."[43]

Superintendent Mitchell was well aware of conditions on the plains. He realized that continued white movement over Indian lands could result in a serious outbreak of violence unless the government took some constructive steps to meet some of the Indian complaints. Yet, whatever the solution, one fact stood out clearly: there would be no stopping the tide of emigration and the Indians must make adjustments in their habits of life. Mitchell favored calling a general council to pacify the tribes until a more permanent program evolved, an idea he probably acquired from his predecessor, Harvey. Like Harvey, both Mitchell and Fitzpatrick (who gave his support to a council now that forts had been established) felt the federal government might quiet the tribes by offering some compensation for the destruction of their natural resources. Mitchell forwarded this suggestion to the Indian Office, recommending that all the prairie tribes be invited to a council. Largely because his proposal coincided with the administration's awareness that all the Indian tribes must be moved away from the routes of communication, Mitchell's suggestion was immediately approved. Indian Commissioner Orlando Brown decided to make the council the occasion for a treaty with the western tribes establishing definite boundaries.[44]

A question of the scope and nature of the proposed treaty soon developed. Mitchell readily adopted Brown's suggestion for establishing boundaries for the plains tribes and in his enthusiasm, he thought he saw a chance to bring peace to the entire west by having all the tribes, including those from the Southwest, attend the council. With all the major tribes represented, Mitchell would first put the chiefs in a good frame of mind by handing out a quantity of presents and guaranteeing substantial annuities in the future as compensation for the loss of their buffalo and timber. In this atmosphere, he expected that the tribes could be brought into a binding agreement with the national government whereby they would agree to quit fighting with each other and accept some limitation on their movements. To justify the large expenditure this would entail, Mitchell assured the Indian Office that the treaty "would do more towards establishing friendly relations with the prairie tribes than all the efforts that have heretofore been made; at all events it would do no harm, and the expense would be less than that of a six month's war on the plains and mountains of New Mexico."[45] Annuities, moreover, promised to guarantee the good behavior of the tribes; once dependent upon the government, the Indians could be threatened with loss of annuity funds for any violation of their treaty. In this way, too, the government had a lever to force tribes into taking up agriculture as a first step in the civilization program.

Brown had some second thoughts on learning the full extent of Mitchell's plan. Such a gathering promised more expense than the department could afford, and he asked Mitchell, on September 20, 1849, if he should concentrate only on the Cheyenne, Arapaho, and other tribes along the Santa Fe road. Were the council held at Fort Laramie, as suggested by Mitchell and Fitzpatrick, Brown expected it to be more expensive. Perhaps the northern tribes really did not need a treaty now that the army was stationed on the Oregon Trail. Brown was quick to stipulate, however, that if Mitchell and Fitzpatrick persisted, he would back their views and ask Congress for the money. Such apparently happened, for by November the commissioner had committed himself to including all the prairie tribes in the proposed treaty.[46]

Meanwhile Mitchell had already proceeded on his own with plans for the treaty. The season already being too far advanced to gather the tribes, Fitzpatrick was ordered at the end of August to notify all the Indians inhabiting the Missouri, Platte, and Arkansas to assemble in the vicinity of Fort Kearny about July 1, 1850. Unfortunately, Fitzpatrick arrived at Fort Leavenworth five days after his expected escort to the Arkansas departed, and when the post quartermaster refused to supply him with transportation, the temperamental agent got into a quarrel with the army over what he considered a deliberate refusal to cooperate with Indian

Office business and returned to St. Louis.[47] This proved the first of many snags.

Fitzpatrick's delay in getting to the tribes failed to daunt Mitchell, who had by now become so enthusiastic about the treaty that he neglected much of his responsibilities for the border tribes. As soon as the Indian Office put its stamp of approval on the plan, Mitchell took over the major responsibility for its success. His first task was to draw up the legislation that would be required. This he did by asking Congress for the unprecedented sum of $200,000, to be spent on presents, transportation, and the purchase of captives. Mitchell, expecting no difficulty, further refined his plans in a letter to Brown on March 9, 1850.[48] He proposed dividing the Indian country into geographical districts— including areas for the Comanche, Kiowa, Apache, Arikara, Mandan, Gros Ventre, Sioux, Cheyenne, Crow, and Arapaho. Once placed on these reserves, the tribes would be held responsible for any depredations committed on their soil. To secure adherence to the treaty stipulations he also recommended that $40,000 worth of annuity goods be distributed to the tribes. All in all, this treaty promised to be the most expensive the government had ever negotiated, but the results seemed worth the price.

With the arrival of decent weather in the spring of 1850, word went out via traders and agents asking the tribes to gather at Fort Laramie. Fitzpatrick himself returned to the Arkansas in February to prepare the southern tribes. He remained in the vicinity of Big Timbers, near the crossing of the river, for several months, holding conferences with Sioux, Cheyenne, Arapaho, and Kiowa. All the chiefs seemed favorable to the proposed treaty and were especially delighted with the government's promise of a generous supply of presents. Of course, the Indians were playing the entire affair by ear, hoping that they could make some accommodation that would stop the disruption of their way of life. Fitzpatrick knew the Indians were anxious for an agreement, and in reporting later to Mitchell, he stated that the time was ripe for a treaty "while the Indians of whom I speak are friendly disposed." The agent suggested that without further delay there should be "some understanding with them in regard to the right of way through their country; and whatever our and their rights may be, let us and them know it, that we may have some data on which to base future proceedings."[49]

Not everyone of the frontier favored the treaty, however. In fact it became an issue of some debate during the summer of 1850. Some Democrats considered the entire affair politically inspired. A far more fundamental question was raised over whether the tribes could be expected to obey any settlement. The editor of the Democratic St. Louis *Daily Union* launched a campaign to discredit the treaty, Superintendent Mitchell, and the Taylor administration. Writing on May 30, 1850, he criticized the federal government for squandering $200,000, saying it was a waste of money to place "wild" Indians on assigned lands before they had been whipped into a respect for American authority. Mitchell reacted quickly to such criticism by writing several long justifications of his plan for the pages of the rival *Daily Missouri Republican*, a Whig paper. It showed his faith in peacefully getting the tribes onto reserves. The superintendent first claimed the *Union* editorials were simply an attempt to make "political capital, by assailing everything that is done, or attempted to be done, by the present administration." Moreover, the idea of chastising the Indians seemed ridiculous. Some 30,000 warriors inhabited the plains, and the most elementary figuring indicated that the cost of defeating these tribes would be staggering.

The Union recommends the whipping of these prairie tribes, with as much non-chalance, as if he was recommending the whipping of a negro baby, that was caught playing with fire. . . . It [the treaty] is intended as a *cheap* experiment—if it fails to secure peace and good will between the whites and Indians, it will then be time to undertake the whipping experiment.[50]

Unfortunately for Mitchell, Congress was at the very time tied up with the slavery issue, and despite very active support from the Indian Office, the House of Representatives, as it did on other matters, refused to discuss variant issues during this period of confusion (Chapter 3). Thus as the time for the council drew near, Mitchell found himself in the embarrassing position of having to tell the tribes that the Great Father had not yet agreed to the council. The disappointed superintendent then postponed the assemblage indefinitely and attempted to quiet the tribes by assuring them that the government had not deserted its red children.[51]

Both Mitchell and Fitzpatrick were worried that hostilities might erupt before the legislators realized the gravity of the situation. Although the tribes remained at peace, numerous indications of a volatile situation continued to flow into the St. Louis office. Of greatest concern was the increased emigration, which had doubled in 1850. W. S. McBride, traveling west that year, paused at Fort Laramie long enough in May to calculate the extent of the migration. As of May 31, "8352 men, 68 women, 39 children, 2266 wagons, 8087 horses, 2744 mules, 1544 oxen, 91 cows," had passed the Fort. "Then suppose," he added, "this was the first fourth of the emigration and that three fourths were yet back & we have 38,840 crossing the plains in one season & this estimate I think is moderate."[52]

Buffalo and other game had all but disappeared from the Platte valley, and although the Oglala and Brulé could still find animals to the north and west, the border tribes were in a precarious situation. Yet if the Sioux were less affected by the loss of game, they suffered more from white disease. Cholera continued ravaging the tribe, and smallpox made a return appearance in 1850. The disease spread to the remotest bands and by the middle of the year death and devastation was rampant throughout the vast Sioux lands from Minnesota to the Platte. Word soon spread among the tribe that the epidemic was white magic designed to accelerate their extermination. This opinion, added to the destruction of game and timber, caused Mitchell a great deal of worry. At any moment the tribes under his jurisdiction might touch off a war.[53]

Mitchell's anxious wait came to an end in March 1851 when Congress, having settled the sectional dispute, turned its attention to the Indian problem on the plains by appropriating $100,000 "to enable the President of the United States to hold a

treaty, or treaties, with the prairie and mountain tribes." The
time and place of the council was set for September 1, 1851, at
Fort Laramie. As the council promised to be the largest gathering
of Indians ever attempted by the United States, it seemed desirable to impress them with the power of their Great Father. The
Indian Office asked the War Department to have ten companies
of troops in attendance at the ceremonies.[54] It soon became evident, however, that the army shared little of the department's
enthusiasm.

Secretary of War C. M. Conrad, seeing no reason to expend
additional funds, suggested that the three companies stationed at
Laramie were sufficient. This lack of cooperation infuriated
Mitchell. By his estimate some 15,000 warriors would gather.
"And when we take into consideration the fact that most of these
tribes have never met—except on the battlefield . . . I think [we]
should have at least one thousand men on the ground."[55] He also
facetiously suggested the army should make an appearance if for
no other reason that to see the faces of the tribesmen they usually
saw only in a cloud of dust.

The superintendent of course proceeded with plans despite
continuing difficulty with the War Department. In early spring
he dispatched runners and circulars up the Missouri, Platte, and
Arkansas rivers informing all the Indians in his jurisdiction to
gather at Laramie. At the same time he made arrangements with
trader Robert Campbell for some $50,000 worth of Indian goods
to be purchased and freighted to the treaty grounds.[56] Certainly
there would be every incentive for the tribes to appear.

The council also offered incentives for white speculators. Merchants, freighters, traders, and general hangers-on all prepared to
get in on the bounty. Robert Campbell, for example, expected to
make additional profit by adding an extra team of oxen to all his
wagons and selling these animals for a premium price at the
council ground.[57] Even the Mormon community in Salt Lake saw
a chance to use the treaty for their own benefit. When Governor
Brigham Young heard of the planned treaty, he decided the Shoshoni Indians in his vicinity must be included. He was looking
for a chance to remove this local tribe, believing they were a

hindrance to settlement. (About this time, George A. Smith and James Lewis, two leading Saints, wrote to President Fillmore that "the soil in some parts of the vallies is rich and fertile and may by the hand of industry some day become valuable but this will be when the government will remove the Indians from the Territory."[58]) Young, serving as ex officio superintendent of Indian affairs for Utah, ordered, on his own authority, H. R. Day, a Mormon calling himself an Indian subagent, to take a delegation of local Indians to Fort Laramie. Commissioner Lea approved of sending the Utah Indians, but not for the reason desired by Young. Jacob H. Holman, a Gentile, who was then on his way to assume the duties of agent at Salt Lake, was ordered to lead the procession. Although Holman was not as concerned with the Mormon settlements as was Day, he did believe the transcontinental trails should be cleared of Indians in order to calm emigrant fears.[59]

As the date for the council neared, it became increasingly clear that the government might have more on its hands than it bargained for. Agent Holman, heading east with sixty Shoshoni chiefs and a large entourage of warriors, women, and horses, encountered a party of Cheyenne headed for Laramie. Old tribal animosities immediately flared up, and the Cheyenne wasted no time in killing several of their long-time enemies. The Shoshoni then refused to go on unless they received protection from the army. Major Holman quickly dispatched his son to Fort Laramie, where he succeeded in finding a small escort, but in the meantime most of the Shoshoni delegation decided to return, and only a small party continued.[60] This encounter portended trouble for any harmonious gathering of such a large group of hereditary enemies.

Tom Fitzpatrick also had troubles with tribal animosities in the south. On April 22, 1851, he departed again for the Arkansas and held a "talk" with all the tribes in the vicinity. "The Camanches, Kiawas, Apaches, Arripahoes, and Cheyennes were there." He explained to each tribe that their Great Father "had it in contemplation to do something for them, and make restitution for any damage or injury which they were liable to, or might suffer hereafter from American citizens travelling through their country."[61] But the Comanche, Kiowa and Apache refused to attend the council, saying they could not trust the Sioux or Crow. "Thus ended the 'Big Talk,'" Fitzpatrick wrote in disgust. Of the southern tribes, only the Cheyenne and Arapaho, who were on friendly terms with the northern tribes, accepted the invitation.

Nor did the Pawnee or any of the other border tribes accept the invitation. They, too, feared that their old enemy the Sioux would use the occasion to destroy them. Consequently, one of the goals of the council—to secure peace agreement between the Sioux and the other tribes—was negated by the persistence of intertribal animosities, which could not be quelled by government pledges.

On May 26, 1851, Lea sent Mitchell final instructions. An analysis of Lea's instructions shows the extent to which the Indian Office was now committed to fixing boundaries and beginning the process of civilization. By this time the Indian Office had had the benefit of advice from agents and observers in Texas, New Mexico, among the border Indians, and on the plains, all seeing the need for reservations. Small wonder Lea saw a chance to begin this policy among a significant portion of the Indian poulation. He therefore ordered that: (1) all tribes were to establish official relations with the United States; (2) the government would purchase a right-of-way and compensate the tribes for the destruction of their resources, payment to be made in stock and agriclutural goods; (3) "the strongest inducements should be held out to the Indians to resort to agriculture & the raising of stock . . ."; (4) a fixed boundary for each tribe should be established.[62]

Mitchell departed for Laramie on July 24. Included in the party were Colonel A. B. Chambers, senior editor of the *Daily Missouri Republican*, and B. Gratz Brown, a reporter, who would keep the nation posted through the pages of the *Republican*. Also included in the party, but traveling separately, was Father Pierre DeSmet. When they arrived at Laramie on August 31, Mitchell noted that the tribes were assembled, "and impatiently expecting my arrival."[63]

Teton Sioux, Cheyenne, Arapaho, Crow, Gros Ventre, Assiniboin, and Arikara stood waiting, perhaps 10,000 in all including women and children. The army had supplied only 270 soldiers for protection, causing much uneasiness to the whites. One soldier, Private Percival Lowe, estimated that the tribes could easily wipe out all the Americans if they took a mind to.[64] But the Indians were more interested in presents, and the real danger came from a collision between the Shoshoni and the other tribes. When Agent Holman and the Shoshoni arrived on the council grounds the anticipated explosion almost occurred. One Sioux warrior decided to avenge the death of his father and headed for the Shoshoni party. Fortunately for all concerned, Jim Bridger and a French interpreter interceded and calmed the situation before shooting began. Bridger, who was with the Shoshoni, explained to young Lowe what would have happened if the Sioux had not been stopped: "My chief would 'er killed him [the Sioux] quick, and then the fool Sioux would 'er got their backs up, and there wouldn't have been room to camp 'round here for dead Sioux. You dragoons acted nice, but you wouldn't have had no show if the fight had commenced—no making peace then."[65]

Tempers cooled somewhat after this episode. Mitchell decided to conduct the official council at Horse Creek, some thirty-odd miles down the Platte, and the commissioners, soldiers, and Indians all moved, the various tribes selecting locations where they could keep an eye on their enemies. Despite Mitchell's optimistic report that all was friendly and that the chiefs were exchanging visits and presents, the atmosphere remained tense.

On September 8, the superintendent called the tribes together to make his talk. He told them their Great Father had listened to his "Red Children's" complaint that their buffalo had been driven off and their grass and timber destroyed by the emigrants, and he would make retribution. For this compensation, however, he expected his children to allow their white brothers free and unmolested passage. And to keep peace he wanted the right to establish military posts in Indian country. There must also be justice and peace among the Indian nations. To accomplish this great task, their Great Father would mark off separate boundaries for each tribe. "In doing this it is not intended to take any of your lands away from you."

[But] your condition is now changed from what it formerly was. In times past you had plenty of buffalo and game to subsist upon, and your Great Father well knows that war has always been your favorite amusement and pursuit. He then left the question of peace and war to yourselves. Now, since the settling of the districts West of you by the white men, your condition has changed, and your Great Father desires you will consider and prepare for the changes that await you.[66]

For these concessions and to help the tribes begin adopting an agricultural way of life, Mitchell promised an annuity of $50,000 per year, for fifty years.

On September 12, with the aid of former traders Fitzpatrick and Bridger as well as DeSmet, the government began drawing the boundaries. The superintendent first decided that the Shoshoni, since they did not technically reside in his supintendency, must be excluded from the council. All he could do on this score was to get the Shoshoni and Cheyenne to shake hands and promise to end their blood feud. More serious trouble came when the whites began dividing up the rest of the lands. The Sioux, Cheyenne, and Arapaho all claimed much of the same territory and had never really recognized any boundaries. The commissioners determined that the Platte would be the dividing line, and in particular that the Sioux must remain to the north. But the Sioux balked. "You have split the country and I do not like it," said Black Hawk, an Oglala, speaking for his people. The chief claimed that the tribe was in the habit of living and hunting from the Platte to the Arkansas and they did not want to be restricted. "These lands once belonged to the Kiowas and the Crows, but we whipped these nations out of them, and in this we did what the white men do when they want the lands of the Indians." Mitchell finally calmed the tribe by explaining to them that they would be able to hunt south of the river as long as they remained at peace. The rest of the boundaries went rather smoothly. The Cheyenne and Arapaho were assigned the area between the Arkansas and North Platte, the Mandan and Gros Ventre to country on the Yellowstone, the Crow a territory near the Powder River, and the Blackfeet their traditional lands at the headwaters of the Missouri.[67]

Without much further ado the treaty was signed. For the first time the tribes of the central plains entered into treaty relations with the United States. In addition, they had agreed in essence to restrict themselves to certain boundaries. But in spite of the hopes of government officials, the treaty did not mark the beginnings of reservations for the plains tribes. The boundaries were rather vague and the participants did not give up the right to hunt elsewhere. Also, the military and economic reasons for restricting these tribes had not yet become imperative to the expanding American nation. Thus no real force backed up the treaty. Accordingly, it was not until the Medicine Lodge treaty in 1867 that the Cheyenne and Arapaho were confined to distinct reservations. The Sioux received their reservations at the 1868 treaty of Fort Laramie. However, the 1851 treaty is a milestone on the road to these reservations. The government had committed itself to the principle of reservations and the treaty would be used to restrict future Indian movements. As Gratz Brown put it: "It is a useful section to the Government in this, that, in recognizing boundaries, it give a locality to each tribe, and enables the Government to hold the tribes responsible for injuries or depredations."[68] Thus for a handful of presents, the Indians were each given a defined land where they were told that they could live "forever" in peace. Little did they realize that in the future this arrangement allowed the Americans to divide and conquer—to force individual groups onto more restricted reserves without upsetting their neighbors.

But neither the government nor the Indian realized this fact in September 1851. To the government the Indian dilemma growing out of the conquest of Mexico and the opening of the continent had been resolved. The Indians had agreed to live on their part at peace with each other and stay separated from the whites. The Americans seemingly had cleared the routes of communication, stopped the border warfare, and guaranteed the Indians indemnity for damage done to their country. To all it seemed a perfect treaty; it appeared to end the certain possibility of a costly war and pave the way for peace. No less important, it offered a humane guarantee of the survival of the prairie tribes. "Humanity," wrote Mitchell at the conclusion of the council, "calls loudly for some interposition on the part of the American government to save, if possible, some portion of these ill-fated tribes; and this, it is thought, can only be done by furnishing them the means, and generally turning their attention to agricultural pursuits."[69] All this he confidently expected the Laramie treaty to accomplish.

8

Epilogue

❦   The signing of the treaty of Fort Laramie is a landmark on the national path to a reservation system for the American Indian tribes. The structure and details of this system were by no means complete or final by 1851, but the collective experience of dealing with the tribes of the plains and Southwest as the old "Indian barrier" disappeared strongly indicated that some sort of tribal reservations and defined boundaries constituted the only practical way for the whites to obtain peace with the remaining Indian population. Events quickly proved, of course, that most tribes were unwilling to be completely restricted. Yet, in a general view, the conclusions were inescapable to those who wanted to help the Indian. With the establishment of continental boundaries, white Americans would be entering that part of the Indian domain that had remained relatively immune. To preserve peace as this invasion occurred, and to provide for the tribes when their means of survival disappeared, government leaders believed that the Indians could no longer pursue their traditional life. If they did, it must inevitably lead to a collision with the interests of white society. Thus from all corners came the same general advice: the tribes had to be gathered at places where they would be out of the path of white expansion and where they could be kept from harming either whites or each other. Both the friends of the In-

193

dians and those who only wanted what he possessed favored this solution.

Although it now seems that the reservation system as it came into operation only benefitted white greed, implicit in the gathering momentum to place the tribes on reservations was the idea that the Indian would be the ultimate beneficiary. Accepting the current doctrines of the desirability and inevitability of progress, American officials predicted that the Indian could survive his encounter with a more civilized society only by adapting to that society. Despite other political and economic interests, much of this was conceived in the utmost good faith. The desire to maintain peace as the nation expanded and progressed was coupled with the notion that it would be of positive benefit to the tribes to segregate them from the whites until they could be civilized. The sincerity of this humanitarian concept must be recognized in any discussion of the foundations of the reservation system. It was not solely an attempt to locate the American native on the most undesirable lands and leave him to rot there.

American culture in the nineteenth century was impregnated with a strong ethnocentrism; so strong in fact that there could be no serious thought of conceding any value to Indian life and society. It was pagan and barbaric, and therefore unacceptable. Even those who sincerely wanted to help the Indian—and there were many—conceived of aiding him by ending his "savage" and uncertain life style and getting him to imitate the white farmer. Reformers had long believed, and would continue to believe, that the choice facing the Indians was one of "extermination or civilization." To most this meant that as long as the Indian retained his old way of life he would not progress. Like the white man, he must labor in the earth. It was this concept that underlay the movement for assigning the tribes reservations. David Dawson Mitchell summed up the collective thought of the age following the Fort Laramie treaty negotiations when he said: "Humanity calls loudly for some interposition on the part of the American government to save, if possible, some portion of these ill-fated tribes; and this, it is thought, can only be done by furnishing them the means, and generally turning their attention to agricultural pursuits."

Almost all government officials acquainted with the Indian during the years of expansion—Medill, Fitzpatrick, Neighbors, Calhoun, Harvey, Lea—predicted that the end result would be exploitation and eventual extermination of the Indian should the nation fail to provide a suitable environment for acculturation. Even at this early date, before the idea of allotment of lands in severalty became generally accepted, reservations were not viewed as an end in themselves. In essence they were intended to protect the native until some point in the future when he would be ready to integrate into American society. In the meantime, the government should concentrate on getting them to agree to restrictions and encouraging them to begin farming. The government bureaucracy would have to be geared to this end. Thus the restricted atmosphere seemed to be pleasing and desirable to everyone—except the Indian, who was not asked.

There are many reasons why the government did not immediately put into operation the system it thought necessary to assure peaceful relations in the future. The period between 1846 and 1851 was largely one of policy formulation and experimentation, not implementation. Only in a relatively few areas, such as with the border tribes, did the situation reach proportions sufficiently acute to demand rapid action. In most other cases on the western frontier, however, government agents did push for as much of the reservation idea as conditions permitted or required. It is accurate to state therefore that the first steps toward reservations were taken in New Mexico, Texas, on the high plains, and elsewhere. Yet the completion of a national reservation system had to await several things that most observers at the time only dimly realized. Even Thomas Fitzpatrick, who was more perceptive than most and predicted that some of the tribes would have to be forced into acting as the government wished never foresaw how much effort it would take to get the frontier tribes on reservations. Most official thinking confidently predicted that once having been shown the white man's way, the Indian would be more than

anxious to lay down the life of the camp and adopt an argricul-
tural economy.

Put in simplest terms, the powerful western tribes, the ones
that have been discussed herein, were undefeated and no peaceful persuasion, no matter how logical and rational white officials
believed it to be, could convince these tribes to give up their
heritage and traditional style of life and begin assimilation. Although the government had basically decided how to handle the
remaining Indian population in the United States, it proved
impossible to put that policy into effect until the tribes had been
forced into submission; something that was not seriously contemplated at the time, but proved a bloody corollary of the program
once inaugurated.

As a consequence, the Indian wars that occupied the western
frontier between 1860 and 1890, and the national scandal and
humiliation that went with them, were in many respects the inevitable result of refinements and enforcement of the ideas first
propounded during the era of Manifest Destiny. Unfortunately,
much of the humanitarian spirit of the first advocates disappeared in the transition—although the protection of the Indian
continued to be a justification for restricting him until the rise of
the allotment movement in the 1880's. As it became clear that
most tribes would resist the logic of white opinion and continue
to block white expansion, the nation decided to put a full reservation system into operation by defeating or starving the tribes
into compliance.

Factors that were not overwhelming during the era of expansion spurred the movement for reservations after 1860. Of primary importance was the fact that white frontiersmen and entre-
preneurs found more and more value to the remaining Indian
lands. Thus the pressure to concentrate the Indians and free the
remaining territory was actively encouraged by settlers, miners,
cattlemen, and railroads. All of these forces had been present in
the late 1840's, and had to some extent influenced the development of the reservation movement, but their power was relatively
minor in relation to what it would become. At mid-century the
lands of the western tribes still remained relatively unknown.

Two decades later the exploration of the West was in full swing and only the Indian stood in the way. The pressure to move the tribes away from lands they were not using for productive purposes increased until the nation found itself in a major war to dispossess the Indian.

In the last analysis, then, the roots of much of what would follow for the American Indian are located in the 1846–51 period. There was considerable soul-searching and experimentation on the part of the government and reformers before the final reservation system evolved, but the debates were over relatively minor details and the essentials remained unchanged. Later attempts to resolve the inherent problems of an Indian population on the frontier—the Peace Policy during President Grant's administration and even the drive to civilize Indians that culminated in the Dawes Act of 1887—are outgrowths of the proposals of the age of expansion. They were more elaborate and more restrictive, but essentially logical progressions. The concentration of all tribes on reservations during the 1860's and 1870's simply fulfilled by force a relatively passive policy that had been decided upon as a response to the end of the barrier philosophy and the national expansion of the 1840's. The beginnings of the reservation system came in the era of Manifest Destiny, when it was looked upon as an alternative to extinction. The brutal and disastrous Indian wars that followed were in essence to fulfill a policy dictated by white response to conditions of an earlier date.

Notes

Notes

Abbreviations

AGO	Adjutant General's Office
CIA	Commissioner of Indian Affairs
HEH	Henry E. Huntington Library
ISL	Indiana State Library, Indiana Division
KHS	Kentucky Historical Society
LC	Library of Congress
LR	Letters Received
LS	Letters Sent
MHS	Missouri Historical Society
NARS	National Archives and Records Service
OIA	Office of Indian Affairs
SI	Secretary of the Interior
SW	Secretary of War
U.S., *Stat.*	United States Statutes at Large

Preface

1. Alban W. Hoopes, *Indian Affairs and their Administration, with Special Reference to the Far West, 1849–1860* (Philadelphia: University of Pennsylvania Press, 1932); James C. Malin, "Indian Policy and Western Expansion," *Bulletin of the University of Kansas, Humanistic Studies* 2 (1921), 1–108.

2. Perhaps the only other time the United States found it necessary to face as many new Indian problems was immediately after the Revolution, when policy had to be formulated from British precedent. Reginald Horsman, *Expansion and American Indian Policy, 1783–1812* (East Lansing: Michigan State University Press, 1967); and Francies Paul Prucha, *American*

Indian Policy in the Formative Years: The Indian Trade and Intercourse Acts, 1790–1834 (Cambridge, Mass.: Harvard University Press, 1962), both contain excellent discussions of the early problems in formulating policy.

Chapter 1

1. Roy Harvey Pearce, *The Savages of America: A Study of the Indian and the Idea of Civilization* (Baltimore: Johns Hopkins Press, 1965), penetrates and discusses the whole attitude of Americans toward the Indians. Many historians and anthropologists have over the last few years examined the development of ethnocentric points of view in American society. See particularly Wilcomb E. Washburn, "The Moral and Legal Justifications for Dispossessing the Indian," and Nancy O. Lurie, "Indian Cultural Adjustment to European Civilization," in James Morton Smith, ed., *Seventeenth Century America: Essays in Colonial History* (Chapel Hill, N.C.: University of North Carolina Press, 1959), pp. 15–32, 33–60; Wilbur R. Jacobs, *Dispossessing the American Indian* (New York: Charles Scribner's Sons, 1972), pp. 1–15, 19–30, 107–125; William Brandon, "American Indians and American History," *The American West* 2 (1965): 14–25, 91–92; Peter Lowenberg, "The Psychology of Racism," in Gary B. Nash and Richard Weiss, eds., *The Great Fear: Race in the Minds of Americans* (New York: Holt, Rinehart, Winston, 1970). pp. 186–201.

2. Bernard W. Sheehan, "Paradise and the Noble Savage in Jeffersonian Thought," *William and Mary Quarterly* 26 (1969): 329, 342, 358–59.

3. Francis P. Prucha, "Indian Removal and the Great American Desert," *Indiana Magazine of History* 59 (1963): 309–22. Prucha convincingly demolishes the old myth that removal was based on giving the Indians unfit lands, by noting that the lands assigned were not desert and that the Indians themselves saw them as being very good. Even accepting this evidence, however, some writers still insist that the nation saw no future use for this land. See, for example, Ralph K. Andrist, *The Long Death: The Last Days of the Plains Indians* (New York: Collier, 1969), pp. 1–12.

4. *Annual Message of the President, 1824*, 18th Cong., 2d sess., Senate Doc. 1 (Serial 108), pp. 16–17; John C. Calhoun to James Monroe, January 24, 1825, *Register of Debates in Congress*, 18th Cong., 2d sess. (1825), vol. 1, Appendix, pp. 370–412; U.S., *Stat.*, vol. 4, pp. 411–412. For an excellent analysis of the Removal Bill and its more immediate consequences, see Annie H. Abel, "The History of Events Resulting in Indian Consolidation West of the Mississippi River," *Annual Report of the American Historical Association, 1906*, 1, 370–412.

5. In 1834 the War Department presented Congress with a map showing the general boundaries for all the transplanted tribes. This map is presented

in "Regulating the Indian Department," 23rd Cong., 1st sess., *House Report 474* (Serial 263), following p. 131.

6. Keokuk's Reservation, as this tract of land was called, was a well-meaning attempt to help these friendly Indians. However, they were surrounded on all sides by whites and found the narrow strip of land untenable. See Alonzo Abernathy, "Early Iowa Indian Treaties and Boundaries," *Annals of Iowa* 11 (1914): 251–52.

7. U.S., *Stat.*, vol. 1, p. 49, vol. 4, p. 735. The entire congressional proposal on the reorganization of the Indian department is given in "Regulating the Indian Department," pp. 2–10. The legislative background of the laws of 1834 is analyzed in Prucha, *American Indian Policy*, pp. 251–69. The office of Superintendent of Indian affairs at St. Louis had been created in 1822, and was specifically continued by the act of 1834. St. Louis was the only full superintendency in 1834.

8. Ruth A. Gallaher, "The Indian Agent in the United States Before 1850," *Iowa Journal of History and Politics* 14 (1916): 37; "Regulating the Indian Department," p. 11; George D. Harmon, *Sixty Years of Indian Affairs: Political, Economic, and Diplomatic, 1789–1850* (Chapel Hill, N.C.: University of North Carolina Press, 1941), pp. 171–72.

9. U.S., *Stat.*, vol. 4, p. 736. Subagents were intended to operate where there were no provisions for an agency, and although subagents were supposed to have the same duties as agents, the low salary of $750 per year and difficult living conditions made it extremely hard to attract qualified men.

10. The full text of the act is presented ibid., pp. 729–37; see also "Regulating the Indian Department," pp. 10–14.

11. "Regulating the Indian Department," pp. 33–37; Annie H. Abel, "Proposals for an Indian State, 1778–1878," *Annual Report of the American Historical Association for 1907* 1 (1908): 97–99. John Quincy Adams, in particular, felt the whole idea was unconstitutional, asking what right the government had to establish a territory solely for the use of Indians.

12. In 1836 Congress tried again to "provide for the security and protection of the emigrant and the tribes west of the State of Missouri," by granting the lands to Indians in perpetuity, but the effort met failure. For a survey of all proposals up to 1848 concerning an Indian Territory, see "Indian Territory, West of the Mississippi," 30th Cong., 1st sess., *House Report 736* (Serial 526), pp. 1–10.

13. *Annual Report, CIA, 1842*, pp. 520–22; *Annual Report, CIA, 1844*, p. 313; Francis P. Prucha, "American Indian Policy in the 1840's: Visions of Reform," in John C. Clark, ed., *The Frontier Challenge: Responses to the Trans-Mississippi West* (Lawrence: University of Kansas Press, 1971), pp. 81–100.

14. Mitchell to Crawford, October 25, 1841, OIA, LR, St. Louis Superintendency; *Annual Report, CIA, 1840*, pp. 241–42. In 1838 another frustrated agent wrote that "These whiskey traffickers, who seem void of all conscience,

rob and murder many of these Indians; I say rob—they will get them drunk, and then take their horses, guns, or blankets off their backs, regardless of how quick they may freeze to death; I say murder—if not directly, indirectly, they furnish the weapon—they make them drunk, and when drunk, they kill their fellow beings." Quoted in Helen Hunt Jackson, *A Century of Dishonor: The Early Crusade for Indian Reform*, ed. Andrew F. Rolle (New York: Harper & Row; 1965), p. 50.

15. Robert M. Utley, *Frontiersmen in Blue: The United States Army and the Indian, 1848–1865* (New York: Macmillan Co., 1967), p. 18.

16. Hoopes, *Indian Affairs*, pp. 10–12; Henry B. Beers, *The Western Military Frontier, 1815–1846* (Philadelphia: University of Pennsylvania Press, 1935), pp. 109–10; Russell F. Weigley, *History of the United States Army* (New York: Macmillan Co., 1967), pp. 159–60.

17. U.S. *Stat.*, vol. 4, p. 554, vol. 5, p. 33. The 1st Dragoons, created 1832, constituted the first mounted troops to be used in the Indian country as a permanent branch of the army. Francis P. Prucha, *The Sword of the Republic: The United States Army on the Frontier, 1783–1846* (New York: MacMillan Co., 1969), pp. 365–95, discusses the activities of the frontier dragoons between 1832 and 1846. A good example of the attempts to revise frontier defenses is Secretary of War Joel R. Poinsett's report to the House of Representatives in March 1840, 26th Cong., 1st sess., *House Ex. Doc. 161*. In 1842 Winfield Scott, commanding general of the army, proposed to increase frontier forces by six regiments, but Congress refused, 27th Cong., 2d sess., *Senate Doc. 248*.

18. *Annual Message of the President, 1848*, pp. 7–8.

19. The term "Great Plains" can very greatly in interpretation and no rigid definition is entirely accurate. For the purposes of this study, however, the rather broad definition of Walter Prescott Webb, *The Great Plains* (New York: Grosset & Dunlap, 1951), p. 8, is the most suitable. Webb's definition of a "plains environment" presents three specific characteristics—level surface, treeless land, and insufficient rainfall. All of the tribes of the plains frontier during the 1840's, with the exception of some of the New Mexican tribes, may thus generally fall into the category of plains Indians.

20. Population figures are especially hard to determine. Harold E. Driver, *Indians of North America* (Chicago: University of Chicago Press, 1969), p. 486, estimates that about 150,000 Indians resided in the territory acquired from Mexico in 1846. There were probably an equal number on the central plains. Driver, pp. 63–65, tends to take a rather conservative population estimate in comparison with Henry F. Dobyns's "Estimating Aboriginal American Population, an Appraisal of Techniques with a New Hemispheric Estimate," *Current Anthropology* 7 (1966): 395–416, who projects much larger aboriginal populations than have been considered in the past. For a convenient survey of the population controversy, see Virgil J. Vogel, *This Country Was Ours: A Documentary History of the American Indian* (New York: Harper & Row, 1972), pp. 250–55.

21. Good general descriptions of these peoples are found in Alvin M. Josephy, *The Indian Heritage of America* (New York: Alfred A. Knopf, 1968), pp. 114–18, 147–53; William Brandon, *The American Heritage Book of Indians* (New York: Laurel, 1964), pp. 303–18, 330–59; Robert H. Lowie, *Indians of the Plains* (Garden City: Natural History Press, 1963).

22. Edward H. Spicer, *Cycles of Conquest: The Impact of Spain, Mexico, and the United States on the Indians of the Southwest, 1533–1960* (Tucson: University of Arizona Press, 1962), pp. 1–8, 152–70, 210–14. Much recent work has been done on the impact of the white man on the Indian's biotic and cultural environment. See especially Driver, *Indians of North America*, pp. 505–29; Jacobs, *Dispossessing the American Indian*, pp. 25, 134, 151–53; Craig MacAndrew and Robert B. Edgerton, *Drunken Comportment: A Social Explanation* (Chicago: Adline Pub. Co., 1969), pp. 13–36; Nancy O. Lurie, "The Worlds Oldest On-Going Protest Demonstration: North American Indian Drinking Patterns," *Pacific Historical Review* 40 (1971): 311–32; James C. Malin, "The Grassland of North America: Its Occupance and the Challenge of Continuous Reappraisals," and Andrew H. Clark, "The Impact of Exotic Invasions on the Remaining New World Midlatitude Grasslands," in William L. Thomas, ed., *Man's Role in Changing the Face of the Earth* (Chicago: University of Chicago Press, 1956), pp. 250–362, 737–56.

23. Frank R. Secoy, *Changing Military Patterns on the Great Plains: 17th Century through Early 19th Century*, vol. 21 of *Monographs of the American Ethnological Society* (Locust Valley, N.Y.: J. J. Augustin, 1953), pp. 86–95; Peter Farb, *Man's Rise to Civilization as Shown by the Indians of North America from Primeval Times to the Coming of the Industrial State* (New York: E. P. Dutton & Co., 1968), pp. 112–19; Clark Wissler, "The Influence of the Horse in the Development of Plains Culture," *American Anthropologist* 14 (1914): 1–25. Wissler maintains, as do other anthropologists, that the horse did not entirely change plains Indian culture, but merely intensified already existing traits.

24. Clark Wissler, *North American Indians of the Plains* (New York: American Museum of Natural History, 1934), pp. 148–51; George Catlin, *North American Indians: Being Letters and Notes on Their Manners, Customs, and Condition, Written During Eight Years' Travel Amongst the Wildest Tribes of Indians in North America, 1832–1839* (Edinburgh: J. Grant, 1926), 2: 2. Roderick Nash, *Wilderness and the American Mind* (New Haven: Yale University Press, 1973), pp. 100–101, notes that Catlin, with his romantic conception of the Indian, was one of the first to suggest some national effort to preserve the wilderness. The attractive physical characteristics of the plains Indians were also consistently noted by the early fur traders and trappers. These men tended to consider all the Indians of the plains handsome. For a discussion of the trader's view, see Lewis O. Saum, *The Fur Trader and the Indian* (Seattle: University of Washington Press, 1965), pp. 115–22.

25. Wayne Gard, *The Great Buffalo Hunt* (Lincoln: University of Nebraska Press, 1959), p. 28. See also John Miller, agent at Council Bluffs, to

Thomas H. Harvey, Superintendent of Indian Affairs, St. Louis, September 10, 1847, in *Annual Report, CIA, 1847*; James C. Olson, *History of Nebraska* (Lincoln: University of Nebraska Press, 1955), pp. 23–24; Martin S. Garretson, *The American Bison: The Story of its Extermination as a Wild Species and its Restoration Under Federal Protection* (New York: New York Zoological Society, 1938).

26. Francis Parkman, *The Oregon Trail* (New York: Washington Square Press, 1963), p. 119.

27. Josephy, *Indian Heritage of America*, p. 120; Lowie, *Indians of the Plains*, p. 125, remarks that even when there were one or two principal chiefs they never made decisions without obtaining popular consent. "In normal times the chief was not a supreme executive, but a peacemaker and orator."

28. S. L. A. Marshall, *Crimsoned Prairie: The Wars Between the United States and the Plains Indians During the Winning of the West* (New York: Charles Scribner's Sons, 1972), p. 7; Lowie, *Indians of the Plains*, pp. 114–119; Driver, *Indians of North America*, pp. 320–24, 328–29; Utley, *Frontiersmen in Blue*, p. 7.

29. Randolph B. Marcy, *Thirty Years of Army Life on the Border* (New York: Harper and Brothers, 1866), pp. 28–29.

30. Bernard Mishkin, *Rank and Warfare Among the Plains Indians*, vol. 3 of *Monographs of the American Ethnological Society* (New York: J. J. Augustin, 1940), pp. 1–7, 57–63; Marian W. Smith, "The War Complex of the Plains Indians," *Proceedings of the American Philosophical Society* 78 (1938): 426. Lynn R. Bailey, *Indian Slave Trade in the Southwest* (Los Angeles: Westernlore Press, 1966), discusses slavery as another major motivation for intertribal warfare. Driver, *Indians of North America*, pp. 322–23, notes that despite the exphasis on bravery, war was not necessarily a game and pehaps has been somewhat exaggerated.

31. Smith, "War Complex of the Plains Indians," p. 431.

32. Reverend P. J. DeSmet to Thomas H. Harvey, December 4, 1848, OIA, LR, Upper Platte Agency.

33. Clark, "The Impact of Exotic Invasion," pp. 755–56; Lowie, *Indians of the Plains*, p. 115; Utley, *Frontiersmen in Blue*, p. 7.

34. Major E. Steen to Colonel John Munroe, Commander, 9th Military Department, Santa Fe, February 5, 1850, AGO, LR, M/181/1850.

Chapter 2

1. Thomas L. Hamer to Medill, October 8, 1845, and W. Ewing to Medill, November 1, 1845, in William Medill Papers, Library of Congress. Medill was born in New Castle County, Delaware, in 1802. After studying law at Delaware College he was admitted to the bar in Lancaster, Ohio, in 1832.

He served as a state representative from 1835 to 1837 and then spent two terms in the House of Representatives (1839–43). Polk appointed him first as 2nd assistant postmaster general and then commissioner of Indian affairs. He later served as governor of Ohio and first comptroller of the federal treasury, 1857–61. See Robert A. Trennert, "William Medill's War with the Indian Traders, 1847," *Ohio History* 82 (1973): 46–62, for some of Medill's activities as Indian commissioner.

2. U.S., *Stat.*, vol. 9, pp. 13–14.

3. Thomas Hart Benton to Medill, April 9, 1846, and Resolution of the Senate (copy), August 3, 1846, in OIA, LR, Upper Platte Agency; LeRoy R. Hafen, "Thomas Fitzpatrick and the First Indian Agency of the Upper Platte and Arkansas," *Mississippi Valley Historical Review* 15 (1928): 374–84.

4. *Congressional Globe*, 29th Cong., 1st sess., p. 1221.

5. Harvey to Medill, December 2, 1846, OIA, LR, Miscellaneous, 1846; Charles Bent to Medill, November 10, 1846, Henry E. Huntington Library, document HM 13230.

6. Mitchell to Harvey, September 11, 1846, *Annual Report, CIA, 1846*, p. 301.

7. Medill to T. P. Moore, April 1, 1846, OIA, LS, vol. 38; Commissioner's Report, *Annual Report, CIA, 1846*, p. 228.

8. "Regulating the Indian Department," pp. 9–10, 27–28. An excellent account of the activities of the traders is contained in a report by Capt. J. R. B. Gardiner, who witnessed the annuity payment to the Sacs and Foxes in 1843, printed in the Washington *Daily Union*, October 20, 1847. Ordinarily the traders used their power to get the chiefs to oppose changes in departmental practices that might hurt profits. Also it was not beyond the realm of possibility for the traders actually to incite hostilities. "These people," wrote one observer, "would not hesitate to get up a . . . war even at the sacrifice of a few lives provided it offered any inducement in the way of profit." See D. D. T. Grant to General P. Whitmore, October 27, 1847, OIA, LR, Miscellaneous, 1847.

9. See, for example, an office memo by Medill dated July 27, 1846, Medill Papers. Other indicators of the situation appear later in Harvey to Medill, June 5, 1847, OIA, LR, St. Louis Superintendency; and Medill to Harvey, August 30, 1847, OIA, LS, vol. 40.

10. *Annual Report, CIA, 1846*, p. 217; Medill to Robert B. Mitchell, January 22, 1847, OIA, LS, vol. 39.

11. T. P. Andrews to Medill, December 24, 1846, Medill Papers. There are indications that Medill was aware of the pressure of traders as early as 1845; see George W. Ewing to Medill, November 19, 1845, in the Ewing Papers, Indiana Division, ISL. It was rather commonplace for traders to have a say in the hiring and firing of Indian agents during this period: see Trennert, "The Fur Trader as Indian Administrator: Conflict of Interests or Wise Policy?" presented at the meeting of the Western History Association, Fort Worth, October 11, 1973.

12. Medill to Col. Thomas P. Moore, April 1, 1846, appointing Moore Indian agent for the Upper Missouri, OIA, LS, vol. 38.

13. Medill to Harvey, October 31, 1846, and March 27, 1847, ibid., vols. 38 and 39; Medill to G. W. & W. G. Ewing, July 17, 1847, ibid., vol. 39.

14. Medill to Marcy, December 30, 1846, "Changes in the Public Service," 29th Cong., 2d sess., *House Ex. Doc. 70* (Serial 500).

15. Medill proposed the following pay scale: superintendents, $1600 instead of $1500; agents to remain at $1200; and subagents, $800 instead of $700.

16. *Congressional Globe*. 29th Cong., 2d sess., p. 366; Medill to Harvey, January 23, April 20, 1847, OIA, LS, vol. 39.

17. U.S., *Stat.*, vol. 9, pp. 203–4.

18. Medill to Harvey, August 30, 1847, OIA, LS, vol. 40; *Annual Report, CIA, 1847*, p. 746.

19. St. Louis *Daily Union*, January 18, 1847.

20. These tribes (Omaha, Oto, Potawatomi) were few in number, generally destitute, and entirely dependent upon the United States for protection from the hostile tribes of the plains. A good description of their condition can be found in a report from Jonathan L. Bean, December 31, 1845, OIA, LR, Council Bluffs Agency.

21. St. Louis *Missouri Republican*, June 5, 1847. The attitude of the frontier newspapers is noted in the Washington *Daily Union*, July 12, 1847.

22. *Daily Union*, June 16, 1847; see also July 12 and November 2, 1847.

23. Both Benton and Webster were very close to the Chouteau firm; Benton from his Missouri background and interest in the fur trade, and Webster from holding financial interests in the company. See Bernard A. DeVoto, *Across the Wide Missouri* (Boston: Houghton Mifflin, 1947), p. 24; Elbert B. Smith, *Magnificent Missourian: The Life of Thomas Hart Benton* (Philadelphia: Lippincott, 1958), pp. 66–67, 80–82; John E. Sunder, *The Fur Trade on the Upper Missouri, 1840–1865* (Norman: University of Oklahoma Press, 1965).

24. Charles Findlay to P. Chouteau, Jr. & Co., August 22, 1847, Chouteau Papers, MHS; P. Chouteau, W. G. & G. W. Ewing, and S. S. Phelps to Marcy, nd [1847], OIA, LR, Miscellaneous, 1847.

25. Report of subagent Alfred J. Vaughan, September 29, 1847. Chouteau Papers, MHS. In 1848 the traders finally claimed $64,000 due from the Potawatomi; see petition to the president, November 20, 1848, Ewing Collection, ISL.

26. George W. Ewing to Marcy, May 8, 1847, OIA, LR, Miscellaneous, 1847; Medill to Benton, May 18, 1847, OIA, LS, vol. 39. Medill indicated in this letter that Benton was acting as agent for Chouteau & Co.

27. W. G. & G. W. Ewing to Medill October 26, 1846, Ewing Collection, ISL; Medill to W. G. & G. W. Ewing, November 20, 1847, Medill to Harvey, August 30, 1847, OIA, LS, vol. 40. An indication of the activities of the traders can also be seen in Findlay to Chouteau, October 1, 1847, and

Willard P. Hall to R. W. Cummins, November 4, 1848, Chouteau Papers, MHS.

28. Joseph Sinclair to Medill, August 7, 1847, Medill Papers, LC; Washington *Daily Union*, October 20, November 2, 1847. That Medill intended to give the companies no aid in satisfying the department is clearly indicated in a letter to George W. Ewing, November 20, 1847, Ewing Collection, ISL.

29. Harvey to Medill, *Annual Report, CIA, 1845*, p. 536.

30. Medill to Harvey, January 23, 1847, OIA, LS, vol. 40.

31. John Miller to Harvey, December 15, 1846, OIA, LR, Council Bluffs Agency; Edward McKinney to John Miller, September 16, 1847, *Annual Report, CIA, 1847*, pp. 926–29. Medill, in some cases, did provide a little money for the immediate relief of the decimated tribes, but this provided no solution to the basic problem. He was extremely niggardly in handing out such funds. See Medill to Harvey, March 7, 1847, OIA, LS, vol. 40.

32. Commissioner's Report, *Annual Report, CIA, 1848*, pp. 386–91. Although not published until November 1848, the commissioner's plan had been in the works for some time and most parts appear to have been general knowledge as early as the spring of 1848.

33. "The Vice-President—The Hon. William Medill," Philadelphia *Pennsylvanian*, February 25, 1848; M. G. Wherfurt to Medill, February 25, 1848, Medill Papers, LC.

34. Douglas, in particular, had introduced numerous bills into Congress to provide a route to the Oregon territory and had long been stressing the need to organize the Nebraska territory. At the same time, the Illinois Senator kept a constant pressure on the secretary of war in regard to the proposed route. See Malin, "Indian Policy and Westward Expansion," pp. 36–40.

35. Most comments about this section of the bill plus the actual text are found in the speech of Robert W. Johnson, July 6, 1848, *Congressional Globe*, 30th Cong., 1st sess., Appendix, pp. 773–75.

36. Ibid.

37. *Congressional Globe*, 30th Cong., 1st sess., pp. 904–7.

38. Ibid., pp. 904–5, Appendix, p. 774. Upon Rockhill's election to Congress, Joseph Sinclair described him as a good Democrat, a strong supporter to Medill, and a man who would not engage in any business with Ewing and gang. See Sinclair to Medill, August 7, 1847, Medill Papers, LC.

39. *House Journal*, 30th Cong., 1st sess. (Serial 513), pp. 1002–3; *Senate Journal*, 30th Cong., 1st sess. (Serial 502), p. 494.

40. *Annual Report, CIA, 1848*, p. 400; Joseph Sinclair to Medill, April 5, 8, May 11, 1848, Medill Papers, LC.

41. Sinclair to Medill, April 29. 1848, Medill Papers, LC. Sinclair lived in Fort Wayne along with the Ewings and had worked for the Indian Office in the past, especially supervising the migration of the Miami Indians in 1846–47. There was no love lost between Sinclair and the Ewings. In November 1845, George Ewing had asked for Sinclair's removal from office as

Fort Wayne subagent because he was a "blaggar and rascal," see Ewing to Medill, November 18, 1845, Ewing Collection, ISL. Besides Marcy and Polk and people like Sinclair, such papers as the Cincinnati *Enquirer* and the Fort Wayne *Sentinel* actively supported Medill.

42. *Annual Report, CIA, 1848*, pp. 400–401, 418–29.

43. Sinclair to Medill, April 29, May 11, 1848, Medill Papers, LC; Petition to the President, November 20, 1848, Ewing Collection, ISL; John Miller to Harvey, September 15, 1848, *Annual Report, CIA, 1848*, p. 465; Willard P. Hall to Richard W. Cummins, November 4, 1848, Chouteau Papers, MHS. Hall, a Missouri congressman, actually urged the Potawatomi agent, Cummins, to disobey the commissioner and aid the traders in collecting their debts.

44. G. C. Matlock to Harvey, October 17, 1847, *Annual Report, CIA, 1847*, p. 852; Otto F. Frederikson, *The Liquor Question Among the Indian Tribes in Kansas, 1804–1881* (Lawrence: University of Kansas Press, 1932), pp. 55–64.

45. Harvey to Medill, *Annual Report, CIA, 1848*, p. 441.

46. Marcy to the governors of Missouri, Iowa, and Arkansas, July 14, 1847, *Annual Report, CIA, 1847*, pp. 767–69; *Annual Report, CIA, 1848*, p. 402.

47. Harvey to Medill, *Annual Report, CIA, 1848*, p. 441.

48. Gerald M. Capers *Stephen A. Douglas: Defender of the Union* (Boston: Little, Brown, 1959), pp. 47–50; Richard N. Current, *Daniel Webster and the Rise of National Conservatism* (Boston: Little, Brown, 1955), pp. 143–44; Hoopes, *Indian Affairs*, pp. 70–71.

Chapter 3

1. *Annual Report, Secretary of the Treasury, 1848*, p. 36.

2. *Congressional Globe*, 30th Cong., 2d sess., pp. 514, 672, 678.

3. Ibid., p. 680; U.S., *Stat.*, vol. 9, p. 395; *Niles National Register*, February 14, 1849. Section 5 of the act provided that the secretary of the interior would assume all duties in relation to Indian affairs formerly held by the secretary of war. Benton and Atchison were among those opposed in the Senate.

4. For a general study of Ewing see Paul I. Miller, "Thomas Ewing, Last of the Whigs" (Unpublished PhD dissertation, Ohio State University, 1933). Ewing's closeness to Zachary Taylor and the patronage issue are discussed in Holman Hamilton, *Zachary Taylor, Soldier in the White House* (Hamden, Conn.: Archon Books, 1966), pp. 153, 163–64; and Albert D. Kirwan, *John J. Crittenden: The Struggle for the Union* (Lexington: University of Kentucky Press, 1962), p. 248.

5. George W. Ewing to John B. Sarpy, March 14, 1849, April 10, 1849, Chouteau Papers, MHS. Ewing started making wholesale replacements on March 30, 1849, when Harvey was replaced by D. D. Mitchell. This replace-

ment was at the intigation of the traders, even though Ewing was being fed information that men bent on deception were misrepresenting frontier conditions. See J. N. Reynolds to T. Ewing, March 31, 1849, Thomas Ewing Papers, LC.

6. T. Ewing to Medill (copy), April 7, 1849, Medill to G. W. Ewing, April 18, 1849, Ewing Papers, ISL; G. W. Ewing to J. B. Sarpy, April 19, 1849, G. W. Ewing to Chouteau, March 28, 1850, Chouteau Papers, MHS; Frankfort (Ky.) *Commonwealth*, October 9, 1849; C. Glenn Clift, ed., "The Governors of Kentucky, 1792–1824, The Old Master, Colonel Orlando Brown, 1801–1867," *Register of the Kentucky Historical Society* 49 (1951): 17; *Congressional Globe*, 31st Cong., 2d sess., pp. 653–58; Trennert, "William Medill's War with the Indian Traders, 1847," *Ohio History* 82 (1973): 61–62. Although the Indian Office did occasionally state that its policy was to continue paying annuities to individuals, in actual practice the old system in many cases was put back in operation. See Medill to Mitchell, May 16, 1849, OIA, LS, vol. 42; P. Sappington and H. H. Jamison to Orlando Brown, November 4, 1849, OIA, LR, Council Bluffs Agency; Mitchell to Luke Lea, September 14, 1850, *Annual Report, CIA, 1850*, pp. 653–54.

7. Regulation of March 31, 1849, OIA, LR, Miscellaneous, 1849; Medill to John Wilson and James S. Calhoun, April 7, 1849, Medill to John C. Hays, April 11, 1849, OIA, LS, vol. 42; J. D. Richardson, ed., *Compilation of the Messages and Papers of the Presidents, 1789–1897* (Washington: Government Printing Office, 1896–99), 5: 19; William H. Ellison, "The Federal Indian Policy in California, 1849–1860," *Mississippi Valley Historical Review* 9 (1922): 45. The Upper Missouri later received a subagency.

8. Washington *Daily Union*, April 18, 1849.

9. Ibid., June 3, July 19, 1849. Several men did use their appointment as free passes to California, but this seems to have been the exception rather than the rule. From letters in the Thomas Ewing Papers in the Library of Congress it is evident, however, that many office seekers wanted assignments in California. It was to the administration's credit that most of these proposals were rejected.

10. Ibid., June 19, July 10, 14, 25, 1849. One of the Democratic arguments was that if the intercourse laws could not be extended over Texas, how could they apply to New Mexico and California, where the position of the government was even more ambiguous.

11. Washington *National Intelligencer*, July 9, 1849.

12. Appointment of Commissioner of Indian Affairs, May 31, 1849, Ewing to Brown, June 1, 1849, Brown to Taylor, June 4, 1849, Orlando Brown Papers, KHS; Crittenden to Brown, July 13, 1849, in Mrs. Chapman Coleman, *The Life of John J. Crittenden, with Selections from his Correspondence and Speeches*, (Philadelphia, J. B. Lippincott & Co., 1871), 1: 340–43. "My present position is in all respects agreeable to me," Brown told the president on accepting office, "my home is also one abounding in every comfort, and there

is no pecuniary inducement that would cause me to leave it."

13. George W. Ewing to P. Chouteau, June 13, 1849, Chouteau Papers, MHS.

14. Cincinnati *Enquirer*, June 13, 1849.

15. Mitchell to Medill. June 1, 1849, OIA, LR, Upper Platte Agency; Medill to T. Ewing, June 15, 1849, OIA, report book #6.

16. Brown to Fitzpatrick, August 16, 1849, OIA, LS, vol. 42.

17. Mitchell to Brown, August 27, 1849, OIA, LR, Upper Platte Agency; Brown to Mitchell, August 27, September 20, 1849, OIA, LS, vol. 42; *Annual Report, CIA, 1849*, pp. 942–43.

18. *Annual Report, CIA, 1849*, p. 946.

19. Ibid., p. 952; *Annual Report, SI, 1849*. Commissioner Medill had recommended full superintendencies as far back as 1846 to remove the office from the personal concerns of agents and governors, but he never suggested more than two superintendencies for the tribes west of the Mississippi.

20. *Annual Report, CIA, 1849*, pp. 954–55; *Annual Report, SI, 1849*, p. 41.

21. *Senate Journal*, 31st Cong., 1st sess. (Serial 548), p. 221. The bill also proposed to include the Indians of New Mexico in the negotiations.

22. Ibid., p. 51. On January 3, 1850, Atchison introduced a bill asking for a right of way through the state of Missouri and implied in the proposal that there would be further extension westward. In June 1850, he proposed that the government grant a railroad from St. Louis to the western boundary of Missouri. Both bills passed the Senate but failed in the House.

23. *Congressional Globe*, 31st Cong., 1st sess., Pt. 1, p. 93; *Annual Report, SI, 1849*, p. 44.

24. *Senate Journal*, 31st Cong., 1st sess., p. 312; *Congressional Globe*, 31st Cong., 1st sess., pp. 1482–83; *House Journal*, 31st Cong., 1st sess., pp. 861, 931, 1210; *Annual Report, CIA, 1850*, p. 41; D. D. Mitchell to Lea, September 14, 1850, ibid., pp. 47–49.

25. King, a Georgia congressman who agreed with Taylor's policy, went to California in June 1849. Colonel McCall was sent to New Mexico in November 1849 by the War Department with instructions to encourage statehood. In addition, the military commanders in both territories were apparently under instructions to encourage statehood in any way possible. See "T. Butler King's Report on California," 31st Cong., 1st sess., *House Ex. Doc. 59* (Serial 577); and "Colonel McCall's Report in Relation to New Mexico," 31st Cong., 2d sess., *Senate Ex. Doc. 26* (Serial 589).

26. Brown to Smith, February 27, 1850, OIA, LS vol. 43.

27. Calhoun to Medill, October 15, 1849, Calhoun to Brown, November 7, 16, 1849, in Annie H. Abel, ed., *Official Correspondence of James S. Calhoun while Indian Agent at Santa Fe and Superintendent of Indian Affairs in New Mexico* (Washington: Government Printing Office, 1915), pp. 48–58, 72–74,

78–81; Brown to Calhoun, April 28, 1850, Brown to S. R. Thurston (Delegate from the Oregon Territory), February 16, 1850, OIA, LS, vol. 43.

28. "Note from the Mexican Minister, Mr. Luis de la Rosa, to Mr. Clayton, Secretary of State, March 20, 1850," 31st Cong., 1st sess., *Senate Doc. 43* (Serial 558); Lea to Rollins, August 9, 1850, OIA, LS, vol. 43; *Senate Journal*, 31st Cong., 1st sess., p. 467. This bill was approved in the Senate on August 23, 1850, but failed in the House.

29. Washington *Daily Union*, February 9, 1850.

30. *House Journal*, 31st Cong., 1st sess., p. 439; U.S., *Stat.*, vol. 9, p. 437.

31. Medill to Mitchell, May 16, 1849, OIA, LS, vol. 42.

32. Brown to Ewing, February 28, 1850, Orlando Brown Papers, KHS; Cincinnati *Enquirer*, September 8, 1849; Frankfort *Commonwealth*, October 9, 1849; Clift, "The Governors of Kentucky," p. 16. As early as July 1849, Brown was hinting at resigning, but Crittenden kept urging him to remain. See Crittenden to Brown, July 26, 1849, in Coleman, *Life of Crittenden*, pp. 346–47. However, by April 1850, Brown was definitely committed to resigning no later than July 1, 1850. See Brown to Hanna, April 29, 1850, Orlando Brown Papers, folder 37, Filson Club, Louisville.

33. The entire affair is discussed in *Congressional Globe*, 31st Cong., 2d sess., pp. 652–56. See also Washington *Daily Union*, April 26, 1850; G. W. Ewing to Chouteau, March 28, 1850, Chouteau Papers, MHS.

34. U.S., *Stat.*, vol. 9, pp. 453–58, 446–52.

35. See the comments of James A. Pierce of Maryland and Thomas J. Rusk of Texas, September 25, 1850, *Congressional Globe*, 31st Cong., 1st sess., p. 1702; U.S., *Stat.*, vol. 9, p. 556; and A. S. Loughery, acting commissioner, to Campbell, Todd, Temple, October 15, 1850, OIA, LS, vol. 43.

36. Taylor to Brown, June 28, 1850, Orlando Brown Papers KHS; Crittenden to Brown, May 18, 1850, Coleman, *Life of Crittenden*, pp. 371–72; Washington *Daily Union*, July 17, 1850; James H. McLendon, "John A. Quitman, Fire-Eating Governor," *The Journal of Mississippi History* 15 (1953):74; D. D. Mitchell to Brown, September 3, 1850, Orlando Brown Papers, folder 37, Filson Club. The new commissioner is not to be confused with his uncle, Luke Lea, who at the same time was Indian agent at Fort Leavenworth.

37. Fillmore to Ewing, July 20, 1850, Thomas Ewing Papers, LC.

38. *Annual Report, CIA, 1850*, pp. 35–36.

39. Ibid., pp. 41–42, 44; *Annual Message of the President, 1850*, p. 11; *Annual Report, SW, 1850*, pp. 3. 5; *Annual Report, SI, 1850*, p. 28. To solve the difficulties with Texas, Lea suggested the Senate appoint a commissioner to negotiate with Texas authorities in order to come to some arrangement allowing the federal government to extend the Indian trade and intercourse laws over that state.

40. Lea to Calhoun, January 22, 1851, OIA, LS, vol. 44; *Congressional Globe*, 31st Cong., 2d sess., pp. 616–17.

41. *Congressional Globe*, 31st Cong., 2d sess. pp. 617–19.

42. Ibid., p. 621. Hall, incidentally, had been extremely active with Atchison in promoting the cause of a northern railroad to the Pacific through the state of Missouri and the Indian country.

43. U.S., *Stat.*, vol. 9, pp. 586–87.

44. Jurisdictional History of the Office of Indian Affairs"; Lea to Mitchell, March 25, 1851, OIA, LS, vol. 44; see also various letters between March 21 and 25, 1851, in ibid. Stephen B. Rose was appointed to Utah, and Abraham R. Wolley, Edward H. Wingfield, Richard H. Weightman, and John Grenier to New Mexico.

45. U.S., *Stat.*, vol. 9, p. 572; Lea to Mitchell, May 26, 1851, OIA, LS, vol. 44. This bill was passed February 27, 1851.

Chapter 4

1. David G. Burnet to Henry R. Schoolcraft, September 29, 1847, quoted in Schoolcraft's *Archives of Aboriginal Knowledge Containing All the Original Papers . . . Respecting . . . the Indian Tribes of the United States* (Philadelphia: J. B. Lippincott & Co., 1860), 1:230; Ernest Wallace and E. Adamson Hoebel, *The Comanches, Lords of the South Plains* (Norman: University of Oklahoma Press, 1952), pp. 31–32.

2. Schoolcraft, *Archives*, 1:518, lists Kiowa and Lipan Apache figures at 1,500 and 500 respectively in 1846. These figures may be somewhat understated.

3. David K. Torrey to Capt. A. Talcott, September 6, 1847, OIA, LR, Texas Agency. Torrey and his brothers were among those chosen by Houston to form one of the trading houses, and they established the only successful operation.

4. George D. Harmon, "The United States Indian Policy in Texas, 1845–1860," *Mississippi Valley Historical Review* 17 (1930):279, notes that at this time the United States was pursuing a policy of creating a territory to belong solely to the Indians, while Texas worked in the opposite direction. For the Texas point of view see George W. Bonnell, Texas commissioner of Indian Affairs, to the secretary of war of the Republic, November 3, 1838, in "Communication from the Commissioner of Indian Affairs and other documents, in relation to the Indians in Texas," 30th Cong., 1st sess., *Senate Report 171* (Serial 512), pp. 38–51.

5. D. G. Wooten, ed., *A Comprehensive History of Texas*, (Dallas: William G. Scarff, 1898), 2, p. 8. The reason the federal government consented to Texas retaining her public lands was the existence of some $10 million in debts that had been run up by the Republic. Since the state of Texas assumed the responsibility for these debts, it was believed she might be able to pay the debt through the sale of public lands.

6. *Annual Report, CIA, 1846*, p. 225.

7. Walter P. Webb, *The Texas Rangers: A Century of Frontier Defense* (Austin: University of Texas Press, 1965), p. 127; A. B. Bender, *The March of Empire: Frontier Defense in the Southwest, 1848–1860* (Lawrence: University of Kansas Press, 1952), p. 130; Albany *Evening Journal*, April 23, 1846, reprinted from the New Orleans *Picayune*, April 14, 1846.

8. Albany *Evening Journal*, June 9, 1846; Grant Foreman, "The Texas Comanche Treaty of 1846," *Southwestern Historical Quarterly* 51 (1948): 313. The original orders were issued in September 1845, after Texas had resolved to enter the Union.

9. Official Report of P. M. Butler and M. G. Lewis to Medill, August 6, 1846, and Lewis to Medill, July 13, 1846, OIA, Ratified Treaties; Austin *Democrat*, May 27, 1846. The treaty was with the Comanche, Aionai, Andarko, Caddo, Lipan, Longwha, Keechy, Tahwacarro, Wichita, and Waco Indians.

10. *Congressional Globe*, 29th Cong., 1st sess., pp. 980–81.

11. Horton to Polk, October 22, 1846, OIA, LR, Miscellaneous, 1846; Medill to Torrey & Brothers, December 15, 1846, OIA, LS, vol. 39; *Annual Report, CIA, 1846*, p. 218.

12. Kenneth F. Neighbours, "Robert S. Neighbors in Texas, 1836–1859: A Quarter Century of Frontier Problems," (PhD Dissertation, University of Texas, 1955), 1: 1–70; Albany *Evening Journal*, February 3, 1847, reprinted from the New Orleans *Picayune*.

13. Medill to Neighbors, March 20, 1847, OIA, LS, vol. 39.

14. *Annual Report, SW, 1847*, p. 70; Medill to David R. Atchison, April 26, 1848, in "Indians in Texas," pp. 26–28; U.S., *Stat.*, vol. 9, pp. 203–4.

15. Medill to Neighbors, March 20, 1847, OIA, LS, vol. 39.

16. Neighbors to Medill, June 22, 1847, *Annual Report, CIA, 1847*, pp. 892–96.

17. *Annual Report, CIA, 1847*, pp. 751–52; Neighbors to Medill, August 5, 1847, ibid., p. 891; Col. John C. Hays to Neighbors, July 13, 1847, OIA, LR, Texas Agency. The company referred to here was most pobably the "Society for the Protection of German Immigrants in Texas," organized by Prince Carl of Solms-Braunfels to settle Germans in Texas. Its grants were between the Llano and Colorado in Comanche country. For more information on these colonies, see Rudolph L. Biesele, *The History of the German Settlements in Texas, 1831–1861* (Austin: Press Von-Boeckmann-Jones, 1930); and Biesele, "The Relations Between the German Settlers and the Indians in Texas, 1844–1860," *Southwestern Historical Quarterly* 31 (1927): 116–29. See also the Houston *Democratic Telegraph and Texas Register*, May 10, 1847.

18. Houston *Democratic Telegraph and Texas Register*, May 17, June 7, 1847; Neighbors to Medill, August 6, 1847, OIA, LR, Texas Agency.

19. Neighbors to Medill, September 14, October 12, 1847, *Annual Report, CIA, 1847*, pp. 899–906; J. Pinckney Henderson to W. L. Marcy, August 22, 1847, OIA, LR, Texas Agency; Utley, *Frontiersmen in Blue*, pp. 70–71; Webb, *Texas Rangers*, p. 127; Wooten, *History of Texas*, 2: 770; W. C.

Holden, "Frontier Defence (in Texas), 1846–1860," *West Texas Historical Association Year Book* 6 (1930): 38–41. Technically the Rangers were volunteers in the U.S. Army during the Mexican War.

20. Neighbors to Medill, August 5, 1847, *Annual Report, CIA, 1847*, pp. 897–98; David G. Burnet to Schoolcraft, September 29, 1847, Schoolcraft, *Archives*, 1: 230–41; Burnet to Neighbors, August 20, 1847, Indians in Texas," pp. 7–8.

21. *Annual Report, SW, 1847*, p. 70; Medill to Neighbors, August 20, 1847, "Indians of Texas," pp. 5–6; Medill to Neighbors, August 31, 1847, OIA, LR, Texas Agency.

22. Torrey to Talcott, September 6, 1847, OIA, LR, Texas Agency. Torrey suggested that Sam Houston be made a commissioner to treat with the Indians. As their friend, he might be able to counsel them to keep the peace.

23. Neighbors to Medill, September 14, October 12, 1847, *Annual Report, CIA, 1847*, pp. 899–906. At the council Neighbors warned the tribes to expect no more presents until the federal government made some permanent decision on the Indians of Texas.

24. Neighbors to Medill, October 1, 1847, OIA, LR, Texas Agency. The agent also suggested that the delay entailed by the visit would give Congress time to act.

25. Neighbors to Medill, November 18, 1847, ibid.

26. Neighbors to Henderson, December 10, 1847, "Indians in Texas," pp. 10–11. One of these citizens was Eliphas Spencer, who flatly refused to recognize the authority of the state and finally had to be bodily removed by Neighbors and Captain Johnson of the Rangers. See also Neighbors to Medill, December 13, 1847, ibid., pp. 12–13.

27. Henry O. Hedgecoxe to Neighbors, February 18, 1847, ibid., pp. 14–15. Hedgecoxe made it plain that the laws of Texas could not stop the venture because "the State of Texas is bound constructively to put us in possession of all the lands included in said grant."

28. Houston *Democratic Telegraph and Texas Register*, August 9, September 6, 1847; Medill to Neighbors, April 10, 1848, "Indians in Texas," p. 26; Lena Clara Koch, "The Federal Indian Policy in Texas, 1845–1860," *Southwestern Historical Quarterly* 28 (1925): 275–77.

29. Neighbors to Medill, March 2, 1848, OIA, LR, Texas Agency; Neighbors to Medill, March 26, 1848, "Indians in Texas," pp. 13–14. Captain Henry McCullough, for one, spread alarm throughout the state by demanding that he be allowed to march on the Indians in retaliation for alleged depredations. According to Neighbors' account, the actions of the Rangers were taken deliberately. Apparently some of the settlers were engaged in selling whiskey to the Indians with the tacit approval of the local Ranger company.

30. Copy of the talks of several Comanche chiefs on the Salt Fork of the Brazos, February 14, 1848, and Neighbors to Medill, March 2, 1848, OIA, LR, Texas Agency.

31. Resolutions of Thomas S. Rusk, *Senate Journal*, 30th Cong., 1st sess., (Serial 502), p. 282. This resolution originated in the Texas state legislature.

32. *Congressional Globe*, 30th Cong., 1st sess., pt. 1, p. 639; *Senate Journal*, 30th Cong., 1st sess., p. 255; William Medill to David R. Atchison, April 26, 1848, OIA, LS, vol. 40. This proposal may have been based on the idea of Sam Houston, who as early as January 1847 had attempted to have a superintendent, agents, and subagents appointed for the Indians of Texas. See *Senate Journal*, 29th Cong., 2d sess. (Serial 492), p. 89. Italics mine.

33. Medill to Atchison, April 26, 1848, OIA, LS, vol. 40.

34. Holman Hamilton, *Prologue to Conflict: The Crisis and the Compromise of 1850* (Lexington: University of Kentucky Press, 1964), 20n. Texans were especially opposed to separate status for New Mexico. See, for example, the speech of David S. Kaufman in the House of Representatives, July 27, 1848, *Congressional Globe*, 30th Cong., 1st sess., Appendix, pp. 783–88; Washington *Daily Union*, April 22, 1848. The Texas Indian bill was reported out of committee on June 3, 1848, and relevant documents presented to the Senate on June 15. After this, all mention of the proposal ceases and it must be presumed that Southern states refused to bring the matter to a vote.

35. Neighbors to Medill, June 26, 1848, OIA, LR, Texas Agency.

36. Eliphas Spencer to Polk, April 18, 1848, Neighbors to Medill, August 19, 1848, David S. Kaufman to Medill, July 21, 1848, ibid.; Medill to Neighbors, August 21, 1848, OIA, LS, vol. 41.

37. S. Highsmith to the Austin *Democrat*, March 30, 1848, Neighbors to Medill, April 10, 1848, reprinted in "Indians in Texas," pp. 51–52; Galveston *Civilian*, April 7, 1848; Neighbors to Medill, April 28, 1848, Charles E. Barnard to Neighbors, n.d. [April 1848], OIA, LR, Texas Agency.

38. Neighbors to Medill, June 15, 1848, *Annual Report, CIA, 1848*, pp. 590–93. Neighbors again recommended that immediate action be taken by the department to prevent hostilities.

39. Neighbors to Medill, September 14, 1848, ibid., p. 593; Neighbors to Medill, September 10, 1848, AGO, LR, N/32/1848. Neighbors again warned that peace was impossible as long as friendly tribes were attacked and their property stolen. He also noted the general fear on the frontier of the Indians and this is confirmed by newspaper accounts. See, for example, the Albany *Evening Journal*, August 25, 1848, which reports the reaction of several Texas newspapers.

40. *Annual Report, CIA, 1848*, p. 408; President's message to the House of Representatives, July 6, 1848, *Congressional Globe*, 30th Cong., 1st sess., p. 901; General Order #49, August 31, 1848, AGO, LS, vol. 25; *Annual Report, SW, 1848*, p. 94. For Texas public opinion see the Albany *Evening Journal*, August 25, 1848.

41. Neighbors to Medill, October 23, November 7, 1848, OIA, LR, Texas Agency. Most of the killings in October and November were reportedly done by the Lipan Apache in retaliation for the raid on their village.

42. Koch, "Indian Policy in Texas," pp. 276–77.

43. R. C. Crane, "Some Aspects of the History of West and Northwest Texas Since 1845," *Southwestern Historical Quarterly* 26 (1922): 31; J. Fred Rippy, "The Indians of the Southwest in the Diplomacy of the United States and Mexico, 1848–1853," *Hispanic American Historical Review* 2 (1919): 336.

44. Neighbors to Worth, March 7, 1849, OIA, LR, Texas Agency. The agent also hoped the reservations would be able to bring civilization to the tribes by providing education in mechanics and agriculture.

45. Worth to Medill, December 27, 1848, Neighbors to Brown, August 13, 1849, OIA, LR, Texas Agency; Brown to Neighbors, August 11, 1849, OIA, LS, vol. 42. Neighbors had gone to Washington to promote his plan when he discovered he had been fired.

46. Rollins to Brown, November 10, 1849, OIA, LR, Texas Agency. Rollins arrived on November 8, but for some months thereafter he did little. Neighbors predicted such an action in a letter to Sam Houston, November 2, 1849, ibid., when he stated that Rollins did not intend to meet the Indians until spring, and therefore Texas would have no effective agent until that time. "I leave you to calculate the consequences," he told Houston.

47. *Annual Report, CIA, 1849,* p. 941; Washington *Daily Union,* January 26, 1850; letter from a Texan, "Publicas," to Senator Jefferson Davis, n.d., printed in the *Daily Union,* July 23, 1850. Brown reported that the outbreak was wholly unexpected and entirely without cause, and that Neighbors had foreseen no difficulty. All Neighbors' reports for the six months prior to the outbreak, however, had predicted such a consequence if the Texans were allowed to continue antagonizing the Indians.

48. Houston *Democratic Telegraph and Texas Register,* August 9, 1894; Philadelphia *Public Ledger,* February 19, June 1, 15, 1849; Washington *Daily Union,* June 3, August 9, 1849.

49. *Annual Report, SW, 1849,* p. 94; Letter from a Major Arnold to the *National Intelligencer,* printed in the Philadelphia *Public Ledger,* June 15, 1849.

50. *Annual Report, SW, 1849,* p. 94; Brooke to Jones, August 11, 1849, ibid., pp. 140–41; *Annual Report, CIA, 1849,* p. 941; Philadelphia *Public Ledger,* June 15, 1849.

51. *Annual Report, CIA, 1849,* p. 942.

52. Crawford to Brooke, June 4, 1849, Brooke to Jones, July 14, 1849, Brooke to Winfield Scott, October 2, 1849, *Annual Report, SW, 1849,* pp. 138–40, 152–53.

53. Captain H. G. Catlett to commissioner of Indian affairs, May 12, 1849, OIA, LR, Texas Agency. After Texas entered the Union, Catlett was for a time employed on the Texas frontier as assistant quartermaster to the U.S. Army. It is unclear whether he was a volunteer (Ranger) or a regular. In any case, he was most sympathetic to the activities and philosophy of the Rangers.

54. Medill to Mitchell, June 14, 1849, OIA, LS, vol. 42; Medill to Ewing, June 4, 1849, *Annual Report, CIA, 1849,* pp. 975–76.

55. Crane, "West and Northwest Texas," p. 31; Utley, *Frontiersmen in Blue*, p. 71. The posts finally established on the Mexican border were Forts Brown, Ringgold, McIntosh, and Duncan. Fort Inge, Meril, and Ewell were placed on Indian trails leading to Mexican territory.

56. Brooke to Jones, August 31, 1849, *Annual Report, SW, 1849*, pp. 139–43.

57. "Report of Lt. W. H. C. Whiting's Reconnaissance of the Western Frontier of Texas," 31st Cong., 1st sess., *Senate Ex. Doc. 64* (Serial 562), pp. 238–44; Crane, "West and Northwest Texas," p. 33; Brooke to Scott, October 2, 1849, *Annual Report, SW, 1849*, pp. 152–53. Whiting's instructions were also to survey the route for a road connecting the posts and record the geographical features of the country. Capt. Randolph B. Marcy also made an expedition across northern Texas at this time and his report confirmed much of what Whiting said.

58. This was specifically stated by Governor Bell in a letter to Brooke, June 4, 1850, printed in Dorman H. Winfrey, ed., *Texas Indian Papers, 1846–1859* (Austin: Texas State Library, 1960), p. 122.

59. Brooke to Jones, January 20, March 7, 1850, *Annual Report, SW, 1850*, pp. 23–24, 26–27; petition from the citizens of Limestone County to the governor, December 25, 1849, P. H. Bell to the Texas legislature, January 10, 1850, *Texas Indian Papers*, pp. 107–8, 110–11.

60. Rollins to Howard, February 26, 1850, OIA, LR, Texas Agency.

61. Resolution from P. H. Bell to U.S. Congress, February 7, 1850, Bell to Brooke, June 4, 1850, *Texas Indian Papers*, pp. 117, 122; *Congressional Globe*, 31st Cong., 1st sess., pp. 294, 808; Catlett to Brown, April 23, 1850, OIA, LR, Texas Agency.

62. Bell to Brooke, June 4, 1850, *Texas Indian Papers*, p. 122.

63. Brooke to Scott, May 28, 1850, *Annual Report, SW, 1850*, pp. 121–23.

64. Orders #27, Headquarters 8th Military Department, San Antonio, June 4, 1850, printed in the Washington *Daily Union*, July 12, 1850; Lt. Colonel W. J. Hardee to Major George Deas, September 14, 1850, *Annual Report, SW, 1850*, pp. 56–59; much of the official military correspondence of the campaign is contained in *ibid.*, pp. 49–61.

65. Washington *Daily Union*, July 12, 16, 1850.

66. Catlett to Lea, September 5, 1850, Brooke to Jones, October 10, 1850, OIA, LR, Texas Agency. "This man Catlett," said Brooke, "is a dangerous person and should be removed, if possible, or, at all events, prevented from going into the Indian country; and I trust the Government of the United States may hereafter exclude him from all connexion [sic] with any public matters. He is not worth the slightest belief or credence." Secretary of War Conrad did ask that the trader's license be revoked for the good of the country. See Conrad to Stuart, November 1, 1850, OIA, LR, Texas Agency. Apparently nothing came of the matter, however, because the United States had no power over traders in Texas.

67. Harmon, "Indian Policy in Texas," p. 384.

68. *Annual Report, CIA, 1850*, p. 44; Report of William M. Williams to

the Texas House of Representatives, August 26, 1850, a copy of which appears in OIA, LR, Texas Agency.

69. Rollins to Brown, May 8, 1850, OIA, LR, Texas Agency; Rollins to Lea, November 2, 1850, OIA, unratified treaties.

70. A. J. Hamilton to P. H. Bell, August 21, 1850, OIA, unratified treaties.

71. Treaty between the United States and the Comanche, Caddo, Lipan, Quapaw, Tawakoni, and Waco Tribes of Indians, December 10, 1850, Rollins to Lea, December 22, 1850, ibid.

72. Indian Appropriation Act, September 30, 1850, U.S. *Stat.*, vol. 9, p. 586. In January 1851 the Senate Committee on Indian Affairs specifically attempted to extend the intercourse laws to Texas again, but the proposal was voted down. See Harmon, "Indian Policy in Texas," p. 388.

73. Rogers and Stem were appointed respectively on November 2 and November 5, 1850, OIA, LS, vol. 44. The three commissioners were appointed in October 1850. See A. S. Loughery to Todd, Campbell, and Temple, *Annual Report, CIA, 1850*, pp. 153–54; see also a letter of Loughery's, October 11, 1850, OIA, LR, miscellaneous, 1850.

74. Lea to Rollins, Rogers, and Stem, November 25, 1851, OIA, LS, vol. 44.

75. Lea to Stuart, February 13, 1851, Orders #69, December 25, 1850, OIA, unratified treaties; *Texas Indian Papers*, p. 137.

76. Campbell to Lea, January 8, 1851, OIA, LR, miscellaneous, 1851.

77. Todd to Stuart, February 13, 1851, Duval to Todd, January 29, 1851, Colonel T. Staniford to Deas, January 28, 1851, Rollins to Brooke, February 18, 1851, OIA, LR, Texas Agency; Todd, Campbell, and Temple to Lea, February 13, 1851, OIA, LR, miscellaneous, 1851.

78. Duplicate memo of a discussion between Todd, Temple, and Governor Bell, March 14, 1851, Todd and Temple to Lea, March 15, 1851, ibid.

79. These boundaries are suggested in Todd to Lea, March 25, 1851, ibid. Agent Rollins made similar suggestions in a letter to Todd of the same date and it is difficult to tell just who determined the exact lines.

80. Lea to Todd, Campbell, and Temple, April 3, 1851, OIA, LS, vol. 44; U.S., *Stat.*, vol. 9, p. 587; Stuart to Todd, May 12, 1851, OIA, LR, miscellaneous, 1851.

81. Report of Todd, Campbell, and Temple, August 23, 1851, OIA, LR, miscellaneous, 1851. This document is also recorded, with editorial refinements, in *Annual Report, CIA, 1851*, pp. 302–6.

82. Rollins and Rogers planned this treaty after the withdrawal of the Todd commission and may have intended it to be part of a general treaty signed with all the Texas Indians. Rollins died during the summer, however, and Rogers took the responsibility for meeting the Comanche. The resultant treaty, signed October 28, 1851, again merely repeated the Butler and Lewis treaty of 1846. Like Rollins's previous treaty, this one was not ratified. For correspondence concerning this treaty, see the files of the Texas Agency and those covering unratified treaties.

83. *Annual Report, SW, 1851*, p. 113.

84. Harmon, "Indian Policy in Texas," p. 389.

85. Stem to Lea, November 1, 1851, *Annual Report, CIA, 1851*, pp. 525–26. See also several letters written by Stem during 1851 in Watt P. Marchman and Robert C. Cotner, eds., "Indian Agent Jesse Stem: A Manuscript Revelation," *West Texas Historical Association Year Book* 39 (1963): 114–54.

86. Hoopes, *Indian Affairs in the West*, p. 189. For an account of these reservations, see Kenneth F. Neighbours, "Chapters from the History of Texas Indian Reservations," *West Texas Historical Association Year Book* 33 (1957): 3–16; Rupert N. Richardson, "The Comanche Reservation in Texas," ibid., 5 (1929): 43–65.

87. The sad end of the reservation idea in Texas is well covered in Hoopes, *Indian Affairs in the West*, pp. 190–99.

Chapter 5

1. Spicer, *Cycles of Conquest*, pp. 161, 166–67; Ruth Underhill, *The Navajos* (Norman: University of Oklahoma Press, 1956), pp. 54, 61, 69–70.

2. John R. Swanton, *The Indian Tribes of North America*, Bureau of American Ethnology, Bulletin 145 (Washington: Government Printing Office, 1952), pp. 334–35; Underhill, *The Navajos*, pp. 72–77; Bailey, *Indian Slave Trade*, pp. 75–79.

3. John R. Bartlett, *Personal Narrative of Explorations and Incidents in Texas, New Mexico, California, Sonora, and Chihuahua* . . . (New York: D. Appleton & Co., 1854), 1: 322–23; Frank S. Edwards, *A Campaign in New Mexico with Colonel Doniphan* (Philadelphia: Carey & Hart, 1848), pp. 61–62. Both Ralph A. Smith, "Indians in American-Mexican Relations Before the War of 1846," *Hispanic American Historical Review* 43 (1963): 34; and Ralph H. Ogle, "Federal Control of the Western Apaches," *New Mexico Historical Review* 14 (1939): 306, consider the Apache the major obstacle to the development of New Mexico. "From 1540 to 1886," says Ogle, "the Apaches were the most important human element in retarding the occupation and development of the Southwest."

4. Ralph E. Twitchell, *The History of the Military Occupation of New Mexico from 1846 to 1851* (Denver: The Smith-Brooks Co., 1909), pp. 38–40. Kearney headed west in June 1846, with an army consisting of 1,558 volunteers. A second regiment was to follow as soon as organized.

5. Adjutant General Roger Jones to Kearny, May 12, 14, 1846, NARS, Record Group 393, Records of the 10th Military Department.

6. "Occupation of New Mexico," 29th Cong., 2d sess., *House Ex. Doc. 19* (Serial 499), p. 19; "Notes of a Military Reconnaissance, from Fort Leavenworth to San Diego," 30th Cong., 1st sess., *Senate Ex. Doc. 7* (Serial 505), pp. 26–27.

7. Proclamation of August 22, 1846, in "Occupation of New Mexico," pp. 20–21.

8. John Taylor Hughes, *Doniphan's Expedition, Containing an Account of the Expedition Against New Mexico & Etc.* (Cincinnati: U. P. James, 1847), p. 40; "Notes of a Military Reconnaissance," p. 33.

9. Washington *Daily Union*, November 25, 1846; Jefferson City (Missouri) *Inquirer*, December 5, 1846; Edwards, *A Campaign in New Mexico*, p. 39; Hughes, *Doniphan's Expedition*, pp. 50–51; Acting Assistant Adjutant General to Lt. Col. C. F. Ruff, September 16, 1846, cited in Frank D. Reeve, "The Federal Government and the Navajo, 1846–1858," *New Mexico Historical Review* 14 (1939): 83; Underhill, *The Navajos*, p. 87.

10. Washington *Daily Union*, November 25, 1846.

11. Susan Shelby Magoffin, *Down the Santa Fe Trail and Into Mexico: The Diary of Susan Shelby Magoffin 1846–1847*, ed. Stella M. Drumm (New Haven: Yale University Press, 1926), p. 111; Edwards, *A Campaign in New Mexico*, p. 41; Washington *Daily Union*, November 25, 1846.

12. The original Spanish version of this proclamation is printed in "Report of Lieut. J. W. Abert of his Examination of New Mexico, in the Years 1846–1847," 30th Cong., 1st sess., *Senate Ex. Doc. 23* (Serial 506), p. 37.

13. Philip St. George Cooke, *The Conquest of New Mexico and California: An Historical and Personal Narrative* (New York: G. P. Putnam's Sons, 1878), p. 77; Fitzpatrick to Harvey, October 19, 1847, OIA, LR, Upper Platte Agency.

14. Kearny to Doniphan, October 2, 1846, quoted in Hughes, *Doniphan's Expedition*, p. 56; Proclamation by S. W. Kearny, October 5, 1846, AGO, LR, K/209–210/1846.

15. Hughes, *Doniphan's Expedition*, p. 64. The details of Doniphan's expedition are best covered in Hughes, pp. 62–72, and William E. Connelley, *Doniphan's Expedition of Conquest of New Mexico and California* (Topeka: n. pub., 1907), pp. 285–99.

16. Hughes, *Doniphan's Expedition*, p. 71.

17. Underhill, *The Navajos*, p. 92, states that the wealthy Navajo agreed to the treaty simply to protect their stock from the Mexicans. The text of the treaty is quoted in Hughes, *Doniphan's Expedition*, pp. 71–72. The treaty itself was never ratified and is not even listed in the NARS collection of unratified treaties, indicating that it never reached Washington. The Adjutant General's Office reported in 1849 that it had not received either the treaty or the full notes reportedly taken by Doniphan and Gilpin. See marginal notes on AGO, LR, D/174/1847.

18. Connelley, *Doniphan's Expedition*, pp. 310–11.

19. Doniphan to Jones, n.d. [1846], AGO, LR, D/174/1847; Letter to the St. Louis *Daily Union*, dated Santa Fe, December 15, 1846, printed February 19, 1847.

20. Bent to Medill, November 10, 1846, HEH, document HM 13230; Bent to James Buchanan, December 26, 1846, AGO, LS, Vol. 23.

21. Sterling Price, after completing his tour of duty in New Mexico, went on to become governor of Missouri (1852–56). During the Civil War he be-

came a major general in the Confederate Army and participated in a number
of major battles.

22. Washington *Daily Union*, April 19, 1847. The revolt had first been
scheduled for December 19, but confusion led to postponement. The army
then got wind of the plot before it could be carried out and rounded up
some of the leaders. Most of the suspected rebels, however, made good their
escape and immediately commenced work on a new revolt.

23. Price to Jones, February 15, 1847, *Annual Report, SW, 1847*, pp. 520–
26.

24. Price to Jones, July 20, 1847, AGO LR, P/133/1847; Jefferson City
Inquirer, July 10, 1847.

25. Capt. W. M. D. McKissack to Major General Thomas S. Jessup, February 16, 1847, NARS, Record Group 92, Office of the Quartermaster General,
Consolidated Correspondence, box 987; Report of Major B. B. Edmundson
to Price on an attempt to capture Mexicans and Indians guilty of committing depredations, June 14, 1847, AGO, LR, P/133/1847, enclosure #1; Price
to Jones, July 20, 1847, AGO, LR, P/133/1847.

26. For a good account of the military importance of the Santa Fe trail,
see Walker D. Wyman, "The Military Phase of Santa Fe Freighting, 1846–
1865," *Kansas Historical Quarterly* 1 (1932): 415–23.

27. Accounts of these depredations are found in the St. Louis *Daily Union*,
May 29, June 16, August 16, 1847; New York *Tribune*, December 4, 1847; St.
Louis *Reveille*, June 3, 1848 (which reported that almost every train crossing
the plains in 1847 was attacked); letter from L. J. E. to the Jefferson City
Inquirer, printed July 31, 1847; Wyman, "Santa Fe Freighting," p. 420.

28. *Annual Report, SW, 1847*, p. 59; Lt. Col. Wharton to Brigadier General Arbuckle, Commanding the 2nd and 3rd Military Departments, August
14, 1847, AGO, LR, W/631/1847.

29. St. Louis *Daily Union*, September 11, 1847. Gilpin also went on to
greater glories, personally serving Abraham Lincoln, and becoming the governor of Colorado Territoy, 1861–63.

30. Post Order #63, Fort Leavenworth, September 20, 1847, issued by Lt.
Col. Wharton, AGO, LR, W/771/1847.

31. Fitzpatrick to Harvey, December 18, 1847, OIA, LR, Upper Platte
Agency; Capt. Pelzer to Gilpin, November 18, 1847, enclosed in the official
report of Col. Garland's investigation, AGO, LR, G/368/1848. Two other
letters describing the event in some detail, by post adjutant Henry L. Routt,
were published in the St. Louis *Daily Union*, January 8, February 9, 1848.
For a general account of Gilpin's difficulties with the German troops, see
Thomas L. Karnes, "Gilpin's Volunteers on the Santa Fe Trail," *Kansas
Historical Quarterly* 30 (1964): 1–14.

32. Fitzpatrick to Harvey, December 18, 1847, OIA, LR, Upper Platte
Agency; Report of the official investigation of Gilpin's command by Col.
Garland, August 3, 1848, AGO, LR, G/368/1848. Pelzer was not actually
brought to trial. Garland decided to accept his resignation because "the

murder of the Pawnee Indians was the result of ignorance, *timidity*, and accident, and not from a premeditated plan or natural desire to commit such a lawless and brutal act."

33. Gilpin to Jones, August 1, 1848, AGO, LR, G/368/1848; *Annual Message of the President, 1847*, 30th Cong., 1st sess., *Senate Ex. Doc. 1* (Serial 503), p. 11.

34. Price to Jones, July 20, 1847, AGO, LR, P/333/1847; St. Louis *Reveille*, August 30, 1847. Fitzpatrick wrote several letters concerning the military situation in New Mexico. Of particular importance are the ones of October 19, and December 19, 1847, and August 11, 1848, OIA, LR, Upper Platte Agency.

35. Newby to Jones, March 20, 1848, AGO, LR, N/46/1848. Newby apparently feared he would be blamed for the deterioration in New Mexico and wanted the army to know of the "insurmountable difficulties" presented him by Price.

36. Santa Fe *Republican*, June 17, 1848.

37. Letter from "Taos" to the Jefferson City *Inquirer*, dated June 25, 1848, printed August 5, 1848; Santa Fe *Republican*, June 17, 1848.

38. Gilpin to Jones, August 1, 1848, AGO, LR, G/368/1848; Gilpin to Fitzpatrick, February 8, 1848, OIA, LR, Upper Platte Agency.

39. Gilpin to Fitzpatrick, February 10, 1848, OIA, LR, Upper Platte Agency.

40. Richard W. Cummins to Harvey, February 27, 1848, and Solomon P. Sublette to Harvey, February 29, 1848, OIA, LR, St. Louis Superintendency; Fitzpatrick to Gilpin, February 10, 1848, Fitzpatrick to Harvey, February 13, 1848, Gilpin to Fitzpatrick, February 14, 1848, OIA, LR, Upper Platte Agency.

41. St. Louis *Reveille*, May 29, 1848; Gilpin to Jones, August 1, 1848, AGO, LR, G/368/1848. Twitchell, *Military Occupation of New Mexico*, pp. 340–41, reports that 253 Indians were killed in the campaigns. The official reports of Lt. Royall (June 21), Lt. Stremmel (June 23), and Capt. Griffin (July 12), tell another story. Although these indicate they killed a good number of Indians, it is obvious that the Indians did very well in these engagements. See *Annual Report, SW, 1848*, pp. 141–49.

42. Marcy to Polk, July 31, 1848, in "Peace Establishment—Numbers of Indians in Oregon, California and New Mexico, &c.," 30th Cong., 1st sess., *House Ex. Doc. 76* (Serial 521), pp. 3–4; *Annual Report, SW, 1848*, p. 77; Gilpin to Garland, August 18, 1848, AGO, LR. G/368/1848; Fitzpatrick to Harvey, October 16, 1848, *Annual Report, CIA, 1848*, p. 471.

43. J. M. Washington to Marcy, November 8, 1848, "Operations in New Mexico, the letters of Col. J. M. Washington," 31st Cong., 1st sess., *House Ex. Doc. 5* (Serial 569); George A. McCall, *New Mexico in 1850: A Military View*, Robert W. Frazer, ed., (Norman: University of Oklahoma Press, 1968), pp. 35–37.

44. Washington to Jones, February 3, 1849, AGO, LR, W/190/1849.

45. What little is known about Calhoun's career has been ably collected by Annie H. Abel, *Correspondence of Calhoun*, pp. xi–xiii. J. Manuel Espinosa, "Memoir of a Kentuckian in New Mexico, 1848–1884," *New Mexico Historical Review* 13 (1937): 7, notes Calhoun's personality.

46. See the report of Major Beall, January 16, 1849, AGO, LR, W/190/1849; Lt. Whittlesy to Beall, March 17, 1849, Orders #2, 9th Military Department, Santa Fe, March 20, 1849, Washington to Jones, March 29, 1849, AGO, LR, W/306/1849.

47. Washington to Jones, June 4, 1849, AGO, LR, W/364/1849; Washington to Jones, July 7, 1849, AGO, LR, W/418/1849.

48. St. Louis *Daily Missouri Republican*, May 17, 1849; William S. Messervy and others to George M. Crawford, July 1849, AGO, LR, M/506/1849; Messervy to *Daily Missouri Republican*, dated Santa Fe, July 15, 1849, published August 25, 1849.

49. St. Louis *Daily Missouri Republican*, September 12, 1849.

50. Washington to Jones, August 5, 1849, AGO, W/488/1849.

51. James H. Simpson, *Navajo Expedition: Journal of a Military Reconnaissance from Santa Fe, New Mexico to the Navajo Country in 1849*, ed. Frank McNitt (Norman: University of Oklahoma Press, 1964), pp. 65–68; Richard Kern Diary, August 31, 1849, HEH MS #4274; Robert V. Hine, *Edward Kern and American Expansion* (New Haven: Yale University Press, 1962), pp. 76–77.

52. Simpson, *Navajo Expedition*, pp. 96–99; the text of the treaty was forwarded by Calhoun to the commissioner of Indian affairs on December 25, 1849, and is printed in Abel, *Correspondence of Calhoun*, pp. 21–25.

53. Copy of a letter from Simpson to Abert, September 28, 1849, printed in the St. Louis *Daily Missouri Republican*, November 17, 1849.

54. St. Louis *Daily Missouri Republican*, November 4, 14, 1849.

55. Calhoun to Medill, October 15, 1849, in Abel, *Correspondence of Calhoun*, pp. 54–55.

56. Calhoun to Brown, March 30, 1850, ibid., pp. 178–79.

57. Calhoun to Brown, November 2, 7, 1849, February 3, 1850, ibid., pp. 69–70, 74, 141; Washington to Jones, September 25, 1849, AGO, LR, W/514/1849; "The Journal and Proceedings of the Convention of delegates who met in Santa Fe on 24 September, 1849 to present a plan for the Civil Government of New Mexico," 31st Cong., 1st sess., *House Ex. Doc. 39* (Serial 581).

58. Calhoun to Medill, October 15, 1849, in Abel, *Correspondence of Calhoun*, pp. 56–57.

59. Ibid., pp. 53–54. If such proposals had been accepted, the Pueblo Indians would have become the first Indian citizens of the United States.

60. Calhoun to Medill, October 29, 1849, Calhoun to Brown, November 16, 1849, in ibid., pp. 65–66, 79–80. Calhoun also proposed that trading houses be established for the Pueblo, that they be given agricultural implements,

and that American blacksmiths, carpenters, and traders of good character be allowed to locate among the Pueblo.

61. Munroe to Assistant Adjutant General W. G. Freeman, October 30, 1849, AGO, LR, M/659/1849; Espinosa, "Memoir of a Kentuckian," p. 7.

62. Calhoun to Medill, October 29, 1849, Calhoun to Brown, November 30, 1849, in Abel, *Correspondence of Calhoun*, pp. 63, 88. An army detachment came upon the Indians who were holding Mrs. White several weeks after the massacre. An attack was ordered and, in the words of Calhoun, "their lodges were destroyed, six Indians killed, and the body of Mrs. White found, yet warm, evidently killed by the Indians."

63. Letter from "S" dated Santa Fe, October 28, 1849, printed in the St. Louis *Daily Missouri Republican*, December 19, 1849.

64. Letter from Santa Fe, dated October 7, 1849, printed in ibid., December 18, 1849.

65. Calhoun to Brown, February 12, 1850, in Abel, *Correspondence of Calhoun*, p. 149.

66. Steen to Monroe, February 5, 1850, AGO, LR, M/181/1850. See also the report of Capt. Croghan Ker, January 27, 1850, and Sergeant W. C. Holbrook, April 7, 1850, AGO, LR, M/157/1850, and M/269/1850.

67. Munroe to Major W. W. Mackall Assistant Adjutant General, March 1, 1850, AGO, LR, M/179/1850. The rejection was recorded by Scott in pencil at the bottom of Munroe's letter. "It is not seen without an augmentation of the Army where additional companies can be found to re-inforce the 9th Department," said Scott.

68. Munroe to Freeman, March 15, 1850, AGO, LR, M/211/1850.

69. Munroe to Jones, May 13, 1850, 31st Cong., 1st sess., *Senate Ex. Doc. 60* (Serial 562), p. 2.

70. Calhoun to Brown, February 2, 18, 20, 1850, in Abel, *Correspondence of Calhoun*, pp. 132–33, 152–55.

71. The proclamation is recorded in ibid., p. 214; "Message of the President Transmitting a copy of the Constitution adopted by the inhabitants of New Mexico," 31st Cong., 1st sess., *Senate Ex. Doc. 74* (Serial 562); St. Louis *Daily Missouri Republican*, August 19, 1850. For a general survey of the statehood question, see Robert W. Larson, "First Attempts at Statehood," *New Mexico Quarterly* 38 (1968): 65–77.

72. Munroe to Jones, July 16, 1850, Alvarez to Munroe, July 13, 1850, Munroe and Calhoun to Caciques and Gobernadorcillas of the Pueblo Indians, June 25, 1850, *Annual Report, SW, 1850*, pp. 92, 95–98, 101–2; "Communication from New Mexico to the Congress setting forth assundry grievances," 31st Cong., 1st sess., *Senate Ex. Doc. 76* (Serial 562). See also McCall, *New Mexico in 1850*, p. 83, who recognized the difficulty. Article 8 of the constitution specified suffrage in the following terms: "Every male of the age of Twenty-one years, or upwards, (Africans or the descendents of Africans and uncivilized Indians excepted,) . . . and who shall have resided in

this state for six months next preceding any election, shall be a qualified elector for such election." The question was whether the New Mexicans would classify the Pueblo Indians as "uncivilized."

73. Crawford to McCall, November 19, 1849, in "California and New Mexico. Message from the President on the subject of California and New Mexico," 31st Cong., 1st sess., *House Ex. Doc. 17* (Serial 573), pp. 280–81; McCall to Crawford, July 15, 1850, AGO, LR, M/650/1850. McCall's instructions were apparently to encourage statehood for the territory, but also "It will be instructive, and probably necessary information, when the people of New Mexico form a constitution and seek admission in the confederacy of the States, to have your observation and views on their probable number, habit, customs, and pursuits of life." For background on McCall see Robert W. Frazer's introduction to McCall, *New Mexico in 1850*.

74. A. B. Bender, "Frontier Defense in the Territory of New Mexico, 1846–1853," *New Mexico Historical Review* 9 (1934): 261–62; McCall to Jones, December 26, 1850, in "Colonel McCall's Report in Relation to New Mexico," 31st Cong., 2d sess., *Senate Ex. Doc. 26* (Serial 589).

75. Sumner to Jones, February 8, 1851, AGO, LR, S/61/1851; Conrad to Sumner, April 1, 1851, *Annual Report, SW, 1851*, pp. 125–26.

76. Abel, *Correspondence of Calhoun*, pp. 300–302.

77. Munroe to Jones, March 30, 1851, *Annual Report, SW, 1851*, pp. 126–27.

78. Calhoun to President Fillmore, March 29, 1851, and Calhoun to Stuart, March 31, 1851, in Abel, *Correspondence of Calhoun*, pp. 305–6.

79. Copy of the treaty of April 2, 1851, and letter from Conrad to Stuart, May 9, 1851, OIA, Unratified Treaties; Calhoun to Lea, April 29, 1851, in Abel, *Correspondence of Calhoun*, pp. 337–38; St. Louis *Daily Missouri Republican*, May 28, 1851.

80. Calhoun to Webster, June 30, 1851, and Calhoun to Lea, June 30, 1851, in Abel, *Correspondence of Calhoun*, pp. 362–63, 369; St. Louis *Daily Missouri Republican*, July 1, 1851.

81. Letter from "a New Mexican," dated Santa Fe, June 4, 1851, printed in St. Louis *Daily Missouri Republican*, July 2, 1851; Calhoun to Lea, June 25, 1851, in Abel, *Correspondence of Calhoun*, p. 388.

82. For an analysis of the Pueblo situation in the 1920's, see Kenneth Philp, "Albert B. Fall and the Protest from the Pueblos, 1921–1923," *Arizona and the West* 12 (1970): 237–54.

83. Conrad to Sumner, April 1, 1851, *Annual Report, SW, 1851*, pp. 125–26. Bender, "Frontier Defense," p. 264, notes that there were some discussions between Quartermaster General Jessup and Conrad as to the most effective distribution of troops. Jessup believed that large bodies should be placed in a few border posts, but Conrad saw the need for permanent posts in the heart of Indian country.

84. Calhoun to Lea, July 30, 1851, in Abel, *Correspondence of Calhoun*, pp. 392–93.

85. Francis Stanley, *Fort Union* (New York, 1963), p. 63; Robert M. Utley, "Fort Union and the Santa Fe Trail," *New Mexico Historical Review* 36 (1961): 41.

86. Sumner to Jones, August 22, October 24, 1851, AGO, LR, S/388/1851, and S/353/1851; Calhoun to Lea, August 22, 1851, in Abel, *Correspondence of Calhoun*, p. 401; *New York Times*, October 10, 1851.

87. Sumner to Jones, October 24, 1851, AGO, LR, S/353/1851; St. Louis *Daily Missouri Republican*, September 13, October 29, 1851. Not everybody was happy with the situation. Richard Kern, who went on the Navajo expedition, thought both Calhoun and Sumner were fools, and he indicated this sentiment may have been shared by others: Richard Kern to Edward Kern, August 2, 1851, Fort Sutter Papers, HEH.

88. *Annual Report, CIA, 1851*, p. 271; *Annual Report, SW, 1851*, p. 113.

89. "Jurisdictional History of the Office of Indian Affairs"; Sister Mary Loyola, "The American Occupation of New Mexico," *New Mexico Historical Review* 14 (1939): 196.

90. Calhoun to Lea, February 29, 1852, and Calhoun to Sumner, April 7, 1852, in Abel, *Correspondence of Calhoun*, pp. 488, 518.

91. Quoted in Reeve, "The Government and the Navajo," p. 101.

Chapter 6

1. George E. Hyde, *Pawnee Indians* (Denver: University of Colorado Press, 1951), pp. 88–89, 137, 147–48. The treaty of 1833 is recorded in Charles J. Kappler, ed., *Indian Affairs, Laws and Treaties* (Washington: Government Printing Office, 1904–29), 2: 416–18. See also John Treat Irving, *Indian Sketches Taken During an Expedition of the Pawnee Tribe, 1833*, ed. John Francis McDermott (Norman: University of Oklahoma Press, 1955), pp. 141–43. Population estimates for the Pawnee during this period usually range in the neighborhood of 4,000.

2. Fitzpatrick to Harvey, June 24, 1848, OIA, LR, Upper Platte Agency.

3. John Miller to Marcy, January 20, 1848, OIA, LR, Council Bluffs Agency.

4. William T. Hagan, *The Sac and Fox Indians* (Norman: University of Oklahoma Press, 1958), pp. 205–9, 215–24; Abernathy, "Early Iowa Indian Treaties and Boundaries," pp. 241–59.

5. Exact population figures for these tribes are difficult to determine. Agent Miller in 1848 estimated that their numbers ranged in the neighborhood of 5,000. This seems excessive. Swanton, *Indian Tribes of North America*, pp. 251–52, 256–57, places the number in the 2,000 to 3,000 range. See also A. C. Fletcher and Francis LaFlesche, *The Omaha Tribe*, vol. 27 of *Annual Report of the Bureau of American Ethnology* (Washington: Government Printing Office, 1911), pp. 622–28.

6. Miller to Harvey, September 10, 1847, and Edward McKinney to Miller, September 16, 1847, *Annual Report, CIA, 1847*, pp. 857–64, 926–29. McKinney came west in 1846 to establish a mission and school for the Oto and Omaha. It was sponsored and supported by contributions from Presbyterian Societies in New York City.

7. Benton to Chouteau, January 22, 30, 1844, Chouteau Papers, MHS; William B. Napton, *Past and Present of Saline County Missouri* (Indianapolis and Chicago: B. F. Bowen & Co., 1910), pp. 126–28; Sunder, *Fur Trade on the Upper Missouri*, pp. 71, 87. Harvey was born in Northumberland County, Virginia, February 22, 1799. After being involved in Virginia politics for some time, he moved to Missouri in 1835. He died in February 1852.

8. "Colonel" John Miller became the agent at Council Bluffs, July 22, 1846. His agency was responsible for many of the border tribes, including the Pawnee, Omaha, and Oto. Matlock was a former trader. Although his agency dealt largely with tribes far to the north, his activities, particularly in preventing liquor on the river, affected the border tribes.

9. Dunbar to Reverend David Green, Secretary of the American Board of Commissioners of Foreign Missions, June 30, 1846, in William E. Connelley, ed., "Letters concerning the Presbyterian Mission in the Pawnee Country, near Bellevue, Nebraska, 1831–1849," *Collections of the Kansas State Historical Society, 1915–1918* 14 (1918): 683–86; Hyde, *Pawnee Indians*; pp. 163–64; St. Louis *Daily Missouri Republican*, May 27, 1846; Miller to Marcy, September 10, 1847, *Annual Report, CIA, 1847*, pp. 857–64.

10. Marcy to Medill, June 15, 1847, OIA, report book #5; Medill to Harvey, December 31, 1846, OIA, LS, vol. 39.

11. St. Louis *Daily Missouri Republican*, January 17, 1847; see also the St. Joseph *Gazette*, December 25, 1846, and the report of John Miller, December 15, 1846, OIA, LR, Council Bluffs Agency. In reporting the incident to his superiors, Miller called it "one of the most shocking scenes I have ever known." Some of the other reports of warfare among the border tribes are found in Miller to Harvey, September 10, 1847, *Annual Report, CIA, 1847*, pp. 860–62; Medill's report in ibid., pp. 742–43; St. Louis *Daily Missouri Republican*, n.d., as quoted in *Publications of the Kansas State Historical Society* 20 (1920): 172.

12. William J. Ghent, *The Road to Oregon: A Chronicle of the Great Emigrant Trail* (New York: Longmans, Green & Co., 1929), pp. 84–85; Parkman, *Oregon Trail*, p. 88; Heinrich Lienhard, *From St. Louis to Sutter's Fort, 1846*, ed. Erwin G. and Elisabeth K. Gudde (Norman: University of Oklahoma Press, 1961), pp. 40–41; St. Louis *Daily Union*, June 21, 1847, and several letters to frontier newspapers, reprinted in Dale Morgan. ed., *Overland in 1846: Diaries and Letters of the California-Oregon Trail* (Georgetown: The Talisman Press, 1963) 2: 591–92, 594, 597.

13. St. Louis *Reveille*, July 20, 1846.

14. Marcy to Medill, June 15, 1847, OIA, report book #5.

15. Harvey to Medill, September 5, 1846, *Annual Report, CIA, 1846,* p. 286.

16. T. P. Moore to Harvey, September 21, 1846, ibid., p. 292; Harvey to Major C. Wharton, Commanding at Fort Leavenworth, April 18, 1846, OIA, LR, St. Louis Superintendency.

17. For a detailed account of this episode, see Robert A. Trennert, "The Mormons and the Office of Indian Affairs: The Conflict Over Winter Quarters, 1846–1848," *Nebraska History* 53 (1972): 381–400. See also Wallace Stegner, *The Gathering of Zion: The Story of the Mormon Trail* (New York: McGraw Hill, 1964).

18. See, for example, Miller to Harvey, September 10, 1847, *Annual Report, CIA, 1847,* pp. 860–61.

19. Dunbar to Green, June 30, 1846, in Connelley, "Presbyterian Missions," pp. 383–86.

20. Thomas L. Kane to Marcy, December 20, 1846, OIA, LR, St. Louis Superintendency. Kane listed the distribution of the Mormons in Indian country as follows: 10,500 with the Omaha, 1,000 with the Ponca, 700 near the Arkansas River, 3,000 with the Potawatomi, and about 1,000 on "the edge of settlement."

21. *Annual Report, CIA, 1846,* p. 217.

22. *Annual Report, CIA, 1847,* pp. 738–40. It was generally proposed that the Winnebago be placed between the Sioux and the Chippewa, who were hereditary enemies. To make room for the Winnebago, Medill suggested purchasing some land from the Chippewa.

23. Kelley to Marcy, February 26, 1847, OIA, LR, miscellaneous, 1847. Medill wrote many of the chiefs personally thanking them for moving so rapidly. See Medill to Chief Laframboise Joseph and other Potawatomi chiefs, January 3, 1848, OIA, LS, vol. 40.

24. Contract between McElroy and Harvey, February 20, 1847, McElroy to Miller, May 17, 1847, McElroy to Harvey, June 10, 1847, Miller to Harvey, September 15, 1847, Miller to Marcy, January 20, 1848, OIA, LR, Council Bluffs Agency.

25. McElroy to Harvey, June 10, 1847, ibid.; Marcy to Medill, June 15, 1847, OIA, report book #5; Fitzpatrick to Harvey, January 3, 1847, OIA, LR, St. Louis Superintendency.

26. St. Louis *Daily Union,* January 1, 1847; Washington *Daily Union,* January 26, 1847.

27. Medill to Harvey, October 19, 1848, OIA, LS, vol. 40; *Annual Report, CIA, 1847,* p. 743.

28. Kenneth W. Colgrove, "The Attitude of Congress Toward Pioneers of the West, 1820–1850," *Iowa Journal of History and Politics* 9 (1911): 284–87; J. T. Dorris, "Federal Aid to the Oregon Trail Before 1850," *Oregon Histori-*

cal Quarterly 30 (1929): 314–20; *Annual Report, SW, 1847*, p. 59. John Quincy Adams, in a speech before Congress on January 12, 1846, stated that posts on the Oregon Trail would be a great expense and could only be interpreted by the British as a warlike move. Completely ignoring the Indian question, he demanded to know why the regiments were necessary when "we are at profound peace with the World," *Congressional Globe*, 29th Cong., 1st sess., p. 127.

29. Albert Watkins, "History of Fort Kearny," *Collections of the Nebraska State Historical Society* 16 (1911): 235–36. A first battalion was organized in March 1847, but it was drawn off to New Mexico, necessitating the formation of a second body.

30. Roger Jones to Commanding Officer, Battalion of Missouri Mounted Volunteers, June 16, 1847, OIA, LR, miscellaneous, 1847.

31. Fitzpatrick to Medill, January 1, 1847, OIA, LR, Upper Platte Agency; St. Louis *Daily Union*, June 21, July 1, 1847.

32. Harvey to Medill, November 22, 1847, and Harvey to Miller, February 5, 1847, OIA, LR, St. Louis Superintendency; Miller to Harvey, January 20, 1848, OIA, LR, Council Bluffs Agency. Miller suggested that two companies be placed at Grand Island, one at the Pawnee Villages, and two on the Missouri River. This, he believed, would "render ample protection to the Oregon emigrants, to the Indians, and to the Western boundary of the Ioway Territory."

33. Miller to Harvey, September 10, 1847, *Annual Report, CIA, 1847*, p. 859; Hyde, *Pawnee Indians*, p. 169; Harvey to Medill, October 13, 1847, OIA, LR, St. Louis Superintendency. The post at Table Creek was also called Camp Kearny. It was abandoned in the spring of 1848 when the troops were transferred to Grand Island. See Lillian M. Wellman, "The History of Fort Kearny," *Publications of the Nebraska State Historical Society* 21 (1930): 214; and Lyle E. Mantor, "Fort Kearny and the Westward Movement," *Nebraska History* 29 (1948): 175.

34. Harvey to Cutler, November 5, 1846, OIA, LR, St. Louis Superintendency.

35. A good description of the background and political activities of Kane is presented in Bernard DeVoto, *Year of Decision: 1846* (Boston: Houghton Mifflin Co., 1961), pp. 242–43.

36. Medill to Harvey, September 2, 1846, OIA, LR, St. Louis Superintendency.

37. Kane to Medill, January 20, 1847, OIA, LR, Miscellaneous, 1847. See also Clyde B. Aitchison, "The Mormon Settlements in the Missouri Valley," *Proceedings of the Nebraska State Historical Society* 15 (1907): 13–14, who discusses the Potawatomi and Omaha welcome to the Mormons and the agreement of the Omaha to allow the Mormons to remain for two years; and Trennert, "Conflict over Winter Quarters," pp. 386–87.

38. Samuel Allis to David Green, February 1, 1847, in Connelley, "Presbyterian Missions," pp. 739–40; Miller to Brigham Young, April 4, 1847, OIA, LR, Council Bluffs Agency; Aitchison, "Mormon Settlements," p. 15.

39. Kane to Marcy, April 20, 1847, and Kane to Medill, April 21, 1847, OIA, LR, St. Louis Superintendency. Kane stressed the loyalty of the Mormons to the United States and said the government should be humane in providing for them. He also suggested one of the Mormons be appointed a U.S. Indian agent because so many of the Saints would be coming into contact with Indians. Medill became quite annoyed over this suggestion.

40. Medill to Marcy, April 24, 1847, ibid.

41. Kane to Medill, April 24, 1847, ibid.; letter from the High Council to the Latter Day Saints on the Eastern Bank of the Missouri, January 10, 1848, quoted in *On The Mormon Frontier: The Diary of Hosea Stout, 1844–1861*, ed. Juanita Brooks (Salt Lake City: University of Utah Press, 1964), pp. 295–96; Stegner, *Gathering of Zion*, pp. 198–99.

42. Moore to Harvey, September 21, 1846, *Annual Report, CIA, 1846*, p. 292.

43. Matlock to Harvey, June 29, 1947, OIA, LR, St. Louis Superintendency; Miller to Harvey, September 15, 1848, *Annual Report, CIA, 1848*, p. 465. Miller reported that whiskey-sellers in Iowa and Missouri were particularly devastating to the Oto and Omaha. Not only did the alcohol take its toll, but the Indians would have to steal from white settlers in order to acquire goods to trade for alcohol.

44. Hiram M. Chittenden, *The American Fur Trade of the Far West* (New York: R. R. Wilson, 1936), 1: 365–68, 381–82; Medill to W. G. & G. W. Ewing, July 17, 1847, Medill to Harvey, March 24, 1847, January 25, April 5, 1848, OIA, LS, vols. 39 and 40; Harvey to Medill, May 27, 1848, OIA, LR, St. Louis Superintendency.

45. Sunder, *Fur Trade on the Upper Missouri*, pp. 89–90; Medill to Harvey, April 14, 1846, and Medill to Chouteau, May 6, 1848, OIA, LS, vols. 38 and 40. Alexander Harvey was the rival trader involved in this incident. He had attempted to compete with Chouteau and had been roughly handled. Consequently, he passed on to the Indian Office his knowledge of Chouteau's activities.

46. Gantt to R. H. Gillet, Solicitor of the Treasury, April 5, 1848, V. Bogy to P. Chouteau, Jr. & Co., May 23, 1848, H. R. Gambel to P. Chouteau, Jr. & Co., May 29, 1848, OIA, LR, St. Louis Superintendency. There were fifteen or twenty witnesses, largely former Chouteau employees. By 1848 most had been rehired and were working on the Upper Missouri, 2,500 miles from St. Louis.

47. Benton to Chouteau, June 23, 1848, Chouteau Papers, MHS; Gantt to Gillet, August 11, 1848, OIA, LR, St. Louis Superintendency.

48. Chouteau to Medill, January 17, 1849, Chouteau to Harvey and Gantt, January 12, 1849, Gantt to Gillet, February 12, 1849, ibid.; Chouteau to Gantt, February 12, 1849, Chouteau Papers, MHS.

49. Fitzpatrick to Harvey, June 24, 1848, OIA, LR, Upper Platte Agency.

50. Report of Harvey, October 4, 1848, *Annual Report, CIA, 1848*, pp. 441–42.

51. *Annual Report, CIA, 1847*, p. 740.

52. *Annual Report, CIA, 1848*, pp. 386–89.

53. Medill to Mitchell, March 30, 1849, OIA, LS, vol. 41; G. W. Ewing to John B. Sarpy, April 10, 1849, Chouteau Papers, MHS; Ray H. Mattison, "David Dawson Mitchell," in *The Mountain Men and the Fur Trade of the Far West*, ed., LeRoy Hafen (Glendale, Calif.: Arthur H. Clark Co., 1965), 2: 241–46; Sunder, *Fur Trade on the Upper Missouri*, pp. 112–13. Mitchell (1806–61) was born in Virginia and began working for the American Fur Company in 1828. He served as superintendent at St. Louis between 1841 and 1843. During the Mexican War he was with Doniphan in New Mexico and Chihuahua.

54. Report of Barrow, *Annual Report, CIA, 1849*, pp. 1076–79; letter from "Pawnee" to the St. Louis *Daily Missouri Republican*, dated Fort Kearny, May 18, 1849, printed June 4, 1849. Barrow noted that the Pawnee were scattering in all directions in an attempt to escape the cholera. "Such was their dread of this terrible scourge that no persuasion could induce them to bury their dead."

55. Report of Barrow, and Alfred Vaughan to Mitchell, September 30, 1849, *Annual Report, CIA, 1849*, pp. 1077–78, 1081–83; Medill to Mitchell, June 9, 1849, OIA, LS, vol. 42; St. Louis *Daily Missouri Republican*, June 4, 1849.

56. Copy of a report by Major Samuel Woods to Lt. Colonel Loomis, October 19, 1849, and Loomis to Headquarters, October 23, 1849, OIA, LR, miscellaneous, 1849.

57. Brown to Crawford, April 19, 1850, OIA, LS, vol. 43; Ewing to Brown, January 21, 1850, OIA, LR, miscellaneous, 1850.

58. Brown to Senator G. M. Jones, February 23, 1850, and Brown to Crawford, April 19, 1850, OIA, LS, vol. 43.

59. *Frontier Guardian*, June 12, 1850; John Gooch, Jr., to A. H. H. Stuart, October 21, 1850, OIA, LR, Council Bluffs Agency. Gooch was the printer of the *Guardian*. See also in this connection a letter from Thomas J. Sutherland to Lea, May 22, 1851, in ibid., and the *Frontier Guardian*, May 16, 1851. Sutherland claimed the Mormons were at fault for any difficulty because of their continual antagonizing of the Indians and the use of small incidents to excite the community against the Indians whose lands they desired. The exact truth of what either side said is difficult to determine.

60. Barrow to Mitchell, October 20, 1850, *Annual Report, CIA, 1850*, p. 71.

61. Mitchell to Lea, October 25, 1851, *Annual Report, CIA, 1851*, pp. 322–23.

62. Malin, "Indian Policy and Westward Expansion," p. 101; Paul W. Gates, *Fifty Million Acres: Conflicts over Kansas Land Policy, 1854–1890* (Ithaca: Cornell University Press, 1954), pp. 14–26.

Chapter 7

1. Copy of the Senate's confirmation of Fitzpatrick's appointment, August 3, 1846, OIA, LR, Upper Platte Agency.

2. Fitzpatrick to Medill, August 11, 1848, ibid.

3. Chittenden, *American Fur Trade of the Far West*, 1: 305; George M. Hyde, *Red Cloud's Folk: A History of the Oglala Sioux* (Norman: University of Oklahoma Press, 1937), pp. 44–45; Alexander B. Adams, *Sitting Bull: An Epic of the Plains* (New York: Putnam, 1973), p. 40; DeVoto, *Across the Wide Missouri*, p. 224. In 1855 Edwin T. Denig, *Five Tribes of the Upper Missouri*, ed. John C. Ewers (Norman: University of Oklahoma Press, 1961), pp. 14–15, estimated the population of the Teton and Yancton Sioux at 11,800. John C. Ewers, *Teton Dakota History and Ethnology* (Berkeley: University of California Press, 1938), pp. 7–8, revised all early estimates and suggests there were between 15,000 and 18,000. About half were probably living along the Platte.

4. David Lavender, *Bent's Fort* (New York: Doubleday, 1954), p. 133 and passim; Fitzpatrick to Harvey, April 30, 1847, OIA, LR, St. Louis Superintendency. Donald J. Berthong, *The Southern Cheyennes* (Norman: University of Oklahoma Press, 1963), p. 132, uses slightly different figures for the same period; 3,150 Cheyenne and 2,400 Arapaho.

5. Report of Lt. Kingsbury in 1835, quoted in Berthong, *The Southern Cheyennes*, p. 77; see also Lavender, *Bent's Fort*, pp. 150–51.

6. Hyde, *Red Cloud's Folk*, p. 58. The first recorded attempt to halt emigration came in 1842 when Dr. Elijah White's party was held up by the Sioux and only allowed to proceed after the intervention of Fitzpatrick. See LeRoy R. Hafen and W. J. Ghent, *Broken Hand: The Life Story of Thomas Fitzpatrick* (Denver: Old West Publishing Co., 1931), pp. 134–37.

7. Colonel Henry Dodge led two expeditions in the mid-thirties. Fremont's 1842 expedition also came into contact with the Cheyenne and Arapaho, and though not primarily intended to keep tabs on these Indians it was meant to display the eagle.

8. Kearny's report on this venture is recorded in "Report of A Summer Campaign to the Rocky Mountains," 29th Cong., 1st sess., *Senate Ex. Doc. 1* (Serial 470), pp. 210–13; see also Parkman, *Oregon Trail*, pp. 196–98; Philip St. George Cooke, *Scenes and Adventures in the Army: or, Romance of Military Life* (Philadelphia: Lindsay & Blakiston, 1857), p. 335; William Goetzmann, *Army Exploration in the American West, 1803–1863* (New Haven: Yale University Press, 1959), pp. 112–15.

9. St. Louis *Reveille*, September 14, 1846. The best account of Fitzpatrick's activities as a guide are in Hafen and Ghent, *Broken Hand*, pp. 127–78. See also Hafen's "Thomas Fitzpatrick," pp. 374–76.

10. John Craig to George Boosinger, Ray County, Missouri, October 4, 1847, in Morgan, *Overland in 1846*, 1: 134; Edwin Bryant, *What I Saw in*

California . . . (Minneapolis: Ross & Haines, 1967), p. 95. Reliable emigration figures are given in Ghent, *The Road to Oregon*, p. 86. For those going to Oregon, see F. G. Young, "The Oregon Trail," *Quarterly of the Oregon Historical Society* 1 (1900): 370.

11. Quotation from a letter by DeSmet, September 27, 1846, in DeSmet's *Oregon Missions and Travels Over the Rocky Mountains in 1845–1846*, vol. 29 of *Early Western Travels*, 1748–1848, ed. Reuben G. Thwaites (Cleveland: Arthur H. Clark Co., 1906), p. 364.

12. Rufus B. Sage, *Scenes in the Rocky Mountains*, vol. 4 of *Far West and Rockies Series*, ed. LeRoy R. and Anne W. Hafen (Glendale: Arthur H. Clark Co., 1956), p. 206.

13. Letter from Oglala and Brulé Sioux to President Polk, n.d. [1846], OIA, LR, Upper Missouri Agency.

14. Harvey to Medill, May 6, 1846, ibid.

15. Medill to Harvey, June 4, 1846, OIA, LS, vol. 30. Medill said there was reason to believe that recent discoveries might change the route of emigration and when some permanent route was decided upon, then perhaps there might be some small compensation.

16. St. Louis *Reveille*, August 10, 1846; see also the report of T. P. Moore, September 21, 1846, *Annual Report, CIA, 1846*, p. 292, and the St. Louis *Daily Missouri Republican*, June 19, 1846, printed in *Publications of the Nebraska State Historical Society* 20 (1920): 159.

17. Moore to Medill, May 14, 1846, OIA, LR, Upper Missouri Agency; Medill to Harvey, August 14, 1846, OIA, LS, vol. 38.

18. Fitzpatrick to OIA, January 1, 1847, OIA, LR, Upper Platte Agency.

19. Fitzpatrick to Harvey, January 3, 1847, OIA, LR, St. Louis Superintendency.

20. Medill to Harvey, January 23, 1847, OIA, LS, vol. 39.

21. Harvey to Medill, February 4, 1847, OIA, LR, St. Louis Superintendency.

22. Harvey to Medill, February 5, 1847, ibid.

23. St. Louis *Daily Union*, July 1, 1847. The emigration figures for 1847 are given in LeRoy R. Hafen and Francis M. Young, *Fort Laramie and the Pageant of the West, 1834–1890* (Glendale: Arthur H. Clark Co., 1938), p. 126; and Ghent, *Oregon Trail*, pp. 91–93.

24. "The Growing Indian War," Independence *Expositor*, reprinted in the St. Louis *Daily Union*, September 27, 1847.

25. July 1847 circular, OIA, LR, St. Louis Superintendency. There were several reports of Cheyenne and Arapaho being with raiding parties. See, for example, the report of Major B. B. Edmundson to Colonel S. Price, June 14, 1847, AGO, LR, P/333/1847; and Fitzpatrick to Harvey, October 19, 1847, OIA, LR, Upper Platte Agency.

26. Fitzpatrick to Harvey, October 19, 1847, ibid.; Hafen and Ghent, *Broken Hand*, pp. 198–200; Lavender, *Bent's Fort*, pp. 302–3.

27. Fitzpatrick to Harvey, September 18, December 18, 1847, February 15, 1848, Fitzpatrick to OIA, October 19, 1847, OIA, LR, Upper Platte Agency; Berthong, *Southern Cheyenne*, pp. 109–11.

28. Fitzpatrick to Harvey, October 6, 1848, *Annual Report, CIA, 1848*, p. 471. Hafen and Ghent, *Broken Hand*, p. 209, estimate that about 400 wagons were bound for Oregon and some 150 persons for California in 1848.

29. Matlock to Harvey, June 6, 1848, OIA, LR, Upper Missouri Agency; Matlock to Harvey, September 25, 1848, and Harvey to Medill, October 4, 1848, *Annual Report, CIA, 1848*, pp. 468, 441–42; Edward Kern, "Diary of First Part of Fremont's Fourth Expedition," November 12, 1848, HEH, doc. #4154; Hyde, *Red Cloud's Folk*, p. 62.

30. Matlock to Harvey, September 25, 1848, *Annual Report, CIA, 1848*, p. 469; Fitzpatrick to Harvey, December 18, 1847, and Fitzpatrick to Gilpin, February 10, 1848, OIA, LR, Upper Platte Agency; Solomon P. Sublette to Harvey, February 29, 1848, OIA, LR, St. Louis Superintendency.

31. Hafen and Ghent, *Broken Hand*, p. 209.

32. Fitzpatrick to Medill, August 11, 1848, OIA, LR, Upper Platte Agency.

33. *Annual Report, CIA, 1848*, p. 389; *Annual Report, SW, 1848*, p. 77; Gilpin to Adjutant General, August 1, 1848, AGO, LR, G/368/1848; Gilpin to Garland, August 18, 1848, ibid., G/398/1848; Karnes, "Gilpin's Volunteers on the Santa Fe Trail," pp. 13–14.

34. Letters from "Nebraska" to the St. Louis *Daily Missouri Republican*, September 9, October 6, 1848, printed in *Publications of the Nebraska State Historical Society* 20 (1920): 180–82, 185–88.

35. Fitzpatrick to Harvey, October 6, 1848, *Annual Report, CIA, 1848*, p. 471. Italics mine.

36. Fitzpatrick to D. D. Mitchell, May 22, 1849, OIA, LR, Upper Platte Agency.

37. DeSmet recorded his fears for the future of the plains tribes in his *Oregon Missions and Travels Over the Rocky Mountains*; See also DeSmet to Harvey, December 4, 1848, OIA, LR, Upper Platte Agency.

38. Harvey to Medill, October 4, 1848, *Annual Report, CIA, 1848*, p. 438.

39. Ghent, *Road to Oregon*, p. 97. The estimate of 20,000 was given by an officer at Fort Kearny who kept a count during the summer. See "Pawnee" to the St. Louis *Daily Missouri Republican*, published August 6, 1849.

40. *Annual Report, SI, 1849*, pp. 14–15; *Annual Report, CIA, 1849*, p. 951; Medill to Mitchell, April 12, 1849, OIA, LS, vol. 42.

41. For a good background on the Loring expedition and the officers involved, see the introduction by the editor, Raymond W. Settle, to Osborne Cross, *The March of the Mounted Riflemen: First United States Military Expedition to Travel the full length of the Oregon Trail from Fort Leavenworth to Fort Vancouver* . . . (Glendale: Arthur H. Clark Co., 1940); General Orders #19, March 15, 1849, printed in the St. Louis *Daily Missouri*

Republican, April 13, 1849; Loring to Jones, May 10, 1849, AGO, LR, L/144/1849; Loring's report on the expedition, October 15, 1849, ibid., L/307/1849.

42. "A report, in the form of a journal, to the Quartermaster General, of the march of the regiment of mounted riflemen to Oregon, from May 10 to October 5, 1849 by Major O. Cross," 31st Cong., 2d sess., *Senate Ex. Doc. 1* (Serial 587), pp. 131, 146. On May 26, 1849, "Pawnee" recorded that 10,000 men and 2,327 wagons had passed Fort Kearny. Loring arrived five days later. See St. Louis *Daily Missouri Republican*, June 16, 1849. Loring's soldiers were no different from other travelers and Cross recorded how once buffalo were spotted entire troops went after the animals. "All seemed eager to have the satisfaction of saying that they had shot a buffalo, if they were not successful enough to kill one." As usual, "in true hunter style," only a few choice portions of meat were taken and the rest left to the wolves.

43. J. S. Chambers, *The Conquest of Cholera, America's Greatest Scourge* (New York: Macmillan Co., 1938), pp. 195–205; St. Louis *Daily Missouri Republican*, March 24, June 2, August 29, 1849; "Exploration and Survey of the Valley of the Great Salt Lake of Utah including a Reconnaissance of a New Route Through the Rockey Mountains by Howard Stansbury," 32nd Cong., special sess., *Senate Ex. Doc. 3* (Serial 608), pp. 42–45.

44. Mitchell to Medill, June 1, 1849, OIA, LR, Upper Platte Agency; Brown to Fitzpatrick, August 16, 1849, OIA, LS, vol. 42.

45. Report of Mitchell, *Annual Report, CIA, 1849*, pp. 1070–71. See also Mitchell to Brown, August 27, 31, 1849, OIA, LR, St. Louis Superintendency.

46. Brown to Mitchell, September 20, 1849, OIA, LS, vol. 42; *Annual Report CIA, 1849*, p. 943.

47. Mitchell to Fitzpatrick, August 31, 1849, and Fitzpatrick to Mitchell, September 8, 1849, OIA, LR, Upper Platte Agency.

48. Mitchell to OIA, October 26, 1849, and Mitchell to Brown, March 9, 1850, "Documents in relation to a treaty proposed to be negotiated with the Indians of the prairie south and west of the Missouri River, to the northern line of the state of Texas, embracing the Indians of the mountains, including those of New Mexico," 31st Cong., 1st sess., *Senate Misc. Doc. 70* (Serial 563), pp. 3–4. The expenditures were broken down as follows: presents, $40,000; transportation, $15,000; delegations from the different tribes, $20,000; purchases of Mexican prisoners, $25,000; Indians of New Mexico, $50,000; first annuity payment, $40,000; contingent expenses, $10,000.

49. Fitzpatrick to Mitchell, September 24, 1850, *Annual Report, CIA, 1850*, p. 55.

50. St. Louis *Daily Union*, May 30, 1850; St. Louis *Daily Missouri Republican*, May 28, June 2, 1850.

51. Mitchell to Lea, September 14, 1850, *Annual Report, CIA, 1850*, p. 47.

52. W. S. McBride, MS "Journal of an overland trip from Goshen, Ind. to Salt Lake City," HEH Doc. HM 16956.

53. St. Louis *Daily Missouri Republican*, October 3, 1850, August 4, 1851; Hyde, *Red Cloud's Folk*, p. 64; Mitchell to Lea, September 14, 1850, *Annual Report, CIA, 1850*, p. 49.

54. Mitchell to Lea, March 22, 1851, OIA, LR, St. Louis Superintendency.

55. Conrad to Stuart, April 7, 1851, and Mitchell to Lea, April 22, 1851, ibid.

56. Mitchell's report on the treaty of Fort Laramie, *Annual Report, CIA, 1851*, p. 288; Mitchell to DeSmet (copy), April 19, 1851, DeSmet Papers, MHS; Campbell to Lea, May 28, 1851, OIA, LR, St. Louis Superintendency; Campbell to Dougherty, February 15, April 28, 1851, Dougherty Papers, MHS.

57. Campbell to Dougherty, April 28, 1851, Dougherty Papers, MHS.

58. Smith and Lewis to President Fillmore, n.d. [1851], OIA, LR, Utah Superintendency.

59. H. R. Day to Lea, August 12, 1851, and J. H. Holman to Lea, September 21, 1851, ibid.

60. *New York Times*, October 14, 1851.

61. Fitzpatrick to Lea, November 24, 1851, *Annual Report, CIA, 1851*, p. 333.

62. Lea to Mitchell, May 26, 1851, OIA, LS, vol. 44.

63. Mitchell to Lea, November 11, 1851, *Annual Report, CIA, 1851*, p. 289; St. Louis *Daily Missouri Republican*, July 25, 1851; Percival G. Lowe, *Five Years a Dragoon ('49 to '54) and Other Adventures on the Great Plains*, ed. Don Russell (Norman: University of Oklahoma Press, 1965), p. 69.

64. Lowe, *Five Years a Dragoon*, p. 68. Estimates ran as high as 60,000 Indians present, but Hafen and Ghent, *Broken Hand*, p. 228, put the figure at a more realistic 10,000.

65. Lowe, *Five Years a Dragoon*, pp. 65–66. Bridger considered himself something of the protector of the Shoshoni and probably overestimated their ability to fight the Sioux. The Shoshoni were, at least, well armed with guns.

66. St. Louis *Daily Missouri Republican*, October 29, 1851; Mitchell to Lea, November 11, 1851, *Annual Report, CIA, 1851*, p. 289.

67. Holman to Lea, September 21, 1851, OIA, LR, Utah Superintendency; St. Louis *Daily Missouri Republican*, October 29, November 9, 1851; Kappler, *Indian Affairs: Laws and Treaties*, 2: 440–42.

68. St. Louis *Daily Missouri Republican*, November 30, 1851.

69. Mitchell to Lea, November 11, 1851, *Annual Report, CIA, 1851*, p. 290.

Bibliography

Bibliography

Manuscript Collections

Manuscript Sources in the National Archives

The manuscript sources of the National Archives are most important to any study of Indian affairs. Most significant for this work are the rich materials found in the "Records of the Office of Indian Affairs" (Record Group 75). During the period 1846–51 these include the "Documents Relating to Ratified and Unratified Treaties"; letters received from the Central Superintendency, Council Bluffs Agency, New Mexico Superintendency, St. Louis Superintendency, Texas Agency, Upper Missouri Agency, Upper Platte Agency, Utah Superintendency, and Miscellaneous; letters sent by the Office of Indian Affairs, vols. 38–44; and "Report Books," vols. 5–6. The "Records of the Adjutant General's Office" (Record Group 94), especially the letters sent and received, are valuable for the military aspects of Indian policy. "Records of United States Army Commands" (Record Group 393), and "Consolidated Correspondence, Office of The Quartermaster General" (Record Group 92) also offer material concerning the military.

Private Manuscript Collections

Manuscript materials found in various collections also offer additional primary information. The most important are as follows:

Filson Club (Louisville, Ky.)
 Orlando Brown Papers

Henry E. Huntington Library (San Marino, Calif.)
 Fort Sutter Papers
 James Clyman Diary, 1844–46
 Edward Kern Diary, 1848

Richard Kern Diary, 1848–49
Richard Kern Diary, 1851
W. S. McBride Journal, 1850

Indiana State Library, Indiana Division (Indianapolis, Ind.)
  William G. and George W. Ewing Papers
Kentucky Historical Society (Frankfort, Ky.)
  Orlando Brown Papers
Library of Congress (Washington, D.C.)
  Thomas Ewing Papers
  William Medill Papers
Missouri Historical Society (St. Louis, Mo.)
  P. Chouteau Maffitt Papers
  Pierre DeSmet Papers
  John Dougherty Papers
  William L. Sublette Papers

Published Primary Sources

Government Documents

Printed government documents are numerous and many are contained in the Serial Set of Congressional Documents. These include the *House* and *Senate Journals* and the many reports in the *House* and *Senate Executive Documents* which are fully cited in the footnotes. The Serial Set also includes the *Annual Reports* of the Commissioner of Indian Affairs, Secretary of War, Secretary of the Interior, and *Annual Messages* of the President. Other printed information includes the *Congressional Globe*, 29th to 32nd Congresses; *Register of Debates in Congress*, 18th Congress; and the *Public Statutes at Large of the United States of America* (1854).

Historical Materials

Bartlett, John Russell. *Personal Narrative of Explorations and Incidents in Texas, New Mexico, California, Sonora, and Chihuahua, Connected with the United States and Mexican Boundary Commission, during the years 1850, '51, '52, and '53.* 2 vols. New York: D. Appleton & Co., 1854.

Bryant, Edwin. *What I Saw in California: Being the Journal of a Tour, by the Emigrant Route and South Pass of the Rocky Mountains, Across the Continent of North America, the Great Desert Basin, and Through California.* Minneapolis: Ross & Haines, 1967.

[Calhoun, James S.] *Official Correspondence of James S. Calhoun while Indian Agent at Santa Fe and Superintendent of Indian Affairs in New Mexico.* Ed. Annie H. Abel. Washington: Government Printing Office, 1915.

Catlin, George. *North American Indians: Being Letters and Notes on their Manners, Customs, and Condition, Written During Eight Years' Travel Amongst the Wildest Tribes of Indians in North America, 1832–1839.* 2 vols. Edinburgh: J. Grant, 1926.

Clyman, James. *James Clyman: American Frontiersman, 1792–1881: The Adventures of a Trapper and Covered Wagon Emigrant as Told in his Own Reminiscences and Diaries.* Ed. Charles L. Camp. San Francisco: California Historical Society, 1928.

Compilation of the Messages and Papers of the Presidents, 1789–1897. Ed. James D. Richardson. 10 vols. Washington: Government Printing Office, 1896–99.

Cooke, Philip St. George. *The Conquest of New Mexico & California: An Historical and Personal Narrative.* New York: G. P. Putnam's Sons, 1878.

——. *Scenes and Adventures in the Army: Or, Romance of Military Life.* Philadelphia: Lindsay & Blakiston, 1857.

Cross, Osborne. *The March of the Mounted Riflemen: First United States Military Expedition to Travel the Full Length of the Oregon Trail from Fort Leavenworth to Fort Vancouver, May to October, 1849.* Ed. Raymond W. Settle. Glendale: Arthur H. Clark Company, 1940.

Denig, Edwin Thompson. *Five Indian Tribes of the Upper Missouri.* Ed. John C. Ewers. Norman: University of Oklahoma Press, 1961.

DeSmet, Pierre Jean. *Oregon Missions and Travels Over the Rocky Mountains in 1845–1846.* Vol. 29 of *Early Western Travels, 1748–1846.* Ed. Reuben G. Thwaites. Cleveland: Arthur H. Clark Company, 1906.

Edwards, Frank S. *A Campaign in New Mexico with Colonel Doniphan.* Philadelphia: Carey & Hart, 1848.

Hughes, John Taylor. *Doniphan's Expedition, Containing an Account of the Expedition Against New Mexico, & Etc.* Cincinnati: U. P. James, 1847.

Indian Affairs: Laws and Treaties. Ed. Charles J. Kappler. 4 vols. Washington: Government Printing Office, 1915.

"Indian Agent Jesse Stem: A Manuscript Revelation." Ed. Robert C. Cotner. *West Texas Historical Association Year Book* 39 (October 1963): 114–54.

Irving, John Treat. *Indian Sketches Taken During an Expedition to the Pawnee Tribe, 1833.* Ed. John Francis McDermott. Norman: University of Oklahoma Press, 1955.

"Letters Concerning the Presbyterian Mission in the Pawnee Country, near Bellevue, Nebraska, 1831–1849." Ed. William E. Connelley. *Collections of the Kansas State Historical Society* 14 (1918): 570–784.

Lienhard, Heinrich. *From St. Louis to Sutter's Fort, 1846.* Eds. Erwin G. and Elisabeth K. Gudde. Norman: University of Oklahoma Press, 1961.

Life and Select Literary Remains of Sam Houston of Texas. Ed. William C. Crane. Dallas: William G. Scarff & Co., 1884.

Lowe, Percival G. *Five Years a Dragoon ('49 to '54) and Other Adventures on the Great Plains.* Ed. Don Russell. Norman: University of Oklahoma Press, 1965.

McCall, George A. *New Mexico in 1850: A Military View.* Ed. Robert W. Frazer. Norman: University of Oklahoma Press, 1968.

Magoffin, Susan Shelby. *Down the Santa Fe Trail and Into Mexico: The Diary of Susan Shelby Magoffin, 1846–1847.* Ed. Stella M. Drumm. New Haven: Yale University Press, 1962.

Marcy, Randolph B. *Thirty Years of Army Life on the Border.* New York: Harper & Brothers, 1866.

Overland in 1846: Diaries and Letters of the California-Oregon Trail. Ed. Dale L. Morgan. 2 vols. Georgetown, Calif.: The Talisman Press, 1963.

Parkman, Francis. *The Oregon Trail.* New York: Washington Square Press, 1963.

Sage, Rufus B. *Scenes in the Rocky Mountains.* Vol. 4 of *Far West and Rockies Series.* Eds. LeRoy R. and Anne W. Hafen. Glendale: Arthur H. Clark Company, 1956.

Simpson, James H. *Navajo Expedition: Journal of a Military Reconnaissance from Santa Fe, New Mexico, to the Navajo Country Made in 1849.* Ed. Frank McNitt. Norman: University of Oklahoma Press, 1964.

Stout, Hosea. *On The Mormon Frontier: The Diary of Hosea Stout, 1844–1861.* Ed. Juanita Brooks. Salt Lake City: University of Utah Press, 1964.

Texas Indian Papers, 1846–1859. Ed. Dorman H. Winfrey. Austin: Texas State Library, 1960.

Newspapers

Civilian (Galveston, Tex.)

Commonwealth (Frankfort, Ky.)

Daily Missouri Republican (St. Louis, Mo.)

Daily Union (St. Louis, Mo.)

Daily Union (Washington, D.C.)

Democrat (Austin, Tex.)

Democratic Telegraph and Texas Register (Houston, Tex.)

Enquirer (Cincinnati, Ohio)

Evening Journal (Albany, N.Y.)

Frontier Guardian (Kanesville, Iowa)

Gazette (St. Joseph, Mo.)

Inquirer (Jefferson City, Mo.)

National Intelligencer (Washington, D.C.)

New York Times (New York City)

Niles National Register

Pennsylvanian (Philadelphia, Pa.)

Public Ledger (Philadelphia, Pa.)

Republican (Santa Fe, N. Mex.)

Reveille (St. Louis, Mo.)

Sentinel (Fort Wayne, Ind.)

Sun (Baltimore, Md.)

Tribune (New York City)

Secondary Sources

Unpublished Materials

Miller, Paul I. "Thomas Ewing. Last of the Whigs." PhD Dissertation, Ohio State University, 1933.

National Archives. "Jurisdictional History of the Office of Indian Affairs, 1823–1880." Washington: n.d. [1967].

Neighbours, Kenneth F. "Robert S. Neighbors in Texas, 1836–1859: A Quarter Century of Frontier Problems." PhD Dissertation, University of Texas, 1955.

Trennert, Robert A. "The Fur Trader as Indian Administrator: Conflict of Interest or Wise Policy?" Paper delivered to the Western History Association, Fort Worth, October 1973.

Books

Adams, Alexander B. *Sitting Bull: An Epic of the Plains.* New York: Putnam, 1973.

Andrist, Ralph K. *The Long Death: The Last Days of the Plains Indians.* New York: Collier, 1969.

Bailey, Lynn R. *Indian Slave Trade in the Southwest.* Los Angeles: Westernlore Press, 1966.

Beers, Henry P. *The Western Military Frontier, 1815–1846.* Philadelphia: University of Pennsylvania Press, 1935.

Bender, A. B. *The March of Empire: Frontier Defense in the Southwest, 1848–1860.* Lawrence: University of Kansas Press, 1952.

Berthong, Donald J. *The Southern Cheyennes.* Norman: University of Oklahoma Press, 1963.

Biesele, Rudolph L. *The History of German Settlements in Texas, 1831–1861.* Austin: Press Von Boeckmann-Jones, 1930.

Brandon, William. *The American Heritage Book of Indians.* New York: Laurel, 1964.

Capers, Gerald M. *Stephen A. Douglas: Defender of the Union.* Boston: Little, Brown, 1959.

Chambers, John Sharpe. *The Conquest of Cholera, America's Greatest Scourge.* New York: Macmillan Company, 1938.

Chittenden, Hiram Martin. *The American Fur Trade of the Far West.* 2 vols. New York: R. R. Wilson, 1936.

Coleman, Mrs. Chapman. *The Life of John J. Crittenden, with Selections from his Correspondence and Speeches.* 2 vols. Philadelphia: J. B. Lippincott & Co., 1871.

Connelley, William E. *Doniphan's Expedition of Conquest of New Mexico and California.* Topeka, Kansas: n. pub., 1907.

Current, Richard N. *Daniel Webster and the Rise of National Conservatism.* Boston: Little, Brown, 1955.

DeVoto, Bernard A. *Across the Wide Missouri.* Boston: Houghton Mifflin Company, 1947.

———. *Year of Decision: 1846.* Sentry Edition. Boston: Houghton Mifflin Company, 1961.

Driver, Harold E. *Indians of North America.* 2nd ed. revised. Chicago: University of Chicago Press, 1969.

Ewers, John C. *Teton Dakota History and Ethnology.* Berkeley: University of California Press, 1938.

Farb, Peter. *Man's Rise to Civilization as Shown by the Indians of North America from Primeval Times to the Coming of the Industrial State.* New York: E. P. Dutton & Co., 1968.

Fletcher, A. C., and F. LaFlesche. *The Omaha Tribe.* Vol. 27 of *Annual Report of the Bureau of American Ethnology.* Washington: Government Printing Office, 1911.

Frederikson, Otto F. *The Liquor Question Among the Indian Tribes in Kansas, 1804–1881.* Lawrence: University of Kansas Press, 1932.

Gard, Wayne. *The Great Buffalo Hunt.* Lincoln: University of Nebraska Press, 1959.

Garretson, Martin S. *The American Bison: The Story of its Extermination as a Wild Species and its Restoration under Federal Protection.* New York: New York Zoological Society, 1938.

Gates, Paul W. *Fifty Million Acres: Conflicts Over Kansas Land Policy, 1854–1890.* Ithaca: Cornell University Press, 1954.

Ghent, William J. *The Road to Oregon: A Chronicle of the Great Emigrant Trail.* New York: Longmans, Green, & Co., 1929.

Goetzmann, William H. *Army Exploration in the American West, 1803–1863.* New Haven: Yale University Press, 1959.

———. *Exploration and Empire: The Explorer and the Scientist in the Winning of the American West.* New York: Alfred A. Knopf, 1966.

Grinnell, George B. *The Cheyenne Indians.* 2 vols. New Haven: Yale University Press, 1923.

——. *The Fighting Cheyennes.* 2nd Ed. Norman: University of Oklahoma Press, 1956.

Hafen, LeRoy R., and William J. Ghent. *Broken Hand: The Life Story of Thomas Fitzpatrick, Chief of the Mountain Men.* Denver: Old West Publishing Company, 1931.

Hafen, LeRoy R., and Francis M. Young. *Fort Laramie and the Pageant of the West.* Glendale: Arthur H. Clark Company, 1938.

Hagan, William T. *The Sac and Fox Indians.* Norman: University of Oklahoma Press, 1958.

Hamilton, Holman. *Prologue to Conflict: The Crisis and the Compromise of 1850.* Lexington: University of Kentucky Press, 1964.

——. *Zachary Taylor: Soldier in the White House.* Hamden, Conn.: Archon Books, 1966.

Harmon, George Dewey. *Sixty Years of Indian Affairs: Political, Economic, and Diplomatic, 1789–1850.* Chapel Hill: University of North Carolina Press, 1941.

Hine, Robert V. *Edward Kern and American Expansion.* New Haven: Yale University Press, 1962.

Hoopes, Alban W. *Indian Affairs and their Administration, with Special Reference to the Far West, 1849–1860.* Philadelphia: University of Pennsylvania Press, 1932.

Horsman, Reginald. *Expansion and American Indian Policy, 1783–1812.* East Lansing: Michigan State University Press, 1967.

Hyde, George. *Pawnee Indians.* Denver: University of Denver Press, 1951.

——. *Red Cloud's Folk: A History of the Oglala Sioux Indians.* Norman: University of Oklahoma Press, 1957.

Jackson, Helen Hunt. *A Century of Dishonor: The Early Crusade for Indian Reform.* Ed. Andrew F. Rolle. New York: Harper & Row, 1965.

Jacobs, Wilbur R. *Dispossessing the American Indian.* New York: Charles Scribner's Sons, 1972.

Josephy, Alvin M. *The Indian Heritage of America.* New York: Alfred A. Knopf, 1968.

Kirwan, Albert D. *John J. Crittenden: The Struggle for the Union.* Lexington: University of Kentucky Press, 1962.

Lavender, David S. *Bent's Fort.* New York: Doubleday, 1954.

Lowie, Robert H. *Indians of the Plains.* American Museum Science Books edition. Garden City: Natural History Press, 1963.

MacAndrew, Craig, and Robert B. Edgerton. *Drunken Comportment: A Social Explanation.* Chicago: Aldine Publishing Company, 1969.

Manypenny, George W. *Our Indian Wards.* Cincinnati: Robert Clark & Co., 1880.

Marshall, S. L. A. *Crimsoned Prairie: The Wars Between the United States and the Plains Indians During the Winning of the West.* New York: Charles Scribner's Sons, 1972.

Mishkin, Bernard. *Rank and Warfare Among the Plains Indians.* Vol. 3 of *Monographs of the American Ethnological Society.* New York: J. J. Augustin, 1940.

Napton, William B. *Past and Present of Saline County Missouri.* Indianapolis & Chicago: B. F. Bowen & Co., 1910.

Nash, Roderick. *Wilderness and the American Mind.* Revised ed. New Haven: Yale University Press, 1973.

Olson, James C. *History of Nebraska.* Lincoln: University of Nebraska Press, 1965.

Pearce, Roy Harvey. *The Savages of America: A Study of the Indian and the Idea of Civilization.* Revised ed. Baltimore: The Johns Hopkins Press, 1965.

Prucha, Francis P. *American Indian Policy in the Formative Years: The Indian Trade and Intercourse Acts, 1790–1834.* Cambridge: Harvard University Press, 1962.

———. *The Sword of the Republic: The United States Army on the Frontier, 1783–1846.* New York: Macmillan Company, 1969.

Saum, Lewis O. *The Fur Trader and the Indian.* Seattle: University of Washington Press, 1965.

Schmeckebier, Laurence F. *The Office of Indian Affairs: Its History, Activities, and Organization.* Baltimore: Johns Hopkins Press, 1927.

Schoolcraft, Henry Rowe. *Archives of Aboriginal Knowledge: Containing All the Original Papers Laid before Congress Respecting the History, Antiquities, Language, Ethnology, Pictography, Rites, Superstitions, and Mythology of the Indian Tribes of the United States.* 6 vols. Philadelphia: J. B. Lippincott & Co. 1860.

Secoy, Frank R. *Changing Military Patterns on the Great Plains: 17th Century through Early 19th Century.* Vol. 21 of *Monographs of the American Ethnological Society*. Locust Valley, N.Y.: J. J. Augustin, 1953.

Smith, Elbert B. *Magnificent Missourian: The Life of Thomas Hart Benton*. Philadelphia: Lippincott, 1958.

Sonnichsen, C. L. *The Mescalero Apaches*. Norman: University of Oklahoma Press, 1958.

Spicer, Edward H. *Cycles of Conquest; The Impact of Spain, Mexico, and the United States on the Indians of the Southwest, 1533–1960*. Tucson: University of Arizona Press, 1962.

Stanley, Francis. *Fort Union*. New York: priv. pub., 1963.

Stegner, Wallace. *The Gathering of Zion: The Story of the Mormon Trail*. New York: McGraw Hill, 1964.

Sunder, John E. *The Fur Trade on the Upper Missouri, 1840–1865*. Norman: University of Oklahoma Press, 1965.

Swanton, John R. *The Indian Tribes of North America*. Bureau of American Ethnology, Bulletin 145. Washington: Government Printing Office, 1952.

Twitchell, Ralph Emerson. *The History of the Military Occupation of New Mexico from 1846–1851*. Denver: The Smith-Brooks Company, 1909.

Underhill, Ruth. *The Navajos*. Norman: University of Oklahoma Press, 1956.

Utley, Robert M. *Frontiersmen in Blue: The United States Army and the Indian, 1848–1865*. New York: Macmillan Company, 1967.

Vogel, Virgil J. *This Country Was Ours: A Documentary History of the American Indian*. New York: Harper & Row, 1972.

Wallace, Ernest, and E. Adamson Hoebel. *The Comanches, Lords of the South Plains*. Norman: University of Oklahoma Press, 1952.

Webb, Walter Prescott. *The Great Plains*. New York: Grosset & Dunlap, 1951.

——. *The Texas Rangers: A Century of Frontier Defense*. 2nd ed. Austin: University of Texas Press, 1965.

Weigley, Russell F. *History of the United States Army*. New York: Macmillan Company, 1967.

Wissler, Clark. *North American Indians of the Plains*. 3rd ed. New York: American Museum of Natural History, 1934.

Wooten, Dudley G. *A Comprehensive History of Texas*. 2 vols. Dallas: William G. Scarff, 1898.

Articles

Abel, Annie Heloise. "Proposals for an Indian State, 1778–1878."*Annual Report of the American Historical Association for 1907* 1 (1908): 82–102.

——. "The History of Events Resulting in Indian Consolidation West of the Mississippi River." *Annual Report of the American Historical Association for 1906* 1 (1908): 235–438.

Abernathy, Alonzo. "Early Iowa Indian Treaties and Boundaries." *Annals of Iowa* 11 (January 1914): 241–259.

Aitchison, Clyde B. "The Mormon Settlements in the Missouri Valley." *Proceedings of the Nebraska State Historical Society* 15 (1907): 7–24.

Bender, A. B. "Frontier Defense in the Territory of New Mexico, 1846–1853." *New Mexico Historical Review* 9 (July 1934): 249–72.

Biesele, Rudolph L. "The Relations Between the German Settlers and the Indians in Texas, 1844–1860." *Southwestern Historical Quarterly* 31 (October 1927): 116–29.

Brandon, William. "American Indians and American History." *The American West* 2 (Spring 1965): 14–25, 91–92.

Christian, A. K. "Mirabeau Buonaparte Lamar." *Southwestern Historical Quarterly* 24 (July 1920): 39–80.

Clark, Andrew H. "The Impact of Exotic Invasions on the Remaining New World Midlatitude Grasslands." In *Man's Role in Changing the Face of the Earth,* ed. William L. Thomas, pp. 737–56. Chicago: University of Chicago Press, 1956.

Clift, C. Glenn, ed. "The Governors of Kentucky, 1792–1824, The Old Master, Colonel Orlando Brown, 1801–1867." *The Register of the Kentucky Historical Society* 49 (January 1951): 5–27.

Colgrove, Kenneth W. "The Attitude of Congress Toward Pioneers of the West, 1820–1850." *Iowa Journal of History and Politics* 9 (1911): 196–302.

Crane, R. C. "Some Aspects of the History of West and Northwest Texas Since 1845." *Southwestern Historical Quarterly* 26 (July 1922): 30–43.

Dobyns, Henry F. "Estimating Aboriginal American Population, an Appraisal of Techniques with a New Hemispheric Estimate." *Current Anthropology* 7 (October 1966): 296–449.

Dorris, J. T. "Federal Aid to the Oregon Trail Before 1850." *Oregon Historical Quarterly* 30 (December 1929): 305–25.

Ellison, William H. "The Federal Indian Policy in California, 1849–1860." *Mississippi Valley Historical Review* 9 (June 1922): 37–67.

Espinosa, J. Manuel. "Memoir of a Kentuckian in New Mexico, 1848–1884." *New Mexico Historical Review* 13 (January 1937): 1–13.

Foreman, Grant. "The Texas Comanche Treaty of 1846." *Southwestern Historical Quarterly* 51 (April 1848): 313–32.

Gallaher, Ruth A. "The Indian Agent in the United States Before 1850." *Iowa Journal of History and Politics* 14 (January 1916): 3–56.

———. "The Indian Agent in the United States Since 1850." *Iowa Journal of History and Politics* 14 (April 1916): 173–238.

Gittinger, Roy. "The Separation of Nebraska and Kansas from the Indian Territory." *Mississippi Valley Historical Review* 3 (March 1917): 442–61.

Hafen, LeRoy R. "Thomas Fitzpatrick and the First Indian Agency of the Upper Platte and Arkansas." *Mississippi Valley Historical Review* 15 (December 1928): 374–84.

Hamilton, Holman. "Texas Bonds and Northern Profits: A Study in Compromise, Investment and Lobby Influence." *Mississippi Valley Historical Review* 43 (March 1957): 579–94.

Harmon, George D. "The United States Indian Policy in Texas, 1845–1860." *Mississippi Valley Historical Review* 17 (December 1930): 377–403.

Holden, W. C. "Frontier Defense (in Texas), 1846–1860." *West Texas Historical Association Year Book* 6 (June 1930): 35–65.

Karnes, Thomas L. "Gilpin's Volunteers on the Santa Fe Trail." *Kansas Historical Quarterly* 30 (Spring 1964): 1–14.

Koch, Lena Clara. "The Federal Indian Policy in Texas, 1845–1860." *Southwestern Historical Quarterly* 28 (April 1925): 259–86.

Larson, Robert W. "First Attempts at Statehood." *New Mexico Quarterly* 38 (Spring 1968): 65–77.

Lowenberg, Peter. "The Psychology of Racism." In *The Great Fear: Race in the Minds of Americans*, eds. Gary B. Nash and Richard Weiss, pp. 186–201. New York: Holt, Rinehart, Winston, 1970.

Loyola, Sister Mary. "The American Occupation of New Mexico." *New Mexico Historical Review* 14 (April 1939): 143–99.

Lurie, Nancy O. "Indian Cultural Adjustment to European Civilization." In *Seventeenth Century America: Essays in Colonial History,* ed. James Morton Smith, pp. 15–32. Chapel Hill: University of North Carolina Press, 1959.

————. "The World's Oldest On-Going Protest Demonstration: North American Indian Drinking Patterns." *Pacific Historical Review* 40 (August 1971): 311–32.

McLendon, James H. "John A. Quitman, Fire-Eating Governor." *The Journal of Mississippi History* 15 (April 1953): 73–89.

Malin, James C. "Indian Policy and Western Expansion." *Bulletin of the University of Kansas, Humanistic Studies* 2 (November 1921), 1–108.

————. "The Grasslands of North America: Its Occupance and the Challenge of Continuous Reappraisals." In *Man's Role in Changing the Face of the Earth,* ed. William L. Thomas, pp. 250–362. Chicago: University of Chicago Press, 1956.

Mantor, Lyle E. "Fort Kearny and the Westward Movement." *Nebraska History* 29 (September 1948): 175–207.

Mattison, Ray H. "David Dawson Mitchell." In *The Mountain Men and the Fur Trade of the Far West,* ed. LeRoy Hafen, 2:241–46. Glendale, Calif.: Arthur H. Clark Company, 1965.

Neighbours, Kenneth F. "Chapters from the History of Texas Indian Reservations." *West Texas Historical Association Year Book* 33 (October 1957): 3–16.

Ogle, Ralph H. "Federal Control of the Western Apaches." *New Mexico Historical Review* 14 (October 1939): 309–65.

Philp, Kenneth. "Albert B. Fall and the Protest from the Pueblos, 1921–1923." *Arizona and the West* 12 (Autumn 1970): 237–254.

Prucha, Francis P. "American Indian Policy in the 1840's: Visions of Reform." In *The Frontier Challenge: Responses to the Trans-Mississippi West,* ed. John C. Clark, pp. 81–110. Lawrence: University of Kansas Press, 1971.

————. "Indian Removal and the Great American Desert." *Indiana Magazine of History* 59 (December 1963): 309–22.

Reeve, Frank D. "The Government and the Navajo, 1846–1858." *New Mexico Historical Review* 14 (January 1939): 82–114.

Richardson, Rupert N. "The Comanche Reservations in Texas." *West Texas Historical Association Year Book* 5 (June 1929): 43–65.

Rippy, J. Fred. "The Indians of the Southwest in the Diplomacy of the United States and Mexico, 1848–1853." *Hispanic American Historical Review* 2 (1919): 363–96.

Sheehan, Bernard W. "Paradise and the Noble Savage in Jeffersonian Thought." *William and Mary Quarterly* 26 (July 1969): 327–59.

Smith, Marian W. "The War Complex of the Plains Indians." *Proceedings of the American Philosophical Society* 78 (January 1938): 425–464.

Smith, Ralph A. "Indians in American-Mexican Relations Before the War of 1846." *Hispanic American Historical Review* 43 (February 1963): 34–64.

Trennert, Robert A. "The Mormons and the Office of Indian Affairs: The Conflict Over Winter Quarters, 1846–1848." *Nebraska History* 53 (Fall 1972): 381–400.

———. "William Medill's War with the Indian Traders, 1847." *Ohio History* 82 (Winter-Spring 1973): 46–62.

Utley, Robert M. "Fort Union and the Santa Fe Trail." *New Mexico Historical Review* 36 (January 1961): 36–48.

Washburn, Wilcomb E. "The Moral and Legal Justifications for Dispossessing the Indian." In *Seventeenth Century America: Essays in Colonial History*, ed. James Morton Smith, pp. 15–32. Chapel Hill: University of North Carolina Press, 1959.

Watkins, Albert. "History of Fort Kearny." *Collections of the Nebraska State Historical Society* 16 (1911): 227–67.

Wellman, Lillian M. "The History of Fort Kearny." *Publications of the Nebraska State Historical Society* 21 (1930): 213–26.

Wissler, Clark. "The Influence of the Horse in the Development of Plains Culture." *American Anthropologist* 14 (1914): 1–25.

Wyman, Walker D. "The Military Phase of Santa Fe Freighting, 1846–1865." *Kansas Historical Quarterly* 1 (November 1932): 415–28.

Young, F. G. "The Oregon Trail." *Quarterly of the Oregon Historical Society* 1 (1900): 339–70.

Index

Index

Abert, Col. John J., 116
Agriculture for Indians, 119, 128, 129; attempted at Ft. Laramie treaty, 188, 190, 192; for border tribes, 132, 137, 142, 157–58; in conjunction with reservations, 56, 60, 113, 117, 153, 182; proposed by DeSmet, 176–77; proposed by Gilpin, 110; suggested by Fitzpatrick, 167, 171–72; suggested by Medill, 31, 153. *See also* Civilization of Indians
Allis, Samuel, 147
Alvarez, Manuel, 123
American Fur Company, 23, 149. *See also* Chouteau, Pierre, Jr.; Indian traders
Annuities: at Ft. Laramie treaty, 182; reform of, 21–22, 24–25, 36–37; reforms overturned, 43, 53–54; trader opposition to, 27–29, 37
Apache Indians, 10, 15, 62, 94–95, 97, 105, 128, 130, 170, 183, 187–88; and White massacre, 119–20; raids in New Mexico, 98, 108, 114, 121; reservations for, 117, 129. *See also* Lipan Apache Indians
Arapaho Indians, 10, 95, 110, 133, 160–62, 171–72, 182–83; alcohol among, 173; at Ft. Laramie treaty, 187–88, 190; raids on Santa Fe road, 170–71
Arikara Indians, 14, 183, 188
Assiniboin Indians, 14, 188

Atchison, David R. (senator), 59, 73; and Pacific railroad, 32, 50

Baird, Spencer M., 129–30
Bannock Indians, 179
Barranger, Daniel M. (congressman), 34
Barrow, John E. (subagent), 154, 157
Bell, Peter H. (governor), 83, 84, 89
Bent, Charles (governor), 19, 100, 103–4
Benton, Thomas H. (senator), 19, 174; lobbyist for traders, 27, 28, 135, 150
Bent's Fort (Colo.), 161, 170–71
Black Hawk, Sioux, 190
Black Hawk War, 134, 174
Blackfoot Indians, 12, 14, 190
Bridger, Jim, 186; at Ft. Laramie treaty, 190
Brooke, Gen. George M., 78, 86, 90, 92; campaigns against Indians, 85; conducts Indian policy, 79–82, 84, 89
Brown, Orlando (commissioner of Indian affairs), 45–46, 53–54, 156; and treaty with plains tribes, 47, 50, 181–82; on reorganization of Indian Office, 48–49, 51–53; on reservations, 47, 79; resigns, 55
Bryant, Edwin, 164
Buffalo: disappearance of, 14, 134, 154, 162, 164–65, 173, 179–80, 185; Indian reliance on, 12

Buffalo Hump, Comanche, 87
Burnet, David G., 69
Butler, Pierce M., 64–65
Butler and Lewis treaty. *See* Council
    Springs treaty

Caddo Indians, 61, 74
Calhoun, James S., 52, 122, 195; ap-
    pointed agent, 113; attitude on
    citizen armies, 121, 125–26; favors
    reservations, 117–18, 128, 130;
    named governor, 124; relations
    with Pueblo Indians, 118–19, 122,
    126–27; treaty with Navajo, 115–16
Calhoun, John C. (secretary of war),
    2, 41
Campbell, Robert, 186
Campbell, Robert S., 88–89
Catlett, H. G., 80, 86
Catlin, George, 11
Central Superintendency, 59
Chambers, Col. A. B., 188
Chapeton, Navajo, 116
Cheyenne Indians, 7, 10, 11–12, 14,
    25, 95, 110, 133, 160–62, 182–84;
    alcohol among, 162, 173; at Ft.
    Laramie treaty, 182–91; raids on
    Santa Fe road, 170–72
Chippewa Indians, 133, 140
Cholera, 78, 154, 180–81, 185
Chouteau, Pierre, Jr., 23, 29, 46; gov-
    ernment case against, 149–51. *See
    also* Indian traders
Civilization of Indians, 1–2, 8, 124,
    127–28, 129–30; and Act of 1834,
    4, 7; for border tribes, 132, 140,
    152–53, 157–58; hindered by whis-
    key, 20–21; in conjunction with
    reservations, 30–31, 56, 59–60, 113,
    117, 182, 193–97; proposed by De-
    Smet, 176–77
Clymer, James, 36
Comanche Indians, 10, 60–61, 69, 80,
    95, 104, 117, 128, 138, 170, 183,
    187–88; Council Springs treaty
    with, 64–66; described by Marcy,
    13; on Santa Fe road, 110–12, 171;
        raids in Texas, 64, 67–68, 75, 78–
        79, 90, 93; relations with Texans,
        70–72, 75; reservations for, 90, 92–
        93; San Saba council with, 87–88
Compromise of 1850, 50–51, 82, 124
Conrad, Charles M. (secretary of
    war), 127, 186; favors reservations,
    57, 92, 129
Council Bluffs (Neb.) Agency, 44,
    113, 154
Council Bluffs (Iowa) Subagency, 20
Council Springs (Tex.) treaty, 64–67,
    69, 87–88
Craig, John, 164
Crawford, George W. (secretary of
    war), 78, 79, 124, 179
Crawford, T. Hartley (commissioner
    of Indian affairs), 7–8, 17
Crittenden, John J., 45–46, 54, 55
Cross, Maj. Osborne, 179–80
Crow Indians, 14, 183, 188; at Ft.
    Laramie treaty, 188, 190
Crowell, John (congressman), 50
Cutler, Alpheas, 146

Dawes Severalty Act, 157, 197
Day, H. R., 187
DeSmet, Father Pierre Jean, 14, 164;
    participation at Ft. Laramie treaty,
    188–90; plans to protect prairie
    tribes, 176–78
Dodge, Gov. Henry, 18
Doña Ana (N. Mex.) army post, 121
Doniphan, Col. Alexander W., 100,
    109, 120; expedition against Nav-
    ajo, 100–103
Douglas, Stephen A. (senator), 32, 38,
    50
Dunbar, Rev. John, 136, 140

Education for Indians, 2, 129, 137;
    and reservations, 31; manual labor
    schools, 7, 31, 132. *See also* Civili-
    zation of Indians
Emory, Lt. William H., 98
Environmental destruction, 10–11,
    162, 164, 178, 180

Ewing, George W., 27–28, 42, 46
Ewing, Thomas (secretary of the interior), 81, 113, 156; and reorganization of Indian Office, 43–44, 48–49, 51–52, 178; and spoils system, 42–43, 44–45, 77, 153; domination of Indian policy, 43, 46; favors restricting tribes, 46–47; favors traders, 43, 53–54; resigns, 56
Ewing, W. G. & G. W., Company, 23, 28, 34, 35–36, 43, 54, 149. See also Annuities; Indian Intercourse Act of 1847; Indian traders
Ewing, William G., 27, 28, 34, 37

Fillmore, President Millard, 56, 86
Fitzpatrick, Thomas (agent), 19, 163, 195–96; advocates military posts, 144, 152, 166, 167, 175, 178; and Upper Platte Agency, 160–61, 163, 170–72; at Ft. Laramie treaty, 189–90; attitude toward Indians, 107, 110, 133, 142, 167, 170–71, 175; conflict with Gilpin, 110–11; criticism of Indian policy, 108, 173–76; preparations for Ft. Laramie treaty, 182–84, 187–88
Fort Bridger (Wyo.), 179
Fort Conrad (N. Mex.), 129
Fort Croghan (Tex.), 82
Fort Defiance (Ariz.), 128–30
Fort Fillmore (N. Mex.), 129
Fort Graham (Tex.), 82
Fort Kearny (Neb.), 151, 174, 179, 182
Fort Laramie (Wyo.), 163, 166, 170, 179, 182, 183, 185
Fort Laramie treaty of 1851, 185–91, 193
Fort Laramie treaty of 1868, 191
Fort Leavenworth (Kan.), 106, 112, 144, 163, 179, 182
Fort Lincoln (Tex.), 82
Fort Mann (Kan.), 106–7, 111
Fort Martin Scott (Tex.), 82
Fort Union (N. Mex.), 128–29
Fort Worth (Tex.), 81, 82
Fremont, John Charles, 162–63

Gantt, Thomas T., 150–51
Garland, Col. John, 107
German Emigration Company, 67
Gilpin, Lt. Col. William, 106–7, 110–12, 171
Gooch, John, 157
Grant, President Ulysses, 197
Grenier, John (agent), 128
Gros Ventre Indians, 183, 188, 190
Guadalupe Hidalgo, treaty of, 52, 75, 112, 127

Hall, Willard P. (congressman), 58
Hamilton, A. J., 87
Hardee, Col. William J., 85
Harney, Gen. William S., 90
Harvey, Thomas H. (superintendent), 19, 22, 25, 37–38, 42, 46, 142, 145–46, 153, 170, 178, 179, 195; activities at St. Louis Superintendency, 135; advocates protection for Indians, 143–45, 168; advocates routes through Indian lands, 29–30, 167; and case against Chouteau, 150–51; on environmental destruction, 138–39, 165, 173; proposes reservations, 152–53; removed from office, 154, 179
Hays, Col. John C., 67
Hays, Robert, 67
Henderson, J. Pinckney (governor), 68, 70
Holman, Jacob H. (agent), 187, 189
Horton, A. C., 65
Houston, Samuel, 62–63, 65, 70
Howard, Volney (congressman), 83, 84
Hyde, Orson, 156

Indian agencies and superintendencies: location of, 4, 18, 43–45, 53, 55–59, 179; proposed changes of, 19, 23–24, 31–34, 48–49. See also names of individual offices
Indian agents. See names of individual agents
Indian annuities. See Annuities

Indian Intercourse Act of 1847, 53, 54, 66; passed, 24–25; trader objection to, 27–29, 35–37
Indian Trade and Intercourse Acts of 1834, 3–6, 8, 19, 23, 45, 53
Indian traders, 34, 86, 154, 161–62; among the border tribes, 134, 148–51; detrimental activities of, 8, 20–22; on Santa Fe road, 111, 112; pressure on Whig administration, 42–43, 53–54; reaction to Intercourse laws, 27–29, 35–37. See also Annuities; Chouteau, Pierre, Jr.; Ewing, W. G. & G. W., Company; Trading licenses
Indian tribes. See names of individual tribes
Iowa Indians, 48

Jackson, Col. Congreve, 99, 101
Jefferson, President Thomas, 2
Johnson, Robert W. (congressman), 33, 57–58
Jones, Adj. Gen. Roger, 109, 125, 128, 144

Kane, Thomas L., 146–48
Kansa Indians, 10
Kearny, Gen. Stephen W., 108, 120; and conquest of New Mexico, 96–100; on the Oregon Trail, 163
Kelley, John M., 141
King, T. Butler (congressman), 51
Kiowa Indians, 10, 61–62, 170, 183–84, 187–88, 190

Lane, Joseph (governor), 39
Lea, Luke (commissioner of Indian affairs), 86–87, 90, 130, 188, 195; advocates reservations, 57, 59, 88–89, 92, 188; appointed, 55
Lewis, James, 187
Lewis, M. G., 64
Lipan Apache Indians, 10, 61–62, 80; warfare with Texans, 75, 78
Loomis, Col. Gustavus, 155
Loring, Col. William W., 179
Lowe, Pvt. Percival, 189

McBride, W. S., 185
McCall, Col. George, 51, 123–24
McElroy, Alexander, 142
McGaughey, Edward W. (congressman), 58
McKay, James J. (congressman), 32, 34
McKinney, Rev. Edward, 30, 134–35
Magoffin, Susan Shelby, 99
Mandan Indians, 183, 190
Manypenny, George (commissioner of Indian affairs), 158
Marcy, Capt. Randolph B., 13
Marcy, William L. (secretary of war), 17, 28, 36, 66, 75; attempts to stop liquor trade, 38; attitude toward Pawnee, 136–37, 138, 142; removes troops from New Mexico, 112, 174
María, José, Caddo, 74
Martinez, Mariano, Navajo, 116
Matlock, Gideon C. (agent), 135, 173
Medicine Lodge (Kan.) treaty, 191
Medill, William (commissioner of Indian affairs), 18, 42, 46–47, 68, 72, 103, 141, 142, 144, 150, 151, 166, 173, 195; and Indian Intercourse Act of 1847, 25, 27; and reorganization of Indian Office, 19–20, 23–24, 32–35; appointed, 17; attitude toward Pawnee, 136–37; favors reservations, 29–32, 39, 153, 158; federal position in Texas, 63, 66–67, 69, 73; opposition to alcohol, 19–20, 37–38; opposition to Mormons, 146–48; opposition to traders, 20–23, 27–29, 35–37; protection of border tribes, 143, 168; reforms overturned, 43; removal from office, 45–46
Messervy, William S., 114
Mexican War, 16–18, 26, 32, 64, 68, 136, 144, 168, 170, 173
Miami Indians, 37
Michigan Superintendency, 18
Miller, John (agent), 133, 135, 154; protection for border tribes, 30, 143, 145; opposition to Mormons, 147

Missouri Indians, 48, 133
Mitchell, David D. (superintendent), 7–8, 135, 153–54, 179; at Ft. Laramie treaty, 188–92, 194–95; proposes severalty, 157–58; proposes treaty with plains tribes, 47, 81–82; preparations for treaty, 59, 182–86
Mitchell, Robert B. (subagent), 20
Monroe, President James, 2
Moore, Thomas P. (agent), 148, 166
Mormons: conflict with Indian Office, 139–40, 145–48; hopes to remove Shoshoni, 186–87; located at Kanesville, 156–57
Munroe, Col. John, 119–21, 125–26; opposition to civilian government in New Mexico, 122–23

Narbona, Navajo, 101, 115–16
Navajo Indians, 10, 62, 97–99; expeditions against, 100–102, 109, 115–17, 128; forts among, 117, 123–24, 128–29; raids in New Mexico, 94–95, 97, 100, 104–5, 108–9, 116, 121; reservations for, 117, 124, 129–30; treaties with, 101–2, 109, 116
Neighbors, Robert S. (agent), 67–68, 79, 195; appointed, 65–66; conflicts with Texas authorities, 71–72, 74; negotiations with Comanche, 67, 69–70, 75; proposes reservations in Texas, 77, 92; removal from office, 77; Texas opposition to, 74
Newby, Col. E. W. B., 108–10, 120
Northern Superintendency, 59

Omaha Indians, 10, 12, 133, 145, 156–57; and whiskey sellers, 134–35; raided by Sioux, 30, 137, 167; relations with Mormons, 139–40, 145, 146–48; reservations for, 48, 158–59
Oregon Trail, 46, 136, 146, 158, 160, 162; fortification of, 18, 143–45, 166, 168, 174, 178, 179, 182
Osage Agency (Mo.), 154, 173
Osage Indians, 11

Oto Indians, 10, 12, 30, 133, 139, 145, 154, 156–57; and whiskey sellers, 134–35; raided by Sioux, 137, 172; reservations for, 48
Ottawa Indians, 133, 140

Pacific railroad, 32, 49, 152
Parkman, Francis, 12, 137
Pawnee Indians, 10, 12, 14, 106, 168, 188; attack emigrants, 25, 137–38; cholera among, 177; driven from homes, 135–36, 142–43; government attempts to protect, 144–45; murdered at Ft. Mann, 107; reservations for, 48, 153, 157; war with Sioux, 132–33, 142, 154, 172
Pelzer, Capt. William, 107
Pillsbury, Timothy (senator), 65
Polk, President James K., 9, 65, 96, 108, 178; opposes expansion of Indian Office, 35; permits Mormons on Indian lands, 146
Ponca Indians, 10, 48, 140
Potawatomi Indians: Mormons settle among, 140, 146–47; removed from Iowa, 133, 155; traders' claims against, 27, 36–37
Powell, Lt. Col. Ludwell E., 145, 151–52, 175
Price, Col. Sterling, 120; commands in New Mexico, 103–5, 108; suppresses Taos Revolt, 104
Provost, Etienne, 150
Pueblo Indians, 94–95, 102, 117, 125; American view of, 99, 118–19; give allegiance to U.S., 98; in Taos Revolt, 104; New Mexican citizenship for, 118–19, 122–23, 126–27

Reid, Capt. John W., 101
Reservations: background of, 3; for border tribes, 152–53, 157–59; for plains tribes, 176–77, 181–82, 183, 184, 188, 189–92; Medill proposes, 29–32, 39; proposed in New Mexico, 113, 117–18, 124, 129–30; proposed in Texas, 77, 79, 81, 83–84, 89, 93; as solution to Indian prob-

Reservations *(cont.)*
lems, vii–viii, 193–97, *passim*; Whig commitment to, 41, 47–48, 56–57, 59–60, 79
Reynolds, Maj. A. W., 110
Ritchie, Thomas, 26
Rockhill, William (congressman), 34–35
Rocky Mountain Fur Company, 161
Rogers, John A. (agent), 88
Rollins, John (agent), appointed, 77–78; favors reservations, 83–84, 92; negotiations with Comanche, 87–88, 89
Rusk, Thomas S. (senator), 72

Sac and Fox Indians, 37, 48, 54, 154, 155; reservations for, 3, 133
Sage, Rufus B., 164
St. Louis Superintendency, 4, 18, 59, 154, 179
Santa Fe Agency (N. Mex.), 44, 113
Santa Fe road, 10, 46, 95–96, 132, 160, 178, 182; defense of, 96, 106–7, 110–12, 128, 171–72, 174; Indian raids along, 105–6, 107, 170–71; liquor on, 111, 174; White massacre on, 119–20
Schools. *See* Education for Indians
Scott, Gen. Winfield, 82, 85, 121
Seminole War, 174
Shanaco, Comanche, 87
Shoshoni Indians, 10; at Ft. Laramie treaty, 186–87, 189
Simpson, Lt. James H., 116
Sinclair, Joseph, 36
Sioux Indians, 7, 10, 147, 151–52, 153, 158; at Ft. Laramie treaty, 188–92; cholera among, 180–81, 185; described, 160–61, 162–63; proposals to restrain, 144–45, 167–68, 169, 174–75; protest environmental destruction, 162, 164–65, 185; raid border tribes, 25–26, 30, 132–33, 134, 135–37, 142, 154, 167–68, 171–72; reliance on buffalo, 12, 14, 176–77; reservations for, 181, 183, 188, 191; whiskey sellers among, 173

Slavery, 16; impact on Indian policy, 35, 38, 43–44, 49, 50, 113, 184–85
Smith, George A., 187
Smith, Hugh N., 51–52, 118
Smith, Jedediah, 163
Snake Indians, 179
Southern Superintendency, 59
Stansbury, Capt. Howard, 181
Stanton, Frederick P. (congressman), 33
Steen, Maj. Enoch, 15, 121
Stem, Jesse (agent), 88, 92
Stuart, Alexander H. H. (secretary of the interior), 56
Sublette, Solomon C. (agent), 173
Sumner, Col. Edward V.: commands in New Mexico, 125, 127–29

Taos Revolt, 104–5
Taylor, President Zachary, 38, 44, 178, 179; death of, 54, 86; influences Indian policy, 43, 51, 113; supports New Mexican statehood, 82
Temple, Oliver P., 88–89
Texas Agency, 24. *See also* Neighbors, Robert S.; Rollins, John
Texas Emigration and Land Company, 71
Texas Rangers: attitude toward Indians, 67; Brooke's opposition to, 81–82; campaigns against Indians, 62, 74, 78, 85; in government service, 68, 70–72, 75–76
Thompson, Richard W. (congressman), 33, 35
Todd, Charles S., 88, 89, 91, 92
Trading licenses, 5–6, 8; attempted revocation of Chouteau's, 149–51; revocation of Ewings', 37. *See also* Indian traders
Tyler, President John, 179

Upper Missouri Agency, 18, 44, 179
Upper Platte and Arkansas Agency, 19, 160, 175

Ute Indians, 10, 99, 130; proposed
fort among, 103, 127; proposed
reservation for, 117; raids in New
Mexico, 95, 97, 104, 114, 121

Waco Indians, 61, 75, 80
Walker, Robert J. (secretary of the
Treasury), 41
Washington, Lt. Col. John M.: as-
sumes command in New Mexico,
112–13; campaigns against Navajo,
115–16; criticized in New Mexico,
114–15, 116–17, 120–21; proposes
forts among Navajo, 117–18; proposes reservations, 113; reports Indian raids, 114; replaced, 119
Webster, Daniel (senator), 27
Western (Okla.) Superintendency, 18,
59
Whiskey sellers, 5, 7–8; among the
border tribes, 133–34, 150–51;
among plains Indians, 111, 161–

62, 173–74; failure to control, 37–
38; Medill's opposition to, 19–21,
22, 35; restrictions against, 24–25
Whitcomb, James (governor), 36
White, John M., 119–20
Whiting, Lt. W. H. C., 82
Whitman, Marcus, 38
Wichita Indians, 10, 61, 75
Williams, William M., 86
Wilmot Proviso, 38, 52
Wilson, John (agent), 179
Wingfield, Edward (agent), 128
Winnebago Indians, 133, 141, 155–56
Wood, George T. (governor), 78
Woods, Maj. Samuel, 155
Wooley, Abraham (agent), 128
Worth, Gen. William J., 77, 78

Young, Brigham, 186–87; dispute
with Indian Office, 145–48

Zuni Indians, 102